My Life In Jazz

My
Life in JAZZ

by MAX KAMINSKY

with V. E. Hughes

HARPER & ROW, PUBLISHERS

New York, Evanston, and London

∎

To my sons, Sam and Matty

MY LIFE
in JAZZ

Chapter 1

It all started back in 1921 when our sixth-grade carpentry teacher told us we could make anything we wanted the last month of school before vacation. Radio was just coming in then, but nobody sat around waiting for Atwater Kent to go into mass production. People bought the parts and made their own receiving sets, following the instructions in the daily newspapers. The minute I caught sight of one of these diagrams from the Boston *Globe* on the teacher's desk I lost all interest in making the usual table or bench, and I set to work on a radio.

My family, a large one, was crammed into the first-floor apartment of a three-family house on Greenwood Street in Dorchester then, but my mother had fixed up a bedroom for me in the attic where I had all the space and privacy I needed for my radio project. The first set I tried to make—a primitive device called a loose-coupler set made out of two oatmeal boxes, one fitting inside the other to act as a condenser—was a failure. I still have the scar on my hand where the chisel slipped. The next crystal set I attempted was successful, but the only station in operation then, KDKA in Pittsburgh, was not on the air all the time, and usually all I could find to tune in on were code signals. Then,

when I made a one-tube radio about a year later, I hit pay dirt.
The first sound I heard when I turned it on was Ted Lewis's
band playing "Tiger Rag." It was like finding diamonds, if you
like diamonds.

But it was the little crystal set that was the start of it all. I had
always wanted to play the trumpet, and from the time I was
seven or eight I had been pestering my sister Mary's husband,
Henry Pollack, who played trumpet in a symphony orchestra,
to give me lessons, but he would just take hold of my chin, pry
open my mouth, and say, "Wait a couple of years till you get
your second teeth." The radio succeeded where all my pleas,
and even my second teeth, had failed. Henry, eying the crystal
set the way I eyed his trumpet, said if I'd make a radio for him
he'd give me a cornet. The first time I blew it I got that sound
out of it. The next morning I woke at dawn, hopped out of bed,
and played "Flow Gently, Sweet Afton" on my new cornet,
reading the notes. I'll never forget how nice it sounded to me.

I was the youngest of seven children, four girls and three boys,
and I was born in Brockton, Massachusetts, on Labor Day in
1908, one of twins. The following winter my twin sister died of
pneumonia, while I, who'd had the same illness, lingered on in a
coma. My mother wrapped me in blankets, clasped me in her
arms, and rushed outside, where she paced back and forth in the
snow until the cold air revived me. Both my mother and I sur-
vived this cure, my mother living to be nearly ninety.

My parents had emigrated to America in the 1880's, from
different villages in the south of Russia, when they were
scarcely out of their teens. They met and married in Boston.
My father owned a grocery store most of his life in America,
and we were poor most of the time. When I was three years
old we were living in Roxbury in an old tenement on William
Street in the heart of the colored section. On Sundays my sister
Rose would take me to the colored church to hear the gospel
singing, and I still remember the street cries of the Negro push-
cart men on summer nights, as they hawked their wagonloads

of watermelon or fresh-caught crabs. I also remember my mother in desperation spraying the inside of the old wooden cupboard underneath the sink with kerosene and putting a match to it to burn out the roaches. We lived by kerosene light then; when we had gaslight a few years later we thought it was a marvel.

I was four when I first heard the song "Jada," and I was so thrilled by it I couldn't wait to sing it to my sister Rose, who, with my brothers Sy and Morris, worked after school in Pa's grocery store, so I took a nickel from my mother's purse, dragged a kitchen chair out to the hall telephone, called up Rose and sang the song to her. Rose and I were always especially close.

Shortly afterward we moved out to the suburbs in Dorchester, which was a nicer neighborhood and closer to the Jewish section, where my four sisters, now in their teens, could meet eligible young men. I loved our house on Morton Street. There was a deep stretch of woods in back of the house, with gnarled old oak trees perfect for climbing and a marsh thick with skunk cabbage and punk and cattails, where I used to roam by the hour with my homemade slingshot and bow and arrow. I never went into the woods without this arsenal, but it never occurred to me to shoot at the birds or squirrels, and they never bothered me either. I loved the peace and the solitude I found there. I was forever lugging home cardboard boxes of acorns which would be so full of maggots inside of a few weeks that I'd have to throw them out, but I never got over the idea that there must be something wonderful you could do with acorns besides grow trees.

In the summertime I lived for my cart, made of a plank of wood and the wheels and axle of an old baby carriage. I'd coast all day long up and down Blue Hill Avenue, and when my mother tired of calling me in for lunch she'd fix up a salmon sandwich in a paper bag and lower it down to me on a string. Hauling the cart up and down the three flights to our top-floor apartment did such damage to the hall plaster that the owners of the house complained to my parents, and my father eventually moved us to another house on nearby Greenwood Street, where we could live on the first floor in peace.

The Dorchester Tigers, a baseball team of teen-age boys in the neighborhood, made me their mascot when I was eight. They bought me a uniform and carried me around on their shoulders and let me sit on the bench with them, but it never occurred to me that the Tigers to a man were so nice to me because of my pretty sisters. Dorchester at that time was mainly a mixture of Jewish and Irish families, and the Tigers would have to break up many a fight when the Irish kids started stoning the synagogues, which were very poor ones, quartered in empty stores. From the time I was in second-grade grammar school I was attacked by a gang of Irish kids on my way to school every day, and as early as the age of seven I automatically learned to protect myself. As soon as they started toward me I'd grab some bricks—there always seemed to be bricks lying around in the streets in those days—and let them have it, and they'd turn tail and run. The trick was not to show fear in any way. I used to lie awake nights and figure out how to fight, and I had learned very quickly to attack first and ask questions later. I had no one to turn to for advice. In those days there wasn't much talking in families; everyone was on his own.

Around this time, when I was eight years old, I was friends with a boy who lived on the floor below us on Morton Street. His family were devout Holy Rollers and they roused the neighborhood every night with their thumping and moaning and wailing. He was a nice kid, though, and I used to tag along with his family every Friday night to the shul, which was in an empty store front, just to be with my pal. One Friday night three new boys came in, and one of them, a big kid named Jackie Marshard, began acting tough and making a racket, mocking the Holy Roller family. No one told him to quiet down, but I couldn't stand to have him make fun of my friend and his odd family, so I spoke up.

"Why can't you show a little respect for the house of God," I said piously.

Jackie looked me over coolly and said, "Come on outside, wise guy, and I'll show you some respect."

Well, I was stuck with it. This kid was two heads taller, but I didn't want my friend to think I was yellow.

When we went outside it seemed to me that the whole congregation and everyone on the block was gathered around, but I didn't waste any time counting the house. I hit Jackie fast and knocked him out with one punch. His older brother Harry caught him as he was going down. I couldn't believe I had done it and neither could the crowd. There was a second of stunned silence, and then they burst into cheers, and while they were cheering I got the hell out of there before Jackie could get up and start over. It was four years before he caught up with me again.

Within a month after I had my cornet I rounded up every kid in the neighborhood who played an instrument and tried to get them excited about having a band. The feeling to play was so strong in me that I couldn't wait till I learned my instrument, I had to have a band at once. I had been brought up in a house filled with music—all my sisters played the piano, and my brother Morris was already playing violin in a band—and I just seemed to know instinctively how a band should sound. The kids I enlisted would run wild through my house until my mother would lose patience and throw us out, and some would come once and never show up again, but after a while I managed to find a pianist, drummer, trombonist, saxophonist, and banjo player who were interested, and then I worked them hard trying to keep us in tune and in time. All I could think about was my cornet and my band. We'd chip in a couple of pennies apiece and each week we'd buy a stock arrangement of a song, and in a couple of months I began looking around for bookings. Then, just as I had the band in shape, my drummer moved away. I was moping along the sidewalk one evening after supper, worrying about where I was going to find a new drummer, when I found myself face to face with Jackie Marshard. It was dark and he hadn't seen me for four years, but he recognized me instantly.

"*You!*" he yelled in awful triumph.

I had heard of a Harry Marshard who played the drums, but until I found myself trapped by Jackie I hadn't associated him with my fight years ago. Now I had to think fast. We were both twelve, but Jackie had grown even bigger and I wasn't much taller than I had been four years ago.

"Sure, I'll fight you again," I said easily, "but first I know a way you can make some money."

This made him pause for a minute, and while he was hesitating about hitting me right away, I talked fast about the band contest on Friday night at the Sarah Greenwood School for which there was a $2.50 prize, and I offered Jackie the job of playing drums for me.

"I don't know how to play the drums," he said, beginning to circle around me. "Come on, put up your mitts."

"It's easy," I said quickly. "Listen, all you have to do is borrow your brother Harry's drums and I'll teach you how to play them."

It took a lot of persuasion before he finally agreed, and then only on the condition that we were to fight right after the job. The next night he showed up at my house with his brother's drums and I taught him to play a waltz and a fox trot. The waltz was easy, but the fox trot was something else again. He never was able to keep real good time, but I soon found out that what he lacked in musical ability he made up for a millionfold in business sense and personality.

We won first prize in the contest that Friday night. As we were leaving the stage one of the kids in the band accidentally pulled loose the snare drum. It fell to the floor with a loud noise, and Jackie made a much louder noise about the snare drum being broken.

"That'll cost two-fifty for a new snare," Jackie said, cool as you please. The snare drum wasn't even scratched, let alone broken, but Jackie spoke with such overwhelming authority that without a word I handed the prize money over to him and walked off the stage. Outside I told the other boys in the band and they accepted it too. We all knew that Jackie's family was poor; his father had died when he was young and his mother worked hard to support the four children, and I guess we felt, what the heck, let him have the money if he feels so strongly about it that he would act like that. We felt a kind of embarrassment that kept us all silent.

Years later, in 1936, when I was working in the Little Club in New York, Jackie came in one night to see me. He was well on his way to success as a society band leader and he was upset to find me working "in a dive like this," as he put it, and insisted that I come in with his band. We talked about it again the next day and I finally agreed to come back to Boston and work for him after I had finished my date at the Little Club. Before he left me Jackie said that the main thing is money: "Money is the most important thing in the world." I couldn't feel like that, even if he was right, but he was so certain about it that I could find no words to tell him that life couldn't be the way he had figured it out to be; that life was for everyone and all things, not just for him and his money.

Well, after Jackie took the whole $2.50 prize money that night he never said another word about fighting me again, and he was sold forevermore on the music business. The next week I arranged for the band to play at the Shawmut Theatre in Roxbury, where they staged a battle of music every Friday night. The manager of the theatre, Harry Goldstein, thought my idea of a kid band was a perfect gimmick, and he told us we'd battle the winning band. This group, which won regularly every week, was a band of professional colored musicians led by a white violinist named Lou Lissack. The prize money was fifty dollars—a fortune.

I named my band the Six Novelty Syncopaters and for our first

appearance I had the kids dress up in tramp outfits. Not only that
—we played lying on our backs. I don't know how much
syncopating we did, but we were novel, and we brought down
the house. I even made little music stands for us, with JAZZ
printed on them. When I heard the applause for our three
numbers—"Yearning," "Dearest," and "Last Night on the Back
Porch"—I was sure we had won hands down.

"It's a draw!" the manager announced when he had the
audience quieted down, "so we'll split the money between Lou
Lissack's band and the Six Novelty Syncopaters."

I couldn't believe my ears.

"I'll take the fifty dollars or nothing!" I said hotly.

Luckily, "Sock" Sochin, my piano player, had the presence of
mind to step up and accept the twenty-five dollars before I
could say another word and spoil it all for us, but I was so certain we had been gypped that I was burnt up all week, and
events later proved I was right.

The manager told us to come back next week, and after
several Fridays of calling the contest a draw, he decided to
have Lou Lissack take over my band and call it the Lou Lissack
Shawmut Syncopaters.

"We're being taken," I said bitterly to the boys. "They're
stealing our own band from under our noses!" But we didn't
know what to do about it. Harry Goldstein bought us sailor
suits and had our picture taken for the billboard, and we became
a regular Friday-night feature all that winter under Lou Lissack's
leadership. In the summer Lissack and Goldstein decided to run
a dance and they had us kids out hustling to sell tickets on street
corners and on trolleys and trains. We even played in an open
truck to advertise the dance, which was a sellout.

"Meet me at the theatre tomorrow at noon," Lou Lissack told
us afterward, "and I'll have your share of the money for you."

We waited outside the theatre all afternoon until five o'clock,
when Lou finally showed up sporting a brand-new plaid suit
and carrying a shiny new violin case. He looked surprised to see

us, but without batting an eye he told us there was no money left for us.

"Go on home, kids, your mothers will be looking for you," he said over his shoulder as he ducked inside the stage door. We turned and shuffled home, and none of us, not even Jackie, said a word. That he could do such a thing so terrified us that we felt lucky to get away with our skins.

We never went back to the theatre, and that summer I arranged for a job for my band at the little beach at City Point on Boston Bay. We were paid a dollar a night, which was pretty good money for those days, and we wore the sailor suits Harry Goldstein had bought for us. Then came the final blow to my career as boy band leader. One evening while I was sitting on my front steps enjoying the evening breeze, Jackie and Sock came up to me and told me they had been talking things over and they had decided Jackie was to be the leader from now on. We had all been shaken by the Lou Lissack incident, and they felt Jackie would be more of a match for the Lou Lissacks of this world than I would. To be fired from my own band was more than I could take. I ran into the house and cried inconsolably until finally my mother came to my room and talked to me.

"People are bad," she said, "but they're bad to themselves and all the harm they do is only to themselves. Wait, and you'll see this is true."

I never forgot her words, but at the time they didn't bring back my band, and I took a job as a waiter in a summer camp at Gloucester for the rest of the summer just to get away from the fellows in the band. In the fall I went into the eighth grade and Jackie moved away. I didn't see him again for six months. In the meantime, I was getting to play more and more with professionals and getting to know about music and musicians, and after a while I was able to chalk up the whole Shawmut Syncopaters episode to experience.

Chapter 2

By the time I was fourteen I had become known around Boston as a hot trumpet player and the local musicians began hiring me for jobs at dance halls and college fraternity houses, the only two places where there was any audience for hot music in those days. One good thing you can say for Boston, there is no scarcity of colleges and universities. But till now I had not even heard the name, let alone the music, of Bix Beiderbecke or Louis Armstrong. My favorite band in those days was Pearly Breed's, which used to broadcast from Shepherd's Colonial Tea Room in Boston, with Warren Hookway on trumpet. These musicians had heard the recordings of Bix Beiderbecke's Wolverines and they tried to play jazz. I thought this was the greatest band I'd ever heard, and up to then it was.

Then my sister Betty bought a phonograph, and on the "race" records that came with it as a bonus I heard for the first time Bessie Smith, Maggie Jones, Ma Rainey, James P. Johnson, Louis Armstrong and others of the great Negro artists. They all sounded wonderful to me, but I wasn't aware of any special difference or distinction in their music, which I swallowed as unquestioningly as I did Pearly Breed's music. All I remember

is my sister Betty singing her favorite blues from a Maggie
Jones record while she dusted the furniture and mopped the
floors:

> Miss Lizzie Green of New Orleans
> Runs a good-time flat.
> The other day I heard her say
> Things are goin' bad:
> Can't sell no whiskey, can't sell no gin . . .

One night that fall, Elliott Daniels, who later played piano in
Rudy Vallee's band, called me to play a dance at the YMHA.
During the course of the evening I became friendly with one of
the saxophone players, Sam Faber, and he asked me whom I
liked in music.

"Pearly Breed and Ted Lewis," I said promptly, and I was
puzzled and a little hurt when he smiled at my answer. I met
Arthur Karle then, too, another saxophone player, who offered
me a job playing weekends down at Cape Cod, during the spring
and summer of 1924. I'd have to leave school early on Friday
afternoons, so Arthur went to the school principal, Mr. Owens,
a distinguished, august gentleman, who to my surprise and joy
granted me permission to do so. The musicians would come by
for me in a Ford touring car and as soon as we were well away
from the school they'd guzzle gin all the way out to the Cape.
They never pressed it on me, though, and they all took good care
of me, especially Arthur.

One of the jobs I especially enjoyed was playing for the silent
movies. In those days the dance halls would often put on a movie
first as an added attraction, and we'd play for that and for the
dancing afterward. Sometimes we'd get swinging so good we'd
forget to keep track of the story. One time when I remembered
to glance up at the screen I discovered we were playing "Tiger
Rag" during a funeral scene. Every musician who has ever
played for the silent movies seems to have had a similar experience. The audience was so gripped with emotion that it was

oblivious to everything but the movie, and it became a regular
gag with the band to tear into "Hold That Tiger" whenever a
heart-rending scene was in progress. We never had a single
complaint.

Then one afternoon I met Sam Faber again on the trolley and
he began talking to me about Bix Beiderbecke. When I said I'd
never heard of him Sam rushed me home with him then and
there to listen to his records. "This is the time to come, while
my father is out," he said. It seemed that his father, who had
a very successful custom-tailor business in Boston, was determined to make a pants cutter out of Sam, and Sam had to sneak
out of the house at night to play in bands.

But although I liked the sound of them, I wasn't too impressed
when I first heard Beiderbecke's Wolverine records at Sam's
house. I listened intently while Sam put on "Jazz Me Blues,"
"Sensation Rag," and "Big Boy," but it was too much for me to
take in all at once, and it wasn't until a year later, when I heard
Beiderbecke in person, that I really got it.

I was seventeen and in my third year of high school when
Bix Beiderbecke came to Boston with Jean Goldkette's band
that spring of 1926. The band was to open at a dance hall in
Newton called Nutting-on-the-Charles, a large rambling wooden
structure built over the tranquil Charles River. It was so flimsy
that when I worked there myself later and the dancers really
began stomping we used to wonder if the building would last
the night. Nutting-on-the-Charles was quite a romantic spot,
with couples in canoes drifting lazily along the river, and it
was very popular with amorous college boys as well as with the
ones who came to dance. There has, in fact, always been great
enthusiasm for dance bands in New England. It was in New
England that many of the big swing bands of the thirties had
their start, and one of the main reasons for this was the Schribman
brothers, Charlie and Sy, who were the owners of a huge chain
of dance halls throughout the northeast. Charlie Schribman, who
especially loved jazz and helped it every chance he had, was

already bringing in jazz bands way back in 1924.

Jean Goldkette's band was one of the first white jazz bands of the twenties, with Beiderbecke, Bill Rank, Tommy Dorsey, Frankie Trumbauer, Don Murray, Doc Ryker, and Izzy Riskin, and their appearance in Boston was something I didn't want to miss. Charlie Schribman was afraid that the public wouldn't get it at first though, so he had two other bands on hand to ensure a successful engagement, which he promoted as a Triple Battle of Music.

I had saved up just enough money at that time to make the down payment on a Model-T Ford, and on Monday, the opening night, I rushed through my supper, shined my shoes, put on my best suit, and rattled out to Newton at twenty miles an hour. Mal Hallett's orchestra, a very popular local band that combined comedy routines with dance music, went on first and nearly knocked itself out putting on a whole big show; then Barney Rapp's band, which was just coming into prominence then, did all its acts; and finally the Jean Goldkette band came on. Charlie Schribman could have saved himself a lot of worry and expense. They opened with "Pretty Girl Stomp," went on to "Ostrich Walk," "A Sunny Disposish," "Clap Yo' Hands," and ended with "Tiger Rag," and they were such a stunning sensation that when the furor died down and it was time for Mal Hallett's band to play again, neither his musicians nor Barney Rapp's men would pick up their instruments.

"How can you follow *that*?" Mal Hallett asked plaintively, and the crowd wasn't bashful about letting him know they agreed with him. Nobody had heard anything like this music before.

Neither had I. It had taken my eyes to open my ears. I understood now what Sam Faber had been trying to tell me with his records. I just sat there, vibrating like a harp to the echoes of Bix's astoundingly beautiful tone. It sounded like a choirful of angels. When I did work up the courage to go over to speak to Beiderbecke during one of the intermissions, I was still so over-

come I could hardly get a word out. After a few minutes I
realized it was a tossup as to who was more shy, Bix or me. He
kept his eyes fixed on his shiny black shoes and solemnly nodded
his round blond head at each halting word as I tried to tell him
how wonderful the band sounded. It was like talking to an
automated toy. Suddenly I remembered having heard that he
liked baseball. Taking a deep breath, I blurted out an invitation
to take him to a game the next day. At the mention of baseball,
Bix's diffidence vanished and he straightened up and looked at
me.

"Sounds fine to me," he said in a soft-pitched Midwest accent.
He told me that Goldkette had rented a house for the band in
Sudbury, a suburb of Boston, and I arranged to pick him up there
the next afternoon. The Model-T never touched the road all the
way home.

The next day I skipped school and drove out to Sudbury
around noon. My high school career at best was a very sketchy
one, but my mother knew what music meant to me and she
understood I wasn't running wild. Most of the time in school
I was so sleepy from playing late the night before that I was
kind of vague about what was going on, and I always felt out of
touch with my schoolmates since none of them knew or cared
about the one thing I was interested in. I seemed to wake
up only during music class, or when, on the stairs between classes,
I ran across Harry Carney, who later joined Duke Ellington's
band; I was always so glad to see him and talk about music.

The Goldkette band was rehearsing when I arrived at Bix's
boardinghouse the next noon, and I stood in a corner at the
back of the room and listened to "Blue Room" and "Riverboat
Shuffle"—a piece Hoagy Carmichael had written for Bix and
the Wolverines. Goldkette wasn't there; in fact, he never appeared on the bandstand; he busied himself entirely with the
booking and managerial chores of his various bands. The ar-
rangers Bill Challis and George Crozier led the band during re-
hearsals. Before we left for Braves Field to watch Casey Stengel's

Braves lose, Bix took me up to his room after rehearsal, where we talked for a while about music. His sympathetic interest so encouraged me that I asked him if he would write out a hot chorus of "Blue Room" for me to practice, and he obligingly fished a piece of manuscript paper out of the pile of sheet music on the littered table next to the bed and wrote out a thirty-two-bar chorus in about three minutes. Even in the heat of improvising Bix was wholly aware of his sequences and afterward he could reconstruct exactly what he had played. When I questioned him about a weird G-sharp that didn't look to me like it had any business being there, he explained about the use of passing tones to give color or tonal accent to a phrase, and he went on to discuss anticipation—playing notes of the melody a hairbreadth before the strict time. The use of anticipation, without rushing, which is all a part of making the music swing, was just getting to be understood then.

I was terribly worried all that afternoon about how to keep a conversation going with Beiderbecke, but eventually I discovered he had no need of small talk; he seemed to be busy all the time with his own thoughts. Aside from music and baseball, he had only one other form of communication, if you could call it that; he'd kind of turn aside and sing a little snatch from a Bessie Smith or an Ethel Waters blues record. "The whole song is right there in that phrase—hear it?" he'd say suddenly. A gentle, silent man with a dreamy, preoccupied manner, he was one of the most fascinating persons to be with that I have ever known, for no reason that can be explained except that his playing cast such a spell over you that you were irresistibly drawn to him, in awe and gratitude and love. He felt that, of course, and he responded to it in his own inarticulate way. All he ever really seemed to care about were music and whiskey. He was a man who was always trying to find a piano. During intermissions Bix would remain on the bandstand and mess around at the keyboard for his own kicks. A couple of years later when I met Bix again in Chicago at a speakeasy called the Three Deuces, he disappeared after a

while and I discovered him later seated at a battered old upright
in a corner of the darkened downstairs dining room, playing to
an audience of empty, checker-clothed tables. I sat down at one
of the tables and listened while he spun out notes from a silver
spool. His piano style had the same crystal purity of tone, the
same perfect taste, and the same melodic grace that flowed from
his horn, but it was more impressionistic. When Bix played
regular jazz piano he sounded exactly like Bix—the same characteristic use of haunting intervals, the same exquisite hot phrasing. He didn't play ragtime style, ever. Bix's modern piano pieces,
such as "Flashes," "Candlelight," and "In a Mist," were composed
in the same feeling as Willie the Lion Smith's impressionistic
studies, such as "Morning Air"—they were a feeling-out for a
new form without scrapping the old.

During one of our talks about music, Bix once told me that
when he was playing the horn he thought like a pianist rather
than a cornetist. He automatically and instantaneously trans-
posed, so that while fingering the B-flat on the cornet he had it
in his mind and ear as the A-flat it was on the piano, and I suppose
that in his head he heard the richer harmonies of the piano tones.
It was characteristic, too, of Bix that he never tapped his foot
to keep time. The tempo and the swing that modeled his phrases
funneled out like steam rising from the spout of a boiling kettle.
Another idiosyncrasy of Bix's was that as a further means of
ensuring the mellow tone he loved he purposely kept his horn
funky, never cleaning out the dried spittle that accumulates in
the valves and mouthpiece. He had no use at all for a hard,
brilliant sound.

Louis Armstrong and Beiderbecke were the ones who gave a
classical form to the crude raw material of jazz. When
Beiderbecke was born in Davenport, Iowa, in 1903, Louis Armstrong was barely three years old, and jazz itself was actually
only a few years older. Of course, it had taken the music a long
time to become jazz—nearly three hundred years of bouncing
back and forth between the black man and the white man—

but the colored brass marching bands in the South and Midwest
had begun to really swing their music only a short time earlier,
a bare decade or so before the turn of the century.

As a child of three Bix was picking out phrases from classical
music by ear on the family piano, and as a boy he heard the
colored jazz bands from New Orleans playing on the Mississippi
riverboats, which docked at his home town, but it was from
phonograph records that he taught himself to play both jazz
and the cornet. The records from which he learned were those
of a band of white New Orleans musicians, the Original Dixieland Jazz Band, who in 1917 made the first jazz records, which
were a sensational worldwide hit. Bix especially admired the
cornet player in this band, Nick LaRocca, who was also self-
taught. The O.D.J.B. band as a whole was pretty primitive and
they played to a ragtime beat, but they did much to popularize
the new music. It wasn't until he was in Chicago in 1921, attending Lake Forest Military Academy, that Bix had a chance to get
a real earful of the Negro jazzmen, including the youthful
Louis Armstrong, who came up from New Orleans the following
year to join King Oliver's band. The Wolverines, a band of
college boys from Indiana which Bix joined in 1923, was the
first jazz band of white musicians in the Midwest.

But back in 1926 I didn't know anything about the music and
Bix except that they both sounded wonderful. A few days after
the ball-game episode the Goldkette band was booked in Salem
at another of Charlie Schribman's dance halls. It was a muggy,
oppressive night, with a storm threatening. My brother Morris
came along with me and at the hall we sat up in the balcony for
a while, but the storm, when it broke, was so violent that it drove
me down by the bandstand where I could hear, and where I
immediately got into trouble. As soon as they saw me, the
musicians, who were all young and enthusiastic, began urging me
to sit in. Torn between desire and despair, I kept saying, "Later,"
in what I hoped was a casual manner. While I was wondering
what to do, the lights blew out in the dance hall just as the band

kicked off with "Sunday," and in the sudden darkness I found
sudden courage. Turning quickly to Bix, I muttered, "I'll sit
in now." Bix handed me his horn at once. When the lights came
on again a few choruses later, the whole band made a big thing
about being surprised to see me on horn instead of Bix, and I
thought my brother Morris up in the balcony would never stop
clapping. I was so exhilarated by the musicians' kindness that
when Bix told me they were playing in Lowell the next day I
promptly offered to drive him there. I would have *made* a car
if I didn't have one—and the devil with the truant officer.

When I arrived at the boardinghouse the following day, Bix
was at the piano, as usual, playing a passage from a new
symphony the musicians were discussing. Beiderbecke's interest
in classical music, especially the modern impressionists—Debussy
and Delius and MacDowell, and Eastwood Lane—intrigued me,
and I began listening to the Sunday symphony broadcasts to find
out what it was all about. On the way to Lowell, Bix said,
"Listen, Maxie, I'm going to leave the band when we finish this
New England engagement, and I'll tell Goldkette to hire you
in my place." I nearly ran into a ditch. I knew I couldn't play
well enough to be in the Goldkette band, and he knew it too, of
course, but this was a thoroughly typical, Bix-like gesture of
generosity and friendship.

By the time we got into Boston he was asking me where he
could latch on to some gin. Though I was too young to care
about drinking myself, I knew where to get it even during
Prohibition, and within a very short while I got hold of a quart
of alcohol and a quart of ginger ale. When we reached Lowell
it was dark and I was starving. Bix was agreeable about it when I
asked him if he minded if we stopped for something to eat, but
he wasn't the man to let food interfere with his drinking. He
contentedly polished off the alcohol, washing it down with
ginger ale, while I devoured a couple of hot dogs. That night
at Lowell he played like an angel.

After the dance I drove Bix to the Hawthorne Hotel in Salem,

and Bix decided that since it was so late I'd better stay with him
overnight. I went right off to sleep with my nose buried in the
pillow to shut out the smell of his dirty socks steaming in the
washbasin, but I had the feeling he didn't sleep much, ever.
That's all part of the legend about Beiderbecke—he's as famous
for all the buddies and fans who have put him up or bunked
with him as George Washington is for having slept here, and he
is equally famous for his avoidance of water, internally and
externally. He had that Huckleberry Finn quality of homeless-
ness and rebelliousness about him, but in spite of the dirt and
the whiskey everybody loved Bix so much they just wanted
to stick around him. I remarked to my sister Rose the next
day, "I love the way he plays, but I can't stand the way he
lives."

I had another glimpse of Bix when I went to New York in
1927 to take a lesson from Mr. Schlossberg, a famous trumpet
teacher who taught all the great legitimate players. I used to have
a lot of trouble with my embouchure in those days, and when I
inquired about a teacher from Johnny Asevido, a trumpet player
in Jacques Renard's orchestra whose control of his horn I had
always admired, he recommended Schlossberg. When I had
enough money saved up for a lesson I came down to New York,
and then I found out that Paul Whiteman was recording that
afternoon in Liederkranz Hall. I made a fast detour to East
Fifty-eighth Street, staying to watch them record two sides—
"Louisiana" and "Lonely Melody." From the record you
wouldn't know Bix was playing the lead. It isn't true, of course,
that Bix couldn't read; but when he played lead horn he didn't
bring his tone way out in front, as if it were a solo, the way
any other trumpet would have done. He had a way of blending
in his tone so melodically and subtly with the other instruments
that it all came out a smooth, solid tapestry of sound. Bix had so
many leads on this date, in fact, that Charlie Margulis, whom
Tommy Dorsey later christened "Gabby" because he couldn't
keep his mouth shut, became miffed and at one point things got

a little flurried. Bix, who used speech only as a last resort, had a
habit of tossing his horn up in the air as a silent way of letting off
steam. When Charlie began riding him, he tossed up one of the
gold-plated cornets Vincent Bach had given him, but being upset
he missed it and it crashed to the floor, denting the bell.

That seemed to me a good moment to duck out and take a
lesson from Schlossberg. About a year earlier I had registered in
the New England Conservatory of Music for lessons from
Herman Klepfil, who used to play first trumpet in the Boston
Symphony. After the first two or three lessons Klepfil told me
he didn't think I'd ever learn to play the trumpet right, and he
advised me to give it up, but instead of giving up the trumpet I
gave up the lessons. After I had played a while for Schlossberg,
he said, "You can play it. The only way to learn is just to go
ahead and blow it out. Getting the feel of the embouchure is hard
—it just takes time." That was my one lesson with Schlossberg,
but it was exactly what I needed to give me the confidence to
keep at it.

In the late spring of 1927, a year after the Goldkette engagement, Bix came to Boston again with Paul Whiteman, who had
taken over most of the Goldkette band when it broke up in the
fall of 1926. The lengthening shadow of Bix's drinking was already beginning to darken his life and he was withdrawing more
and more into himself, but I had no way of knowing this. Four
years later, at the age of twenty-eight, he would be dead.

Whiteman had chartered a bus to take the band to the Cape
for a one-night engagement. The road to the Cape wound
through Dorchester, and as the bus rounded the curve on Seaver
Street, Bix's cornet case was jolted loose from the shelf and fell
out of the window without anyone noticing it. A few seconds
later, my cousin Hy Benjamin, who was on his way to his store,
found the case in the middle of the street, and the next day my
sister Alice called me up to tell me that Hy had found a cornet
in the street and to ask what they should do.

The minute I saw the horn I knew it was Bix's. I knew he had a gold Bach cornet, for one thing, but mostly it was that being with him was such a thrilling experience that you noticed everything about him, and I felt I would have known any matchstick he threw away. I dashed down in a sweat of excitement to the Metropolitan Theatre, where the Whiteman band was playing that afternoon. The band was off the stand, but the other musicians told me I'd find Bix in a speakeasy up the street, listening to the ball game in comfort. He was curiously diffident when I told him about my cousin finding the cornet, but I was so elated at the remarkable coincidence that I didn't think anything about it. After Bix finished his drink we took a cab back to Seaver Street. When Bix picked up the cornet and blew a few golden notes, I exclaimed absurdly to my cousin Hy, "See, can't you *tell* it's his!" Later, back at the speakeasy, Bix remarked suddenly that a lot of kids were always stealing Frankie Trumbauer's mouthpieces, and it was only then that I realized Bix was harboring the suspicion that in some mysterious way I had swiped his cornet. But I was still too enthralled by the whole coincidence to feel brought down, or even very much aware of Bix's strange notion.

He was right, though, about the extremes to which a youngster will be driven in his passion for the music. A few months after I first heard Bix play, I was working down at the Cape for the summer, and one Sunday night on the train going back to the Cape, I met Howie Freeman, a drummer from Boston, who immediately showed me a brand-new recording he had just bought of Bix's "Singing the Blues" and "Clarinet Marmalade."

"Howie, old pal," I croaked in a voice hoarse with almost unbearable longing, "let me buy it from you." I peeled dollar after dollar from my thin wad, but Howie wouldn't part with the record at any price. By the time the train pulled into my station I had turned from an ordinarily sane, responsible young man into a demon. After I had gathered up my belongings with sneaky casualness, I turned to say good-bye to Howie, and in the next second I snatched the record out of Howie's hand and

raced off the train with it. And that night when I sat in the
little room in my boardinghouse playing the record over and
over, my only thought was, "It was *worth* it." Remorse did
begin to set in a day or so later, and Howie did eventually forgive
me. "I know how it is," he said. But in time I became so ashamed
of my action that I hated to think of it. Another musician, one
of the most talented jazz trombonists around, recently told me of
a similar incident. He was around fifteen when he heard his
first Teagarden record on a jukebox in an ice cream parlor, and
he went so wild that he seized a chair, smashed the glass front of
the jukebox, snatched the record and fled before anyone knew
what was happening. He was from a well-to-do family, with no
more excuse or explanation for his behavior than I had.

The last time I saw Bix was in 1929, after I had returned from
Chicago. Milt "Mezz" Mezzrow, who was very popular in
Harlem in those days, had a booking for a band at the Renais-
sance Ballroom and he put together a pickup group composed
of Bix, who had just come out of the sanitarium after one of his
alcoholic breakdowns, Bud Freeman, Tommy Dorsey, Jimmy
Dorsey, Joe Sullivan, Gene Krupa, and myself. It was quite an
unusual thing in those days to have white musicians play for a
colored dance, but it was a dreadful night for me. It was bad
enough that the other musicians were older and more experienced, but the thought of playing with Bix had me so nervous I
couldn't even speak. At one of the intermissions, when Bix came
over and asked me what was wrong, I didn't know what to say,
besides *Help*! I don't remember Bix playing much that night
either; it was all so mixed up with all the different styles of
playing.

Except for one or two other occasions, such as when I heard
Bix play at Roseland Ballroom in New York, and at Tommy
Dorsey's house on Long Island, this was the extent of my
acquaintance with Beiderbecke. Few as these occasions were,
they left an indelible impression, and I never met anyone who
had known Bix who didn't feel the same way about the man and

his music. Hoagy Carmichael was so inspired by Bix's music and friendship that he switched from a law course in college to a music career. Paul Whiteman summed it up best: "Bix was not only the greatest musician I have ever known, he was also the greatest gentleman." Bix's tone was so pure, so devoid of any tinge of sentimentality or personal ego, that it was the nearest thing to perfect beauty I have ever heard. Aside from the adulation of a tiny group of musicians and fans, he had only two write-ups in his life, neither of them particularly laudatory; his obituary in his home-town paper concluded with the opinion that "Bixie will be forgotten as quickly as the popular songs he played," and no one ever thought to even record his voice, but I, and all who knew him, will never get over Beiderbecke.

Louis and Bix are the two great originators of jazz. I'm not arguing about Louis, this has nothing to do with Louis and his greatness. There was the ethereal beauty of Bix's tone, with its heart-melting blend of pure joyousness and wistful haunting sadness. There was his sense of form, his hotness, his shining fresh ideas, his lyricism, his swing, his perfect intonation, and his impeccable, matchless taste. His intervals were so orderly, so indescribably right, like a line of poetry. Listen to those intervals and try to explain how Bix could think to play like that. Whom did he have to hear? Bessie Smith? Louis? They knew what they knew, but who could teach Bix what he knew? Bix *knew*.

Bix's whole background of jazz was essentially white, and his whole conception of jazz was based primarily on his white musical heritage. But that's not to say that Bix was a pale carbon copy of an alien Negro art. This is the point at which most people go astray. The point is that the Negroes did fashion a wholly new music, but its roots were embedded in European music as well as in the Negro. Without the American Negro there would be no jazz, and without the white man there would be no jazz. Jazz has never existed in Africa, and it doesn't exist there today. It was formed from the two musical cultures: from the African, which has the highest development of rhythm in the world, and from the European, which has the greatest development of harmony in the world; and it happened in America.

And it was not only European music, but the European religion, the Bible, that made jazz, just as it was the Bible, the
Judaeo-Christian religion, that was the basis of all the great art
of Europe—the painting and the architecture and the classical
music. People forget that it all came out of the church. Just as
jazz did. Jazz's beginnings were just as respectable as classical
music's beginnings. Jazz came from the gospel songs, and from
the work songs and the blues, just as the European classical music
is a blend of church and folk music. All the colored musicians
know that their music has its wellsprings in gospel singing, but
they forget their gospel songs are based on the Bible, and that
the frame for their gospel songs came from the old English and
Scottish psalm singing, from which the early Negro slaves
learned the basic harmonies of the white man's music. The Bible
gave those poor, bewildered, uprooted Negro people an identity
—they were God's children—and they took to that Bible like a
duck to water, and in taking to the Bible, and to the harmonies,
they eventually came up with jazz. The American Negroes not
only took to the Bible from the very start; they're showing the
white man today how to live up to what the Bible teaches.

In taking for granted the most obvious of the obvious—the
fact that without the European harmonic development there
would be no jazz at all, no orderly frame on which to build the
beat—a very confused view of the whole situation has grown
up. The ones most guilty of this confusion are the ones closest
to and most familiar with the European musical tradition—the
European jazz writers, who idealized the Negro jazz artist and
scorned the white jazzmen as mere imitators—a sort of reverse
racial prejudice.

An innate feeling for harmony is just as ingrained and natural
to the white man as rhythm is to the colored. Barbershop harmony is the great white American pastime. Every time a group
of white people get together at a party they inevitably end up

around a piano, harmonizing their hearts out. Imagine if jazz had been created the other way around, by white Americans sold into slavery in Africa. The white men would have gathered together in the evenings in the slave quarters and harmonized their troubles away with "Down by the Old Mill Stream" and "Sweet Adeline" and the African boss would have shaken his head wonderingly and said, "Man, what a marvelous gift for harmony those poor white bastards have. It's just *born* in them!"

Chapter 3

The summer of 1928 seemed endless. I didn't know how to break out of the vacuum I was in. Here I was nineteen years old and though I had always had my own little way of playing, I still felt I couldn't play the way I wanted to. There was only one thing I was sure of—that it was hopeless for jazz in Boston— and when I wasn't worrying about the music, I was mooning away the days dreaming about becoming an aviator like Charles Lindbergh and having all the girls admire me, or owning a Stutz Bearcat and having all the girls admire me. The rest of the time I spent glued to my little wind-up Victrola playing the latest records over and over and asking myself as I listened to each one: Is this it?

And as I listened and wondered, another question kept popping up too— the burning question one asks oneself at nineteen: What am I going to do with my life? Then one day while listening to one of Louis's Hot Five records, I suddenly found at least part of the answer. If this was the kind of jazz going on in Chicago, then Chicago was the place to be. I had no clear idea of what I expected to do there or how I'd even get there, but as the summer droned wearily on, just thinking the words "I'm going to Chicago" was like discovering a New World.

In August I had a job in Hartford, where there was even less interest in jazz than in Boston. The musicians in the band used to laugh at me when they heard my Louis records; to them it was just a lot of clatter. The picture was very bleak, not to say pitch black, when I met Charlie Joindreau at a party given by some of the guys at my rooming house. After most of the others had left, Charlie, in a mellow mood from all the home-made beer, began talking about Sonny Greer, the great drummer in The Washingtonians, Duke Ellington's new band, which was playing at the Kentucky Club in New York. Charlie played drums himself in the pit band at the Capitol Theatre in New York, but he came back to Hartford every Sunday to see his family. When he discovered I knew about Louis and Bix, he reacted like a prospector who has struck gold, and he'd make a beeline for my room every Sunday evening to listen to records and talk about jazz. It wasn't long before I was telling him about my wanting to go to Chicago. "But I don't know anyone there," I ended up.

"I do," Charlie said. It was as simple as that. The next thing I knew we were down at the railroad station buying two tickets to Chicago.

I had been helping to support my mother and father with my cornet for several years now, as my father's grocery store never did very well and most of my brothers and sisters were married and had families of their own. My parents were alarmed when I told them I was going to look for work in Chicago, but there was nothing much they could say since they knew I'd send them whatever money I could. I packed my tuxedo, my phonograph, and my records, grabbed my cornet case, and caught the train to Chicago with Charlie Joindreau, just in time to catch the tail end of all the great jazz that had been played there from the early twenties.

I didn't know Charlie very well. The few Sunday afternoons we had spent together we had talked about nothing but music and musicians. He was an easygoing handsome blond fellow in his middle twenties who didn't seem to have a care in the world, but on that endless train ride we got to talking more personally, and although he didn't go into particulars I gathered he was having domestic troubles. I realized then that for Charlie, going to Chicago was a way of running away from his troubles, which is why he jumped at the idea so quickly. I felt sorry for him because he seemed such a nice clean guy, but I never did get a chance to know him much better. We no sooner arrived at Union Station in Chicago the next afternoon when Charlie took off on some private business of his own.

"I'll meet you later at the musicians' union," he called back over his shoulder.

There was nothing to do but check my valise and phonograph at the station, look up the union's address in the telephone book, and wend my way down there to wait for Charlie. After a couple of hours, I began counting the bricks in the building across the street. When the union closed for the night, I was meditating on the problem of how many bricks a man could lay in one day and how long it would take to do the job. Around midnight, hunger drove me to a crummy little restaurant across the street, and I spent the rest of the night on a bench in the little park nearby, still mentally counting bricks. I didn't have sense enough to check into a hotel; all I could think of doing was to wait for Charlie. At dawn I had breakfast in the same little joint, cleaned myself up as best I could, and went back to sit on the front steps of the union again. When Charlie finally showed up around noon, looking as if he hadn't slept all night either, I was so tired of bricklaying that I forgot to be mad at him.

In the course of his evening, Charlie had found out about a rooming house at 2400 North where we could rent a couple of little rooms at four dollars a week, and after we had picked up our bags from the station, hung up our tuxedos, and put Louis's "Mahogany Hall Stomp" on the phonograph, Charlie produced a bottle of gin. One drink later, the wonderful excitement of being in Chicago began to flood over me again; four drinks later, I couldn't see. It was my first experience in being temporarily blinded by bootleg gin. I began to have my doubts not only about Chicago, but about Charlie.

"We'll go to the musicians' union today to look for work," Charlie announced the next afternoon when we crawled out of bed.

"Great!" I croaked, surprised that I could stand up, let alone speak. My knees were jelly, my head was splitting, and my stomach was very undecided, but I could see again—at least, I could when the room stopped whirling.

"But first I have a little business to attend to," Charlie said, squinting at the mirror with a pained expression as he struggled with his bow tie.

My heart sank.

"You go on ahead," he continued, "and I'll meet you at the union. Honest!" he added quickly as I opened my mouth.

I shut my mouth and took the trolley downtown to my old stand on the union steps. I was deep in construction problems again when a dapper young fellow in a majestic black derby strolled past me up the steps, stopped, and came back. I thought he was at least the owner of the Palmer House, he had such an imperiously elegant air about him.

"Who," he intoned in a richly cultivated voice, "are you?"

I told him my name, where I was from, and why I had left Boston. I was kind of interested in hearing the story myself— by this time I'd almost forgotten why I'd come to Chicago.

"Young man," he said when I had finished, "this is your lucky day. Bud Freeman is the name. Come with me." And taking my elbow, he ushered me into the union hall.

Of all the aspiring young white musicians in Chicago in the twenties, I couldn't have picked a more enthusiastic and encouraging friend than the one Fate sent along that day in the person of Bud Freeman. He promptly took me under his wing, and more than anyone else it was due to Bud Freeman's unflagging interest and help that I got anywhere in Chicago. He not only got me all the work then and for years afterward, but above all Bud made me feel like something when I wasn't anything.

Bud had met Charlie Joindreau earlier that summer when he was in New York with Eddie Condon, who was still there, and when Charlie came along a few minutes later it was old home week. After we registered at the union for temporary work permits, Bud jotted down our address and promised to call us when he had any work. The next day, Charlie took me down to radio station WGN to hear another of Jean Goldkette's bands, with Sterling Bose on trumpet and Max Farley and Bill Green on saxes. Sterling Bose's playing sounded marvelous; of all the trumpeters influenced by Beiderbecke, he was the one who sounded closest to Bix. Charlie stayed around to chew the fat with his many friends in the band so I took myself off to a movie and watched Ronald Colman being noble with Vilma Banky who, I felt sure, would bring out the noble streak in Simon Legree.

Charlie wasn't in his room the next day, or the day after, and finally I went back to the radio station to see if the Goldkette men had word of him. They told me he had left for a job in Texas for Goldkette. The fact that he had left word he would send for me didn't do much to cheer me up in the meantime. As unreliable as Charlie was, he was my only link with home in this strange new city, and his desertion hit me harder than the bootleg gin.

I never saw Charlie again. I guess Chicago wasn't far enough away for him, but neither was Texas. A few months later he committed suicide there. It took me a long time to get over the shock of it.

After I became reconciled to the idea of being on my own now that Charlie had left town, I spent the next few days wandering around the city in a daze of bewildered excitement. Although I was all alone in a little beat-up room in a strange city with no work in sight, I felt I was living just being in

Chicago. The signs that plastered the trolley cars and elevated trains advertising Chicago as "The Paris of America" kept reminding me that if Lindbergh could make it alone to Paris I should be able to make out in Chicago. While Chicago didn't exactly look like my idea of Paris, I was in no mood to quibble, and I don't think I even noticed the miles and miles of low, ugly tenements huddled on the flat land under an empty prairie sky, or the cheap hurly-burly of the Loop, or the moody Chicago River winding its dark-green way through the city. I was too busy absorbing the bursting feeling of life in the city, engendered by the hordes of eager young people from midwestern farms and small towns who swarmed into Chicago by the thousands; by the multitudes of Negroes who poured in from the dying cotton and sawmill towns of the deep South, bringing with them their gospel hymns and their earthy blues and work songs and back-country shouts and hollers; and by the excitement sparked by the new writers and artists and musicians caught up in the ferment of discovery of themselves and of the newly emerging American art. In the wake of the tide of immigrants from the hinterlands came the gamblers, the promoters, the bootleggers, and the gangsters, to make Chicago a wide-open, riproaring town, where cattlemen and hillbillies rubbed shoulders with poets and G men, tycoons and politicians, baseball players and B girls, racketeers and reformers.

And in the midst of all this bubbling, yeasty stew, the new phenomenon of jazz was quietly simmering on its own burners. The Mississippi, the Father of Rivers, had been helping to spread the new music to the cities and towns that lined its shores and had been disgorging jazzmen, Negro and white, into Chicago from the South for well over a decade now. The first jazz band heard by the young white Chicago schoolboys who were to take up the torch of jazz was the white New Orleans Rhythm Kings, with Paul Mares, George Brunis and Leon Rappolo, who came to Chicago in the early twenties. When they weren't sneaking into the Blue Friars Inn to hear the N.O.R.K. band

in person, these aspiring young musicians were grouped around
a phonograph at one of the boys' homes teaching themselves to
play, bar by bar, from the N.O.R.K. records. When they discovered King Oliver's Creole Jazz Band, with the young Louis
Armstrong on second cornet, at the Lincoln Gardens on the
South Side, they nearly went crazy with excitement. Then Bix
came along with a still different style, and they not only went
wild over him, they later played and recorded with him. Along
with all this, they also listened to the great blues singer, Bessie
Smith, and it was from all these sources that the young Midwesterners evolved their own style and feeling, which came to
be called the "Chicago style."

   That chance meeting with Bud Freeman opened the door for
me into this seething world of new ideas, new sounds, and new
thinking that was Chicago in the twenties as I began to meet
some of these young white musicians who were to contribute
so much to jazz—Frank Teschmaker, George Wettling, Dave
Tough, Jimmy McPartland, Jess Stacy, Gene Krupa, Wingy
Manone, Muggsy Spanier, Benny Goodman, Rod Cless, Floyd
O'Brien—all extraordinary men, dreamers and artists. It began
with a phone call from a fellow named Charlie Pierce, whom
Bud had told about me. Charlie Pierce, who worked in his
father's butcher shop when he wasn't playing alto sax and booking jobs and record dates for musicians, turned out to be a great
big fat guy with a genial, expansive nature and a mean, swinging tone on his horn. Charlie was running regular Sunday-
afternoon dances at the Cocoanut Grove restaurant at Sixty-third
and Cottage Grove out on the South Side, and he hired me for
the coming Sunday.

   There were three reeds in the band, with Rod Cless and
Charlie Pierce on saxophone as well as Bud Freeman, and when
we kicked off the first set with "Avalon," I couldn't believe what
was happening. Now I knew how Lindbergh felt, only better.
For the first time in my life I was playing with musicians who
could swing—this was like flying *without* an airplane.

Charlie Pierce had another band working during the week at the Cinderella Chinese restaurant at Cottage Grove. George Wettling, Frank Teschmaker and Floyd O'Brien were in the band, and if I had thought my cup was full on Sunday, it was now overflowing. To play with George Wettling on drums in those days was one of the greatest thrills I ever had. The crush roll of the Chicago drummers was unheard of back East, where they were still playing oompah and ricky-tick, breaking up the rhythm into choppy syncopation instead of keeping a steady beat you could play against. George had soaked up the rhythm as a kid, making the rounds of the South Side colored cabarets every evening on his bicycle and listening out on the curb to the Negro bands. And the marvel of it all was that I fitted in with these musicians as naturally as a baseball bat fitted into Babe Ruth's hands. Though barely in their twenties themselves these men had been deeply immersed in the music for six or seven years, absorbing it firsthand from the New Orleans jazz-men while developing their own style and feeling, whereas I had heard it only in tantalizing dribbles and snatches. Being welcomed as one of them the first time they heard me play was not only like coming home, it was feeling that the candle had been kept burning in the window for me all those years.

That nervous, ragged, ricky-tick beat of the white dance bands of the twenties—that was one of the factors that had been at the bottom of my confusion when I listened to my records back home in Boston, trying so desperately to unravel the puzzle of jazz. None of the white musicians I heard on them could keep time. None of the early white popular bands had really understood the beat yet. And that was why the Chicago gang instinctively latched on to me the first time around, for ignorant and inexperienced as I was, I had the innate feeling of the beat and of playing the melody simply and purely without all the little flutings and corny licks that were regarded as "hot" in those days. When I think of those twenties bands with that dreadful twenties beat that Bix was usually trapped in (except when

Eddie Lang was on guitar), it's no mystery to me that he drank
himself to death.

Chicago was vibrating with that great jazz beat. The Negro
pianists who congregated there in the twenties were the innovators of the boogie-woogie style of playing, with its lack of
interest in harmony and melody, but with its marvelous rhythmic
power and complexity. Jimmy Yancey, Pine Top Smith, Meade
Lux Lewis, Albert Ammons, and Pete Johnson were the boogie-
woogie kings of Chicago's South Side. And Earl Hines, the
Pittsburgh-born pianist who played with Louis Armstrong, was
busy evolving his lean revolutionary "trumpet style" piano.

In the following months it seemed as though every day was
the Fourth of July. After the Sunday dances at the Cocoanut
Grove, which were over about eight o'clock, Bud used to take
me with him down to the Loop in a cab. Many of the taxis then
were reconverted limousines, and their air of luxury and intrigue
added a special zing to the thrill of hurtling along the wide,
windy boulevards and to the anticipation of the evening ahead—
of what we thought was man-of-the-world "wine, women, and
song" stuff.

I don't know if it was because I was young, or if it was different in those days because so few people knew about the music
and those who did felt close to one another, but everyone seemed
to go out of his way to be encouraging. After I'd take a chorus,
Teschmaker would shake his head unbelievingly and say, "What
a tone!" and I'd be torn between the elation of believing him
and the misery of feeling I could hardly play yet. Wingy
Manone invited me to his big apartment over on the North Side
for many a sizzling pot of red beans and rice, gumbo, shrimp
creole, and huge platters of ham and eggs. Though Wingy had
lost his right arm as the result of a streetcar accident when he
was a boy down in New Orleans, he was a most independent
and resourceful fellow. I have never heard Wingy refer in any
way to his difficulty in playing the trumpet with one hand, and
he no more let his loss stop him from playing his horn than

he let it interfere with his hospitality. Cornetist Jimmy McPart-land, who had replaced Beiderbecke in the Wolverines when Bix left the band, was always ready to give you a boost, and when I played a job on Christmas Eve with jazz pianist Jess Stacy, Jess went out of his way to make sure I reached home safely from the South Side, which was especially wide open on Christmas Eve. Stacy, growing up in Cape Girardeau, Missouri, one of the steamboat stops on the Mississippi, had early fallen under the spell of the riverboat jazz bands, and he was scarcely out of short pants before he was playing in a riverboat band himself. Stacy's clean, crisp style later helped swing the great Benny Goodman and Tommy Dorsey bands, but he is to this day nowhere as well-known as he deserves. I first met Stacy on a date for which Charlie Pierce had optimistically booked me to lead a band with Muggsy Spanier, Wingy Manone, Stacy, and Wettling. How I managed it I'll never know. The interest in jazz was so keen in those days that when a couple of the musicians took me to a swanky speakeasy to hear Mildred Bailey, the men in Spike Hamilton's band invited me out into the kitchen between sets to hear me play.

Chicago was a great town for clarinets in the twenties. There used to be talk in those days that Teschmaker could play Benny Goodman off the stand. Benny was great in those days, too, but as great as Benny was, Tesch had it over him then. The young Teschmaker, who was killed in a car crash in 1932, was one of the leading spirits who helped mold "Chicago" jazz. Both he and Bud Freeman always had a highly individual, peculiarly personal tone to their horns, and their temperaments and styles were completely opposite. Tesch reminded me a good deal of Beiderbecke with his quiet, manly way and his complete in-volvement with the music, although he was much more solemn and serious by nature. When he wasn't practicing on the clarinet and alto sax, he was busy with the violin and the cornet. He had a soulful, Bix quality that was very musical in spite of its wry "toughness." It's too bad that Tesch had a phobia against making records; he'd freeze up in the studio, but if he had recorded more he would have overcome it.

Bud Freeman, on the other hand, was so outgoing and enthusiastic that he was apt to rear back and laugh aloud from pure joy after taking a chorus, whether he was in a recording studio or at a noisy dance hall. And when you heard his records, even the big-swing-band records of the late thirties, you knew that that fervent personal sound that colored the four-man reed section could only be Bud. Along with Fats Waller, he has one of the happiest sounds in jazz, with his witty ideas, his great biting attack and good hard swing. I guess we all got some of that bite from Dave Tough. Once you had played with Dave you had to play that hard, biting style to keep less experienced musicians playing on time. Nowadays there isn't such a need for that bite since everybody can keep time—even the rock 'n' rollers. The "hard-boiled" urgency so characteristic of the Chicago style was also characteristic of Chicago itself, especially in the twenties, just as the relaxed, easygoing New Orleans style came from the slower-tempoed, easygoing southern port.

Though Tesch and his wife had only a one-room apartment, they had me stay over many times, putting me up on the couch after a late night, and we used to do a lot of talking and thinking about the music into the small hours. I was always wondering about the two schools of jazz—the Louis school and the Bix school—and Tesch and I agreed that Bix was the one we liked best. I knew Louis was great, but I actually knew very little about him then. Bix had heard a lot of Louis and Bessie Smith and he was getting the feeling from the colored music, but it came out so different and so individual that I wondered how this could be. Jazz was so new; we were all so interested and it was a wonderful, thrilling thing to us—the idea of these two great players who were leading the way in the music. There never was any question of anyone else leading the way. These were the two giants in a whole era of great music that was developing naturally, forming and shaping itself by the men who were creating it, with no critics around yet to spoil it all. None of the critics had ever heard this music while it was being made, and they never got over it. When the critics, foreign and domestic, came along a decade later and called it Art, they substituted Art for the music, and between them they nearly strangled one of the best things that ever happened to keep people sane. It came out of America, and it was as great as even the electric bulb. Just imagine that the U.S. has lighted up the world with electricity and with jazz!

As thrilling as it was then in Chicago, it wasn't smooth sailing for me in every department. This was the era of Ben Hecht and Ring Lardner, Sinclair Lewis and Sherwood Anderson, H. L. Mencken and Hemingway, F. Scott Fitzgerald and Eugene O'Neill, and it seemed to me—who up to now had seldom cracked open a book—that all the fellows in the Chicago crowd were on a genius kick. Dave Tough was our ringleader. The son of a well-to-do Oak Park physician, Dave was a brilliant, multitalented young man with a passion for learning. He had just returned from Paris and he was on fire with the excitement of the new thinking that came out of the first World War. After playing all night, Bud and his brother Arnie, Dave, and I would sneak into Bud's house as soon as his father, who was a widower, left for work in the morning, and instead of sleeping we'd stay up all day talking about writers and literature and painting and music and all the great new ideas that were in the air. Or, rather, they'd talk and I'd listen. I never said anything; I came to be *known* for not saying anything. I didn't speak for years. I didn't know what to say about all this, for one thing, and I just wanted to hear what was going on.

Bud was always extremely impressionable and he had the most sensitive aesthetic sense. Dave was more critical and probing. Bud was in love with the theatre and with literature, but Dave wanted to master everything he was interested in. I guess the only trouble with Bud and Dave was that they thought they were the only ones who felt that way, which usually happens with people who are so wrapped up in themselves. But it was wonderful for me to be around them because I wanted to know why I felt that way, too. I could see myself in them—they expressed all my feelings for me. America was still so young and new then and we all had the feeling of wanting to do something great.

The Chicago crowd taught me much by telling me about the books and the writers, and later on, back home in Boston, I found the books and read them all so I could understand it better. Dave Tough wouldn't be in a band a week before he had the whole band showing up for work with books under their arms. He was always intrigued that I could read for enjoyment rather than for learning. He thought I was funny, and he'd ride me about it—Dave had his devastatingly caustic side, too—but I didn't let it bother me too much for I always felt there were other ways to learn besides from books.

It was all very heady stuff for me, discovering there was an exciting new world going on in the thinking and the writing as well as in the music , and I soaked it up like a sponge. I didn't do very well in another line of intoxication, though. Not that I didn't like whiskey, and not that I didn't try, but my system didn't burn it off quickly and it would take me a whole day to straighten out where they'd be fine the next morning. Besides, I never felt I could play well when I was loaded, and that always brought me down. But it didn't stop me from emulating them in that department, too.

It was a fast city and a fast life, a "toddlin' " town, with the bootleg whiskey, the gambling, the whorehouses, the reefer smoking, and the speakeasies, but mostly we were able to keep out of trouble. Almost everyone in Chicago in those days was sooner or later, in one way or another—mostly another—involved with racketeers and gangsters, but I had only one brief brush with the Chicago underworld when George Wettling had a call one afternoon to audition for a job at the Wigwam Club, which was run by a big-time gambler. Six of us piled into

George's blue Nash and drove down there, and after we had played for about an hour the gangster removed his cigar from his puffy lips long enough to say the band was hired.

"You guys be here tonight at eight," he paused, and added menacingly, out of sheer habit, ". . . *or else!*" We broke the world's record for packing up our instruments and we didn't show up at eight that night or ever.

In spite of all the enticements and distractions of Chicago in the roaring twenties, what we were interested in was playing and learning how to play. We played for dancing—the one-step, the Charleston, the fox trot, the shimmy, the Black Bottom, the Lindy Hop—and we played mainly the pop tunes of the day. Everybody danced in those days, and ballrooms bloomed in every town and city. It wasn't until I joined the Summa Cum Laude band in the late thirties that I learned the standard Dixieland repertoire of marches and rags and blues and stomps. All the musicians—Jimmie Noone, Earl Hines, Baby Dodds, Louis Armstrong, King Oliver, Barney Bigard, Johnny Dodds—just played their music to enjoy it and have a good time, and—in the first place—to make a living. Several years later, I asked Lil Armstrong, Louis's former wife, how they all had felt about Louis's playing then, in the Sunset Café days in Chicago with King Oliver. "We didn't think anything about it," Lil Armstrong said. "He just played like that and we liked it fine, but it wasn't until the white folks started writing about it later on and saying it was so artistic that we really thought about it as unusual or special." But although our writers and painters and musicians were beginning to discover America, the public still thought anything not imported from Europe wasn't culture, so we were safe from the critics for a while.

It wasn't until January of 1929, after I had been in Chicago nearly five months, that I finally heard Louis Armstrong play, when Wingy Manone and George Wettling took me to the Savoy Ballroom on the South Side. Louis was playing in Carroll Dickerson's band, with Zutty Singleton on drums, and there

were two other bands, McKinney's Cotton Pickers and Tubby
Hall's band with Kid Ory on trombone. When Louis came over
to the table to greet Wingy and George, I was introduced to
him. From listening to his records I already had some inkling
of the warmth and power of the man, but I was totally unprepared for that remarkable penetrating awareness underneath
the genial, easygoing manner. All his senses seem to receive impressions of you; you feel he's not so much sizing you up as
opening his mind to you, like a receiving set. You can't fake it
with Louis. He can tell.

I was just as unprepared for the full impact of his playing,
too. When the Carroll Dickerson band went on the stand, Louis
started off with the introduction to "West End Blues," and he
broke the place up. He broke me up, too. I sent one quivering
look at Wingy and George and took my leave. The sheer loveli-
ness of Bix's tone and feeling had captured me, but the combination of Louis's dazzling virtuosity and sensational brilliance of
tone so overwhelmed me that I felt as if I had stared into the
sun's eye. All I could think of doing was to run away and hide
till the blindness left me.

Louis is *the* great creative jazz genius. He is the sum total of
all the parts—they all add up to Louis. Above all—above all
the electrifying tone, the magnificence of his ideas and the
rightness of his harmonic sense, his superb technique, his power
and ease, his hotness and intensity, his complete mastery of his
horn—above all this, he had the swing. No one knew what swing
was till Louis came along. It's more than just the beat, it's con-
ceiving the phrases in the very feeling of the beat, molding and
building them so that they're an integral, indivisible part of the
tempo. The others had the idea of it, but Louis could do it; he
was the heir of all that had gone before and the father of all
that was to come.

Louis's singing, too, set the standard for popular ballad singing. In the early days, his voice had little of the gravelly tones
it acquired later; it was a sweet tenor, in perfect pitch, and it

was from Louis's intonation, his phrasing, and his swing that everyone else learned how it should be done.

This roly, rotund brown-skinned man with his marvelously expressive face, the comfortably broad-nostriled snub nose, the lips scarred from all that blowing, the wise, knowing, and innocent eyes, radiates warmth and energy like a cozy fireplace. But unaffected and unphony as he is, Louis has always been king. The white people didn't know about him for a long while, but he always had an enormous following among the colored people right from the start. He was always regal; from the very beginning the musicians, colored and white, always came to *him*, and he'd hold court wherever he happened to be—backstage at a theatre or night club, between takes at a recording studio, or soaking in a steaming tub in his hotel bathroom.

With all his genius, he has never lost his perspective. Louis knows who he is. Not only that, he knows who you are, and though he is the most approachable, most genuine person in the world, and though his charity is legendary, you can't mess with Louis. He has kept straight with himself because his trumpet comes first—that's Louis's first law. To him his playing is a gift, and he'll just sit there and think about the horn before he gets ready to play—accepting his gift, he calls it. World-famous and wealthy as he has been for over thirty-five years, Louis has never forgotten what he wants to do—just play that music—and in doing just that he has done everything.

In the early days, jazz wasn't considered an art, it was a song-and-dance music. In 1926 at the Sunset Café in Chicago, Louis and three other musicians, including Earl Hines, used to close the floor show by doing the Charleston—and they really did it. Sometimes Louis and Zutty Singleton would do a specialty number that broke the place up, with Zutty dressed up as a tough waterfront woman sashaying down the aisle to interrupt Louis's song. Louis had a preacher act, too; he'd call himself Reverend Satchmo, put on a frock coat, and deliver a mock sermon. These jazzmen thought of themselves as entertainers and they used comedy routines as a regular part of their performances.

A week or so after I first heard Louis play, I had a letter from my sister Rose saying that my parents missed me and wanted me to come home. The last thing I wanted to do was to leave Chicago, but this was the first time I'd ever been away so long and in spite of the excitement I was a little homesick by now and worried about my parents. At home I found my mother and father living in a couple of dark little rooms in back of Pa's grocery store. Within a day I found a comfortable, bright little apartment for thirty-eight dollars a month, and my parents lived there until they died.

Back on the jobs in Boston, everyone began talking about me, for I was no sooner on a job than I started trying to teach the drummer how to keep time. I was dying to play the way I played in Chicago but I couldn't do it in a band that couldn't keep time. I didn't make myself very popular, but even so, my reputation around Boston as a jazz trumpet was enhanced.

Then, one rainy afternoon less than a month later a telegram arrived from Charlie Pierce. It was a fifty-word wire about a job at the Persian Ballroom in Chicago, giving all the particulars, when the job was to start, how much it paid, who the other musicians were, what the hours were, and saying that they'd send me the money for the train fare. I didn't have to think twice to wire back my one-word answer—"YES"—which the musicians still kid me about.

"If it makes you so happy, go," my mother said, coming to the door while I packed, "only take care of yourself and don't stay so long this time."

I didn't stay in Chicago very long this time and I didn't take very good care of myself, for as it turned out, I ended up in the hospital with a broken arm. Everything seemed to go wrong on this second trip right from the start.

First of all, the job fell through because the Chicago union wouldn't let me work. All the time I was in Chicago I was allowed to work only two or three nights a week, since union regulations require six months' residence before you can take a steady job. Charlie Pierce rang up NO SALE on the butcher-shop cash register and took out the money for my return fare, but Josh Billings and Dave Tough had more adventurous ideas. "Don't waste the money on railroad fare," they said. "Let's buy us a car and drive back to Boston. Who knows what we might run into on the way."

The thought of Dave Tough in Boston was intriguing. A few minutes later, we drove out of a used-car lot in a rattletrap 1923 Ford that must have been used for plowing. And since there were still a few dollars left over we drove straight to George Wettling's house where there was always a card game going on. Buying the car had lifted me out of the dumps and I came in very strong.

"These guys play rough, Maxie," George said, looking worried.

"So do I," I said. I pulled up a chair and they dealt me in. I was a card player from way back and I was full of confidence and in about three minutes I lost all my money. I should have known better. Tesch was a card shark from further back than I was. All he did between sets was play cards, and when we played at the Chinese restaurant at Sixty-second and Cottage Grove he used to take on the waiters—and the Chinese are the original card sharks of all time.

It was a very cold winter, that winter of 1929. At dawn Dave and Josh and I, penniless, left George's and went outside into the freezing night, cranked up the Ford, and wheezed over to Bud Freeman's house where we shivered in the car till Bud's father left for work. The next week we were really scratching. One night Dave and I drove to a friend's house at suppertime. His wife fixed Dave a plate of food. They didn't have much, so I said I wasn't hungry, but whenever she'd leave the room I'd grab a fork and take a fast turn eating from Dave's plate. A night or so later when we were trying to start up the old Ford, the final catastrophe struck. Frank Veneer got in the car to start the motor while I cranked. He made the mistake of pulling the spark down, making the car buck, and it crashed down on my arm, breaking my wrist. Josh rushed me over to his house where his father, who was a doctor, put it in a temporary splint before taking me over to St. Vincent's Hospital to have it set.

I was really in a pickle now, with no money and my arm in a cast. The next day I wired my family for train fare home, explaining about my arm. My mother and father came themselves and took me back home by train to Boston.

Chapter 4

"She won't go to Harlem in ermine and pearls. . . ." Lorenz Hart's lyrics, written in 1937, reflected the post-depression social consciousness, but in the twenties everybody went to Harlem—society people, theatre people, literary, artistic, and sports figures, politicians and gamblers and businessmen—and the more elite the customers and the more elegant their finery, the more it added to the merriment. For despite the drab poverty, the rotten housing, the menial jobs, the low pay, and the discrimination and segregation, Harlem was the first great chance for the thousands of southern Negroes who poured into New York after World War I, and though they were held down, they had the hope of better times. In the twenties, the colored people of Harlem were just glad to be living—never mind for the moment about the freedom. Harlem hummed around the clock as it went about its business of making ends meet, and while the respectable, hard-working core of day-employed folk who wanted no part of high life—or low life, especially jazz—took their rest, another part of the population was up all night running their night clubs and speakeasies and restaurants and cooking their pigs' feet and fried chitt'lin's and barbecued spare ribs and brewing

45

their bathtub gin and corn whiskey and throwing their im-
promptu house-rent parties and all-night card games—and making their music.

In this stage of their struggle, the people of Harlem were not
only cheered and elated at the idea that they had something the
white folks admired, they naturally welcomed the nightly flood
of cash customers the music attracted. And though their own
deep sense of pride and injustice burned undiminished, and
though certain white artistic circles went in heavily for a kind
of phony cultural mystique of the Negro, and though there was
an element of titillation at the sight of black and white partners
on the dance floor, the over-all spirit was the innocence and the
optimism of the twenties. The Harlem musicians, who took
special joy in astounding the white musicians, used to swing so
hard that smoke almost came out of their horns, and the m.c. at
the Saratoga Club used to make it a special point after each
show "to thank the white musicians for coming up here to see
us," although it was obvious that the shoe was on the other foot.

Plain everyday people went to Harlem, too, to dine in the
excellent uptown restaurants. Greenwich Village and Harlem
were the two places to eat in those days. And though Chicago
was the focal point of jazz in the mid-twenties, Harlem wasn't
exactly dormant then, either. Musicians like Fletcher Henderson,
Don Redman, and William McKinney had bands at one time
or another in the Lenox Club, Small's Paradise, and Dickie
Wells'. Chick Webb had a little band in The Nest before he
had his big band jumping at the Savoy Ballroom. And the Big
Three in Harlem in the late twenties—the Cotton Club, Connie's
Inn, and the Saratoga Club—were rocking the rafters night after
night. Although the tab at the Cotton Club was too steep for
me ever to get in to hear Duke Ellington's band, I didn't feel
underprivileged by having to hang out in the Saratoga Club,
which, while not a big, fancy show place like the others, had a
late, late show around 4 or 5 A.M., and all the musicians used
to drop in after work to hear Luis Russell's great orchestra, with

Henry "Red" Allen, J. C. Higginbotham, Albert Nicholas, Paul Barbarin, Charlie Holmes, and Pops Foster.

Gene Krupa, who was working in the pit band of George Gershwin's *Strike Up the Band*, in 1929, would round up Bud Freeman, Dave Tough, Eddie Condon, and me on payday, when he was flush, and take us up to the Saratoga to hear Luis Russell's band swing the floor show. Dramatically handsome with that black shock of hair and flashing white smile, Gene was as good inside as he looked outside in those days, and he has never changed. The job in *Strike Up the Band* was his first big break in New York. Gershwin was crazy about his playing, and no wonder, because Gene was the first white drummer in a Broadway pit band who could swing the beat so that the chorus girls could kick in time.

The floor show was the big thing in those days. To hear Louis Armstrong swing the floor show at Connie's Inn in 1929 was *really* something. He'd get that chorus line of shapely young sepia-skinned girls stepping high, wide, and I mean hot. The next year, in 1930, Louis was appearing downtown on Broadway in the *Hot Chocolates* revue, playing and singing "Ain't Misbehavin' " and getting himself known to the white world.

But one of the greatest things going on in Harlem then was the piano players, who were in the throes of originating the Harlem stride piano style, developing it out of the old ragtime style by working out a richer chordal structure and a more flowing melodic and rhythmic line, free from the choppiness of ragtime. Fats Waller, James P. Johnson, and Willie the Lion Smith seemed to be running all the house-rent parties in Harlem in the twenties. The charge was a dollar admission for all the pigs' feet, home-fried potatoes, and fried chicken you could eat, and if you wanted more action than listening to the fabulous piano and drum or guitar combo, you could cut yourself into the card game going on in one room or the crap shooting in the next. Pod's and Jerry's at 133rd Street had Willie the Lion Smith as its regular pianist, but some time between midnight and dawn

James P. Johnson or Fats Waller or Luckey Roberts or all three
would come rolling in and the cutting contests would be on.
Cutting contests are good, clean, bloodless manslaughter, committed in the deepest sincerity. For men to whom music is a
way of life, these contests separate the men from the boys. When
one musician cuts another on his instrument, the loser submits
to his master, because he is so sincere himself. "Man, you
showed me! You really *showed* me tonight!" But the loser lives
for the next session when *he*'ll cut the master and be king again.

You'd hear a lot of marvelous girl singers in the clubs along
135th Street, too. In the course of going from table to table, a
singer would take about fifteen choruses of a song, and the con-
stant repetition would drive her to fool around with the phrasing
and the beat, thus taking the evolution of jazz singing another
step along the way toward breaking out of the rigid confines of
the tune. Some of the singers displayed other talents, in their
way of picking up their tips while going from table to table,
and some of the singers were exotic Negro female impersonators.
One of the most renowned of these, a glamorous creature in
polished satin and flashing jewels who called herself Gloria
Swanson, was one of the big attractions at Dickie Wells' night
club.

While I was still recuperating from that ill-fated second trip
to Chicago, Bud Freeman sent for me again to play a job in
Binghamton, New York. Although my broken wrist was still
in a sling, there was nothing wrong with my lip, as I explained
to my mother while she helped me pack. At the end of our first
week in Binghamton, the manager ran off with the money, in
time-honored show-business tradition, leaving us stranded until
the ever-resourceful Bud bailed us out by borrowing our fare
home from one of his friends up there. A short time later I was
in New York, and when I heard Louis was playing up in Harlem
I went up to hear him. Although I had met Louis only a couple
of times by then, he came over to my table to say hello, and in
about two minutes I was telling him about my experience in

Binghamton. You just naturally spill your troubles to that warm-hearted man, but I was completely unprepared for him to put his hand in his pocket and pull out some bills. "We're all entitled to our ups and downs in this life," Louis said gruffly, "but a cat has to hold up his head. Here, pops, tuck this away." I kept refusing and he kept insisting until I finally agreed to a couple of fives on the condition that he would let me pay him back. It wasn't until a year later that I had the chance. I used to frequent a place in Boston called the Railroad Club, a boarding-house for professional Negroes, where I used to sit in with a piano player named Henry. One night while I was there, Louis, who was in town for an engagement, came in to catch a quick meal before his show, and I went over to his table and tried to pay back the ten dollars. Now it was his turn to refuse and mine to insist, until finally he growled that he'd take it on one condition—"if you autograph it for me, daddy." I felt as big as Rockefeller as I carefully wrote my name on a ten spot, which Louis gravely tucked away in his wallet.

During the course of 1929, I became acquainted with some of the other Chicago musicians I hadn't met there the previous year. Around June, Benny Goodman, who was in Ben Pollack's band at the Park Central Hotel, got a one-night job on his own to play Princeton, and Bud Freeman recommended me for the trumpet spot. The train from Boston arrived so early in the morning that I sat around in Central Park until it seemed a decent hour to telephone Benny and find out when and where to meet him that evening. Benny had hired about twenty men to play the job, but it wound up with only four of us who could keep going—Dave Tough, Joe Sullivan, Benny, and me. This was the first date I ever played with Dave as well as with Benny, who turned out to be a very unassuming, plain, quiet fellow, until he started to play. Benny was highly complimentary about my playing, and when we returned to New York he put me up overnight at his apartment. When I woke up the next afternoon, limp as a wet rag, the apartment was empty. Benny had gone off to a rehearsal, but he had left a note enclosing a five-dollar bill for my breakfast and thanking me for helping out. I felt fine.

Then a couple of weeks later I went on a tour of New England with Red Nichols. The only memorable thing to me about this job was that it was where I first met Pee Wee Russell and Eddie Condon. The twelve-piece band had Bud Freeman, who, as usual, had recommended me for the job; Pee Wee and Milt Mezzrow on saxes; Tommy Coonin, Red Nichols, and me on trumpets; Pete Peterson and Herb Taylor on trombones; Joe Sullivan on piano; Dave Tough; Sammy Levitan on bass; and Eddie Condon on guitar.

We were out on the road for three or four weeks, playing dance halls and colleges. We all worked hard in this band, and sometimes we sounded pretty good, but there was a basic conflict between Red Nichols and the band that eventually led to disaster. The Chicago boys couldn't read very well, it's true, and they did drink a lot, but even with Mezz around there was very little marijuana smoking going on. These men were all trying to make something of the band, and above all they had a great feeling for jazz. Red McKenzie had suggested these musicians when Nichols asked him for ideas, and McKenzie told him these were not only the best jazzmen around, they were out of work and available. They wanted to work but no one would hire them.

To put it bluntly, Nichols loathed us and we returned the compliment. The Chicago musicians had been brought up on Louis and Jimmie Noone and Earl Hines and Johnny Dodds and they had all played with Beiderbecke. Red Nichols loved the way Bix played and he tried to copy Bix, but now he was playing with men who knew Bix better than he did. On his part, Nichols was disappointed in this bunch of renegades and was continually frustrated by their unrestrained, free-swinging approach to jazz. At that time Bud was the only one who had real command of his instrument; the rest of us were still learning and we had our good days and our bad days, and, as far as Red

was concerned, our bad ways. Pee Wee was playing third alto
sax and he didn't have much chance to do anything in this band.

We went on the road in two old Cadillacs reminiscent of the
ones the gangsters used, one a seven-passenger black sedan and
the other a touring car with isinglass windows. Our luggage
was strapped on the running boards and we'd flip a coin every
day to see who'd have to sit on the jump seats. One evening in
New Hampshire we stayed overnight in some broken-down little
cabins beside a muddy little lake, and the next morning we
dunked ourselves in the coffee-colored water and baked in the
sun before piling back into the cars. On the road again we ran
into a violent thunderstorm which seemed to have the same
itinerary, with lightning playing tag with us for miles. That
night we were sore and stiff and painfully sunburned, and when
we unstrapped our bags from the running boards we discovered
that the cheap cardboard suitcases had melted and the color from
the red sweaters we wore on the stand had stained our shirts an
angry pink. On the bandstand that night we were a study in
reds and pinks, and when Nichols tried leading this group of
tired, sunburned guys who were so disgusted that they could
barely play, his patience lasted about two numbers before he
stalked furiously off the stand, yelling to me to take over. In a
little while everyone suddenly woke up and began swinging,
and when Red came back and heard us he got even madder. He
thought we had been holding out on him, like it was a mutiny
or something, and he took it personally. By that time we were
all so beat none of us could think straight, and Red fired the
whole band on the spot, and that was the end of that tour.

There is nothing like music for making friends—and for
making hard feelings—and the band was just as responsible for
the whole fiasco as Red was—maybe more so, since he was the
leader and it was his band. A highly proficient and well-schooled
cornetist with a great command of his horn, Red loved jazz so
much that he turned his back on a career as a legitimate trumpet
player. He has done a great deal for jazz, and he was one of the

first to record some of the then unknown jazz greats, such as
Beiderbecke, Teagarden, Teschmaker, Trumbauer, Eddie Lang,
Pee Wee Russell, Bud Freeman, Joe Sullivan, Gene Krupa,
Adrian Rollini, and Glenn Miller.

After the tour, we straggled back to New York, where several
of us checked into the Riverside Towers, at Eightieth Street
and Riverside Drive. Dave Tough and Josh Billings and I were
all squeezed into Josh's room one afternoon—all our rooms were
about the size of a closet—worrying about where our next meal
was coming from, when Gene Krupa, who was living there too,
poked his head in the door.

"I just had a call from B. A. Rolfe," he said to Dave. "He
needs a drummer to fill in tonight, but I can't make it. How
about it? You can all go over"—he nodded at Josh and me—
"and get a free meal out of it, too."

"Yes!" Josh and I said in unison before Dave could open his
mouth. "He'll take it." Dave was always fussy about whom he
played with, and we weren't taking any chances on his turning
it down.

In those days the bands used to go on the stand at six o'clock
and play for the dinner crowd. Dave and I dashed to our own
cells to get cleaned up and at five-thirty we were sitting at a
table at the Palais Royal, a huge Chinese restaurant, now the
Latin Quarter, which was Paul Whiteman's old stamping ground
in the twenties. We had ordered our dinners and were devour-
ing the celery and black olives when Dave went up on the stand
to play the first set. Rolfe gave the down beat and proceeded
to lead the band the way all leaders did in the twenties, pumping
his arms up and down with all the animation of a tin soldier.
Dave must have played all of three bars before a look of sheer
incredulity spread over his face. The next second he quietly laid
down the drumsticks and walked off the stand. He resembled a
sort of young George Arliss in those days, and he did everything
with immense, deliberate dignity. Just as Dave had stopped playing, the waiter appeared at our table, puffing under the weight

of the tray loaded with our dinners. Josh gave an agonized moan as the aroma of the sizzling steak wafted past his nose, but I grabbed him by the collar and pulled him out of his seat.

"Don't run, but don't take all day getting out of here," I whispered.

"But couldn't you have stuck it out for just *one* set?" Josh pleaded with Dave when we were safely outside.

Dave turned around and stared at us. "Didn't you *hear* them?" he said, his voice shaking with outrage. Though Josh and I were shaking with hunger, there was nothing we could say. We all felt a dedication in those days, beyond reasonable or practical considerations, for what we considered the real, true thing.

But we were practically alone in our feeling about jazz, and after a couple of more weeks of pulling in my belt until it nearly circled me twice, I returned home at the end of the summer and landed a job in one of Leo Reisman's bands to play in the new Bradford Hotel. The people who managed the Brunswick Hotel, which housed the famous Egyptian Room where Leo Reisman had reigned as Boston society's favorite maestro, had just taken over the Bradford, and they asked Leo to put an orchestra in there. Leo was now waving his baton at the Central Park Casino in New York, where Mayor Jimmy Walker, Barbara Hutton, Mark Hellinger and all the high-living society of the glittering twenties hung out, but Leo came back to Boston to put the Bradford Hotel band together. About fifty musicians showed up to audition for the band, and while I waited for my turn I began planning how I could do something different to catch Reisman's attention. Louis Armstrong's record of "I Can't Give You Anything But Love, Baby" had just come out. Of all the beautiful things on that record, aside from Louis's wonderful playing, I had been particularly struck with the way the band had held long sustained chords behind his chorus. When it was my turn to audition, I asked the saxophones to do the same while I played the melody very simply and straight.

"Sign him up!" Leo yelled to his manager when I had finished. He had never heard anything like that before, and from then on he was fascinated with me because I had dared try something unusual for those times.

Although I had been on the road with Pee Wee Russell that summer, I didn't get to know him well until he came to Boston later that fall. The Bradford Hotel job, which was one of my first big jobs, paid seventy-five dollars a week, a lot of money in those days, and I worked there all that winter, so when Pee Wee decided to quit the band he had come to Boston with, I was able to invite him to stay at my house.

Pee Wee was always the same—a shy, mournful-looking man, suffering the tortures of the extremely sensitive, so that he was often taciturn and uncommunicative, and when he did talk it was the same as his playing—he'd talk in sudden, swooping little bursts and slide in a wry remark with a shrug, crossing and uncrossing his long, nervous legs and hunching his bony shoulders or screwing up his long, sad face. My mother took one look at Pee Wee's skinny frame and headed for her kitchen. It never occurred to Pee Wee to eat when he was on his own but he docilely and absent-mindedly ate everything she put before him. Then my mother, who never touched spirits in her life, startled me by taking me aside and whispering, ". . . but Pee Wee is a man who needs his liquor," and though it was still Prohibition she got him his gin somehow. Pee Wee used to ask me where she got it, but I was as mystified as he was, and when I asked her she would just wink and say, "You think you're the only one around here has big connections?" I reported back to Pee Wee that it came from somebody's bathtub, but I couldn't say exactly whose.

I was always a great walker, and Pee Wee used to unwind himself from the rocking chair with groans and whimpers and come along with me. Our apartment was on the outskirts of town on Columbia Road and there was a way of getting to the city via a whole series of little parks. The Franklin Park Zoo was three blocks away from my house, and at night the lions roared me to

sleep. As we strolled along, Pee Wee would tell me about the
days in 1926 when he played in Bix's band at the Arcadia Ballroom in St. Louis, his home town, and we'd exchange anecdotes
about Bix by the hour. After a few months, Pee Wee took an
apartment of his own when he landed a job at the Crescent
Club, a speakeasy which opened from midnight to 5 A.M. I used
to love to stop in and hear him play the pop tunes of the day—
he played them marvelously.

By 1931, as the reverberations of the stock market crash faded
away and the country found itself sunk in a paralysis of fear, un-
employment, and want, everything slowed down to a sickening
standstill. Wall Street brokers had ceased to dive out of windows,
the unemployed were selling apples on the streets of New York
and standing in bread lines, the Lindbergh kidnaping, the Dust
Bowl, and Dillinger filled the headlines, and anybody who had a
spare dime played miniature golf to forget his troubles for half
an hour. People stayed home at night and listened to their radio,
or opened their windows and listened to their neighbor's radio
if theirs was in hock, and on Saturday night everyone went to
the movies, where Joan Crawford, Carole Lombard, William
Powell, and Clark Gable brought glamour and romance to drab
lives. On the radio everyone listend to Amos 'n' Andy, Fred
Allen, Jack Benny, Eddie Cantor, and Will Rogers, while new
young singers began sprouting up with fifteen-minute programs
each evening and attracting huge followings: Bing Crosby, Russ
Columbo, Kate Smith, Ruth Etting, and the Boswell Sisters and
Morton Downey and Lanny Ross.

The top composers—George Gershwin, Irving Berlin, Jerome
Kern, Rodgers and Hart, Harold Arlen, Vernon Duke—besides
turning out some of the all-time great show tunes for Broadway
musicals, began writing for the movies. But in the main, jazz took
a nosedive along with the blithe spirit of the twenties. The public
didn't have the heart for the never-say-die attitude of hot jazz,
and the sweet, soothing strains of the Wayne King, Guy Lombardo, Rudy Vallee, and Fred Waring bands took over the

scene. Louis Armstrong and Duke Ellington took their bands
to Europe, the young white jazzmen took jobs in the commercial
bands, and the Harlem musicians kept their hand in by playing
at house-rent parties. In the Midwest, however, especially around
Kansas City, where the Prendergast mob was in power, things
were still romping, and the gangsters who owned the night clubs
were hiring jazzmen like Sammy Price, Lester Young, Count
Basie, and Jo Jones to keep things happy.

As the months and years of 1931-32 and most of '33 dragged
by, I even wondered sometimes if I had dreamt the wonderful
times in Chicago and Harlem. The only way I managed to get
through those long, lonely years was to start off the day by
walking the mile around Franklin Park two or three times until
I was at peace with myself and could face another day with its
discouraging prospect of no work. Day by day I walked through
the depression years, and I'd think to myself, "Here I am, just
a little guy with a name like Max Kaminsky, living in Boston,
the deadest city in the world, and the only thing I know about
is playing the trumpet, and if I can only sweat this out maybe
someday I can make it and people will like me in spite of my
name and how I look." So for three years I scrambled and
scratched and worked when I could, and the rest of the time I
just waited, while I baby-sat for my niece Shirley. Prosperity
—and jazz—were just around the corner, and along with
"Brother, Can You Spare a Dime?" the other song people were
singing in the bleak, cheerless days of the depression was "Life Is
Just a Bowl of Cherries . . . Don't take it serious, it's too mysterious . . ."

Although I practiced a little and found places to sit in and
play when I had no work, playing seemed to come so naturally
that it never occurred to me to study. I remember one of my
mother's favorite sayings: "It's very simple. If you want to do
something, just *do* it," but I never thought of studying. All I
knew about was trying to find work, and even then my mother
had to help out sometimes. During the Jewish holidays when

we didn't want my father, who was very pious, to know I was going to work, I used to stroll nonchalantly out of the house, my coat collar flipped up to hide my tuxedo, and as soon as I was safely outside I'd whip around to the side window, and my mother would hand me my trumpet case. We weren't really fooling my father, of course, but he never said anything as long as we did it behind his back and didn't involve him in it.

In 1933 things were so bad I didn't get a single gig the entire summer. Even my father, who was always so silent that when he occasionally said something as ordinary as "good morning" a pall of nervous apprehension would fall over the house, felt called upon to remark one night, "No work, humm?" There was no reproach in it, for although my father had been against my becoming a musician at first, he accepted it later on. My jobs were a big help to my parents, and when he saw how I loved the music, there was never any argument about it.

One thing I did do was to listen regularly to the Boston Symphony broadcasts on Sunday afternoons as well as to the records of the new classical innovators: Stravinsky, Milhaud, Bartók, Mähler, Schoenberg. I fell in love with Delius and used to listen to his *Appalachia* and *Brigg Fair* for endless hours, wallowing in the tender, sad yearning these pieces used to make me feel. But when it came to playing, this wasn't what I wanted to do. This music sounded new and strange in those days but jazz was even newer and much harder to play—it was scarcely formed yet. The beat and the melody and harmony were still in the process of being welded together.

When I did find jobs during those years, they were often out of town and the experience of traveling all around New England in all kinds of weather and playing under all kinds of conditions with all sorts of musicians taught me how to take care of myself and get along. In fact, it was usually in Boston that I'd get myself into trouble, like the night when I was out with Slappy Wallace. Slappy, a long, lanky Negro, was not only one of the greatest dancers I've ever seen, he was one of the nicest guys I ever knew.

He had all the class of Bill Robinson, with a dash of Bert Williams' whimsey, and he was so marvelous that when Duke Ellington came to Boston he always hired Slappy to dance on the same bill with his band. But Slappy never could be persuaded to come to New York because nothing could convince him that one day the Atlantic Ocean wasn't going to sweep over Long Island and drown the city.

Slappy was built like a question mark, a tall, loose-limbed arrangement of bone and muscle, topped with a wonderfully kind brown face. When he danced, his vague looseness was transformed into quicksilver, and he could make a statue smile with his bodily wit and grace as he ad-libbed to the music. We used to meet late at night after work and go to a restaurant in the colored section for some fried chicken while Slappy limbered up to the records on the phonograph. This jukebox had an automated violin in the glass-enclosed top and when you inserted a nickel the bow would scrape out the tune. Slappy would take off to the music and the customers would throw coins on the floor, which he was glad to get.

Through the years I came to know Slappy quite well. One night when I was in the fried-chicken joint with Russell O'Brien, a friend from high-school days who always loved jazz, Slappy invited us to come with him to visit two girls with whom he had worked as dancers in a night club. Their apartment was in a dilapidated old wooden tenement in the heart of the colored section, and as soon as we got there Slappy sat down on the floor and started strumming softly on his ukelele while the girls went into their show routine. This was such a decrepit old house and they made such a rumpus in their high heels with their tapping and their strutting, they shook the whole building and bits of plaster showered down on us from the walls and ceilings, but we were all oblivious to everything but the music and the dancing. All of a sudden the door burst open and a policeman, with half a dozen other cops crowding behind him, rushed in with drawn guns. The sight of Slappy on the floor with his uke and the girls

halted abruptly in midstep, and Russell and me lounging peace-
fully in a couple of rickety old chairs, drew them up short.

"Slappy!" exclaimed the first cop. "What the hell is going
on here?"

"Why, I'm just giggin'!" Slappy said mildly. The policeman
misunderstood him, however, thinking he had said, "I'm just
kidding."

"Well, *I'm* not kidding!" he said angrily. "Come on, get out
of here, you guys, break it up!"

Slappy and Russell and I got up fast and walked downstairs,
and I'm telling you there were at least five squad cars down there
and a vast, buzzing crowd of people milling around. We walked
out like nothing happened, and here it looked like the President
had been assassinated or something, but we didn't stop to ask
any questions. Later on we found out that a few hours earlier, a
few blocks away, a Chinaman had chopped up a white woman,
and he had made quite a lot of noise doing it. The whole city
as well as the police force was very jittery that night about any
kind of noise, and I guess the neighbors, on hearing the whole
commotion with the building shaking on its foundations, thought
the same mayhem and butchery were going on in there, too. That
little episode cured me for a while from seeking any social life,
and I went back to my solitary walks and to driving around Boston and talking about life till all hours of the night with my two
buddies, Louis Rosenthal and Sidney Epstein.

Like most young men who are ambitious or have a dream, I
was terrified of marriage. My mother would drop hints about
eligible girls in the neighborhood, but I avoided them like a
Guy Lombardo arrangement, and the girls whose company I
frequented were not the ones you'd bring home to mother. Behind the dread of getting trapped into marriage and waking up
one day to find myself working in my father-in-law's hardware
store, was the yearning to have a girl of my own, but it took a
while before I had the gratification of knowing the girls liked
me. I had gone through an agony about my small size a few years

earlier when I was in my teens. "What girl is going to look at a little half-pint like me?" I used to groan to myself in a misery of torment. I even went through a spell where I hated to leave the house. When I was around seventeen I became so desperate that I went to a shoe store and asked for a pair of shoes with built-up heels. The salesman brought out a pair of light-tan "yellow" shoes with sharp, pointed toes a mile long and heels about four inches high, shaped like the heels on cowboy boots.

"I'll take them," I said, though I could scarcely walk in them. I got as far as half a block away from the store before I tottered into a doorway and howled out loud, "What am I *doing* to myself!" The shoes not only were killing me, but when I had caught glimpses of myself limping past store windows, I realized that all you could see was a long, dazzling pair of pointed yellow shoes with a little blur of a person on top of them. They made me look five times shorter than I was. Not even my mother, let alone a teen-age girl, could have kept a straight face at the sight of me. I crawled home by way of back alleys and the minute I reached my room I took a hammer and chisel and pried off the heels before taking them to the shoemaker.

"Wot happen to da heels?" the shoemaker yelled, waving the loathsome shoes at me. "Oh, a friend gave them to me like that," I muttered. "Put on a pair of regular heels and shine them with the darkest brown polish you have." After that experience I swore to myself I was going to be what I was, and the hell with anyone who didn't like it.

During this time, tall, handsome Jackie Marshard, whom I'd come to be friends with since our boyhood fights, was working as a drummer for society band leaders in Boston. His striking Robert Taylor good looks and his outgoing personality made him a favorite with the society girls and their families and it wasn't long before he was getting offers to play for their coming-out parties. Jackie took to the business end of music like pretzels to beer, but he was a natural showman, too, and at times he was torn between wanting to be either a great drummer or a successful businessman. He always looked so blooming, with his immaculate clothes and his strict regimen of no smoking and no drinking, that it was hard to picture him struggling and scratching the way I knew you had to in order to stay with the music. "You'd better go into the business end," I told him, sticking my hands in my pockets to hide my frayed cuffs. "You haven't the heart to suffer with the music. If you really wanted to be a musician you wouldn't have to ask anybody's advice. Nobody and nothing could stop you."

Chapter 5

In the fall of 1933, faint signs of life finally began to stir in the
nation. "Who's Afraid of the Big Bad Wolf?" was the theme
song when FDR took office as President and his energy began
radiating out to the people like the sun itself. With the repeal
of Prohibition, the speakeasy era passed into oblivion and jazz
climbed another rung up the ladder of respectability as it freed
itself from guilt by association with the illegality and licentious-
ness of the bootleg era.

Around this time Mezz Mezzrow, who had always had the
idea in the back of his head of a big band, gathered together a
large group of jazzmen, including Pee Wee, Bud Freeman, and
Eddie Condon. I came down from Boston, and Floyd O'Brien
came in from Chicago. While Mezz was trying to find work for
us, we were all so broke that three or four of us had to stay at
Mezz's apartment up in the Bronx, and it was awful. Mezz was
married and had a son, and I don't know how his wife stood it,
because even I couldn't stand it. The apartment had only one
bedroom; the rest of the sleeping accommodations consisted of
another bed in the living room, and the floor, and there was no
money and no food. Mezz tried very hard with this band, but

although we had a few little jobs, nothing much happened except for a record date in the spring of 1934, when we made "35th and Calumet"/"Old-Fashioned Love" and "Sendin' the Vipers"/ "Apologies." Mezz used a mixed group on this date, adding Benny Carter, John Kirby, Willie the Lion Smith, and Chick Webb, who used just a snare drum, a top cymbal and a high-hat cymbal, the same equipment the boppers use today.

But I like to eat, and I like at least a certain amount of privacy, and when I couldn't take the gypsy-caravan life any longer, Mezz found me a room with a family on 144th Street. If I had thought it was rugged at Mezz's house, I hadn't seen anything yet. My room was separated by flimsy French doors from another rented room occupied by a Russian opera singer who bellowed his scales from dawn to dark, with a few folk songs from the steppes thrown in after supper. That did it. I told Mezz I had to quit the band and find work so I could get some sleep. In a few days I landed a job with Leo Reisman again. About five minutes after I received my first pay check I was packed and out of that room and was writing my name in the register at the Lismore Hotel on West Seventy-second Street. I was no sooner unpacked when Eddie Condon moved in with me. Eddie liked to eat, too, occasionally.

Leo Reisman, who had made a cross-country tour earlier that year with George Gershwin, was on the air twice a week on the Philip Morris and Mincemeat radio shows then, and when I went over to the old NBC building at 711 Fifth Avenue to see if I could get work with him, he made me audition for him again. Leo never trusted anybody; for Leo you always had to audition, no matter how many times you had worked for him before. If he had been the manager of the Metropolitan Opera he would have made Caruso himself audition before each season. I wasn't a member of the New York local then, but Leo obtained permission from the union to use me as a featured performer to play just the themes at the beginning and end of his programs. Leo used to like the way I growled, and for one of his theme songs,

"What Is This Thing Called Love?," I had to growl only for
about six bars at the beginning and end of the song. Sometimes
I'd get so bored during the programs that I'd sneak in a few
bars with the rest of the band, but whenever Leo caught me, he'd
shake his finger ferociously and hiss, "You're *playing!*"

Leo, who had been an institution as a society band leader in
Boston during Prohibition, was perfect for the twenties. John
O'Hara once wrote about "that minor phenomenon called Leo
Reisman," whom he dubbed "the Spirit of Expensive Fun," and
though the band's style, he said, was mannered and affected, it
had a great vitality and was "rowdy after a certain polite fashion." That last phrase brings to my mind the picture of Leo
lying on his back on the bandstand and kicking up his legs to
mark the beat for the band—a position he resorted to when he
became tired of waving his baton.

Leo was all dramatics, all the way. He affected the maestro
look, with his long bushy hair which was always falling over
his eyes, and his beat-up, crushed hats. Those were the days of
full-dress suits and satin evening capes, but instead of a silk
topper, Leo always wore his old, broken-down black fedora,
an affectation that probably dated from his days with the Baltimore Symphony Orchestra. All the musicians looked up to band
leaders like Leo Reisman and Paul Whiteman in those days. They
did everything in such grand style, but Paul Whiteman was the
greatest of them all in the twenties. Whiteman was lavishly generous to his men; when he took over the defunct Goldkette band
and brought them out to Hollywood to make the movie *The
King of Jazz,* he arranged to have a Ford car available for each
musician while they were there. When Beiderbecke was too sick
to play, Whiteman kept his band chair empty in homage to
Bix's greatness. Whiteman tried to make jazz acceptable and
respectable by attempting to raise it to a symphonic level, and
though this wasn't the real thing, Whiteman was a tremendous
factor in bringing it to public attention and creating interest in it.

As for Leo, he made the Egyptian Room in the Brunswick

Hotel a living legend of the glory of the twenties. People came
from all over the country to see him there. He did the same thing
for the Central Park Casino. As a kid I had always thought the
Egyptian Room was beyond anything I could ever hope to see,
but one day when I was about fifteen I ventured inside the Brunswick and took a peek at the fabulous room where all this music
was being played, and for months afterward I couldn't believe
I had actually walked into that room. It wasn't the idea of its
elegance so much as that it was the place where the new music
was being played. It was all so exciting, this beginning of the
feeling of a little jazz seeping into the white man's orchestra,
and Leo even pre-dated Whiteman. Of course, their music
wasn't "hot," but Leo himself did have a feeling for jazz, con-
sidering the bands of those days, especially the society bands.
Although Leo thought the jazz of Louis Armstrong was too
free and untrammeled, he did admire Duke Ellington for his
wonderful dynamics and his musical sense of the dramatic. And
he was right in that, for the Duke is *the* real jazz composer so
far. He knows all about the art of orchestration and he has the
taste and knows how to make use of all the instruments, but
the main thing he never forgets is the real jazz feeling.

I liked working with Leo, in any case, and I always loved
working in New York. Leo never knew exactly how to treat me,
or even what to call me, and since I was little he somehow hit
on calling me Ukulele. For my part, I never knew what Leo
was going to say or do next. One night I invited Eddie Condon
to come down to the radio station to see the show, and after I
unpacked my horn I ducked into the washroom to comb my
hair. Eddie came wandering in after me, and after a minute Leo
popped out of a booth. I'd been working for him for four months
now but when I said, "Hello, Leo," he stared at me as if he'd
never seen me before and exclaimed in a tone of utter astonishment, "What are *you* doing here, Ukulele?" and then he bustled
out, leaving Eddie and me gaping at one another. I've never been
able to think of an answer to that remarkable question. I do think

that underneath all his carrying on, Leo was a very timid man, afraid to trust his feelings with anyone, and he covered up his timidity with a brusque manner and by trying to put fear into his musicians.

When the job with Leo Reisman was over at the end of January, 1934, things really got rough for me, and naturally for Eddie, too, since the job with Leo had been paying the rent at the Lismore. Condon, in those days as now, was a bantam-sized, cocksure little guy, with an impudent Irish face, a quicksilver mind, and a lethal tongue. Bow-tied, debonair, tight-mouthed, and gimlet-eyed, he still preserves today, in a kind of pickled way, the jaunty looks of a perennial youth of the twenties. He always seemed so sure of himself. All the Chicago gang always had that same air of devastating assurance. I used to tell them they were all trying to be characters in a James T. Farrell novel. Maybe they had to be that tough to make it. Each time I return to Chicago nowadays I see the city more clearly—as it is and not through the haze of nostalgia of the past—and when I look at those endless stretches of appallingly ugly, barren streets I think of the Chicago musicians as schoolboys struggling to play the music and holding on to it as something to believe in, something beautiful they were starved for. The Midwesterners, isolated on that vast, empty prairieland, have always been starved for culture, for art and music and architecture and learning. They're the great travelers, the prototype of the American tourist, in search of the beauty of the ages, the things and places and thoughts of mankind. They are so lonely—at least they were. Now they have television.

Eddie was like an owl—he never came to life till the sun went down. If he was up and about at two or three in the afternoon, which was seldom, he'd be silent and morose and take refuge behind a newspaper or a book. As the sun set his star would rise, and he'd become his witty, fascinating, entertaining self. The cockiness and the wisecracking covered a dogged honesty, a

loathing of sham and pretentiousness of any kind, and a pro-
found modesty. He always had great charm for me. One flat-
tering word from Eddie would make me feel I'd been knighted,
and I'd keep hanging around him, hoping to hear more. When
Eddie compliments you, you feel more than satisfied—you feel
justified.

Eddie's special talent, aside from his devotion to jazz and his
wonderful beat-keeping guitar, lay in organizing; he was one
of the first to bring the colored and white musicians together on
record dates, but there weren't always opportunities for doing
this. Nineteen thirty-four was one of the coldest and snowiest
of the depression winters. A snowstorm was a welcome event,
though, because at least then the unemployed could get a job
shoveling snow for the Sanitation Department and take home a
couple of dollars to feed their families. On February 14th, with
the temperature at four below, we found ourselves locked out
of my room at the Lismore for nonpayment of rent. No figures on a theromometer can make you feel colder than having no
place to go and no one to take you in. After several desperate
phone calls around midnight we finally found a Samaritan in
Gene Krupa, who took us in on what we found out later was
his wedding night.

The next day Eddie took me downtown and introduced me
to his friend Sid Jacobs, who was playing drums with Joe
Venuti's band at Delmonico's, at Fifty-first Street and Broadway,
underneath the old Roseland Ballroom. I sat in for one set and
Joe hired me then and there.

The whole experience of playing in Joe Venuti's band was
sheer pleasure. To begin with, I never knew a finer, kinder man
than Joe Venuti. He had that knack of making you feel he was
on your side all the way, and he treated you royally as few men
could. When Wingy Manone came to town that spring, I
brought him over to the bandstand and introduced him to Joe.

"Have him sit in with the boys," Joe said, and after one number

he hired Wingy on the spot, adding another trumpet player to
the band just like that. Later I got Bud Freeman into the band
exactly the same way.

Joe had his wild side, though; in fact, he was as wild as he
was generous—and that's saying a lot. With Joe, to feel was to
act, and his humor was laced with extravagant violence. You
never knew what he was going to do next, and when he did it
you couldn't believe it. He was famous for his pretended loathing of bass players. He claimed they were always goofing off,
and he'd try to catch them at it so he could swoop down on a
poor guy, and with that familiar mad glint in his black eye, he'd
seize the bass and heave it out on the dance floor. There was
another little Jimmy Durante-type bit he was fond of doing, too.
He'd come out with a cheap violin, and after playing it so
beautifully that it sounded like a Stradivarius, he'd fly into a fury
at it and smash it to bits, swearing a blue streak in vaudevillian
broken Italian. On the golf course, when his game was going
badly, he'd throw his clubs, his golf bags, and his caddy, if he
wasn't nimble, into the water hazard, and if his partner wasn't
wary he'd land there, too. On Wingy Manone's birthday, Venuti
sent him a little box containing one cuff link, and some years
later, on Bing's birthday, he sent Crosby, who had his own
racing stables by then, the gift of a moth-eaten, sway-backed,
ancient yellow nag. Once he had the sax player take chorus
after chorus until the poor guy was exhausted. After he had
fallen back into his seat, weak as a kitten, Joe came over and
slapped him on the back to congratulate him. Then he took a
key ring out of his pocket. "My car has a flat. How'd you like
to hop outside and change it for me, kiddo?" he proposed to the
limp musician. Enrico Caruso had made the country *Pagliacci*-
conscious in the twenties, and some nights Joe would give
way to his overwhelming desire to be a clown and would appear
in a harlequin suit and bellow "Ridi, Pagliaccio," before a startled
audience. The Pagliaccio of the Violin, we called him.

But despite the constant frenzy and furor he created around

himself, Joe Venuti was first and foremost a great artist. If he had played any other instrument than the violin he would have become one of the great jazz stars. As it is, he is one of the greatest jazz violinists of all time. Joe had worked in the Goldkette band and had played with Beiderbecke; when the Goldkette band broke up in 1927, he and the guitarist Eddie Lang joined the jazz band led by Roger Wolfe Kahn, son of the millionaire Otto Kahn, and later they went into Paul Whiteman's orchestra, along with Bix. The records Venuti made in the late twenties with the marvelously gifted Eddie Lang were uniquely beautiful, and they were way ahead of their time. These two men were so attuned to each other musically that they composed as they went along as if they were one mind. Both men had been born in Philadelphia and had known each other as kids. Eddie Lang's death in 1933, at the age of twenty-seven or twenty-eight, was a great loss to jazz. He was one of the rare two or three musicians with whom Beiderbecke recorded who was equal in musicianship to Bix. For instance, on the Okeh record of "Singing the Blues," made in 1925, Lang not only plays magnificent ensemble and counterpoint to Bix's cornet; he is the only one in the band who is keeping time. I have never understood how Django Reinhardt could have been so highly praised—except, of course, that he lived some twenty-five years longer than Lang—and Eddie Lang's genius so neglected. And though the Django Reinhardt-Stephane Grappelly records did have a good flavor and a good sound to them, they were regarded by many musicians as merely hillbilly versions of Venuti and Lang.

We worked very hard in that band, from 6 P.M. to 4 A.M., with two two-hour floor shows nightly, and radio broadcasts two or three times a night. Everybody used to go to Delmonico's to see Joe Venuti—there was always something going on with Joe. Mildred Bailey was a regular visitor when she was in town, and Joe would put her on the air with the band during our broadcasts. And Joe could swing like a demon. His was the first big white band I know of that was really trying to swing. I loved the swinging feeling in this band. There weren't many trumpet players around then who could ad-lib the lead and swing a floor show, and if you could do it, there weren't many leaders who would let you do it. It just wasn't the accepted style in white bands. Of course, anything different—good or bad—is usually frowned on at first. Max Farley, the great alto sax man, was in that band, too, and he was writing music in the twelve-tone system—secretly, because very few others were interested in it then.

So I enjoyed every minute of working in Joe Venuti's band, and I was going with a girl who worked across the street in the Rockettes, and all in all, life was good. I used to walk to work through Central Park every evening, and when the weather was bad I'd hop a trolley car in front of the Lismore at Seventy-second Street and ride in pleasant comfort down to Fifty-first and Broadway. As far as I was concerned, the depression was over.

But it wasn't over for a lot of other jazzmen, and I had my own private bread line outside of Delmonico's every night that spring of 1934. Promptly at nine o'clock, during intermission, I'd be at the side door with a pocketful of fifty-cent pieces for the out-of-work musicians waiting in the cold: Pee Wee Russell, Eddie Condon, Bud Freeman and his brother Arnie, Buzzy Drootin's brother Al, Freddy Goodman, Benny Goodman's brother—sometimes it seemed like everybody and his brother. In those days you could get a good meal for fifty cents at the Automat, and on one occasion I was able to provide some even more welcome fare, when Joe Venuti had a birthday party after hours at Delmonico's. The waiters arranged the tables in a huge horseshoe, and we had great mountains of spaghetti and enough kegs of whiskey and gallon jugs of cocktails to get an army drunk. At the nine-o'clock line-up that night I tipped the boys off about the party, and at 1 A.M. Pee Wee and Eddie and Chelsea Quealey were waiting outside while I slipped out to them all the liquor I could get my hands on. One great thing about that club—there were all kinds of handy side- and back-door exits.

After the party Joe Venuti and I took one of the gallon jugs
of whiskey sours and walked over to the Ho-Ho Chinese restaurant on Seventh Avenue, where we drank the whiskey sours in
fragile little teacups to wash down the chow mein while we
talked over the party. Everyone had entertained, and Joe had
behaved himself until one of the male singers sang a romantic
ballad. This tenor was an extremely handsome guy, with a fancy
little mustache, and all the chorus girls adored him. In the middle
of his song, Joe's Mack Sennett humor got the best of him and
he let the poor guy have it with a head of lettuce right in the
middle of high C, knocking him cold. Joe didn't like sentimental
singers, even on his birthday.

In the meantime, the fellows, Pee Wee and Eddie and company, had gone back to my room at the Lismore, and that was
the last I saw of them for four days. Since I had to work every
night I didn't dare go up there and get loaded with them, but
every evening I'd check by ringing my room at the hotel to see
if they were still there. On the fourth night there was no answer
and I decided it was safe to go home. I had to wade through
what looked like a mountain of empty bottles and kegs, but I
finally was able to get a good night's rest in my own bed. Sometimes it seems I have spent half my life trying to find a place to
sleep and the other half trying to get to sleep once I found a
bed.

It was in 1934, too, that I made "Home Cooking"/"The Eel,"
with Joe Sullivan, Bud Freeman, Pee Wee Russell, Floyd O'Brien,
Eddie Condon, and Big Sid Catlett. Although I had recorded
in 1929 with Red Nichols, and with the Chocolate Dandies as
well as with Mezz's band, this was the first time I felt I made any
kind of a record. I had never met Big Sid Catlett until he showed
up in front of the Brunswick studio at 1776 Broadway, where I
was waiting for the rest of the guys. Big Sid was so big that instead of shaking hands he simply picked me up bodily, as if I
were a toy, and when I was on eye level with him he said, most
politely, "Man, I'm glad to know you." It was so spontaneous,

and he was such a nice, plain guy in such nice, plain clothes that
he was tops with me from then on. Every time I looked over at
Sid during the recording session and saw that grin of his, it gave
me confidence.

On "Home Cooking" Sid had no bass drum, just a cymbal and
snare, but he made it sound like a full set. On the other hand,
though he was such a big, powerful fellow, he could play very
lightly and delicately without sounding weak. He had such
finesse, and such an infallible sense of right time and touch, in
such perfect swing, that he gave you a tremendous lift when you
played with him because the time was just so right.

One of the most difficult instruments to play is the drum, and
one of the most difficult things to do on the drums is to shade
them. When Big Sid was with Louis's band in 1942, I heard
him play the introduction to the floor show on the tom-tom
with such shading and color that it sounded like timpani. Dave
Tough didn't have the variety or the great facility of playing
so many different kinds of things, but Dave had the instinct for
keeping miraculous time and for getting the sound and the right
volume. Most drummers have the fault of not knowing the right
volume to play; when they play loud they get very heavy and
slow up the beat, and when they play soft they change the time
along with the volume. But Sidney and Dave had the ability to
keep proper time at any volume.

The really great drummers can play the top part of the beat
and not rush. Most amateurs play at the bottom part of the beat,
where it's most heavy. The beat is just a stroke of time but it has
so many vibrations to it that the stroke can be hit at the top or
middle or bottom. Most all the early jazz bands played at the
bottom of the beat, and that's why Louis used to call out, even
on records, "Swing, man, *swing!*" He meant to hit it on the
top.

In all music the three basics are rhythm, harmony, and melody,
but in jazz the rhythm is foremost. Without the perfect time the
other parts can never be right. Big Sid could feed you so you'd

play on top of the beat without rushing it—that's swing. And rhythm in jazz is not only keeping the proper time—you can keep perfect time and yet not swing. You can also keep perfect time and swing without having the right shading and taste and color and accent. For instance, Gene Krupa actually made Benny Goodman's band. He, too, knew how to feed the musicians; the truly great drummer knows what to play with all the different solos. Gene knew exactly what little different shading or color or tone or rhythmic figure to play behind each instrument. Jo Jones in Count Basie's band and Sonny Greer in Duke Ellington's orchestra both knew how each man's different style requires a different thing; they just have that instinct of knowing exactly what is needed, for when a musician is playing a solo, the more perfectly a drummer plays the beat and backs him up with the right kind of sound, the easier it is for the soloist to phrase the way he would like to.

There are some great drummers today who can do it, like Ed Thigpen, Morey Feld, Charlie Persip, and Sam Woodward, now with the Duke. Though most of these are rated as drummers of the modern school, they still play that drum as it should be played. The drum has to be played right in any school of jazz— or it's not jazz. For though a lot of modern musicians claim that they have the swing, they really don't. They have a kind of continuous shuffle beat, and though the time is even, the swing is missing.

After Delmonico's closed for the summer of 1934 Joe Venuti took the band into the Brooklyn Paramount for a week's engagement. Wingy Manone sat right behind the microphone, and just before the curtain rose on our first show Venuti cautioned Wingy against swearing.

"Promise me you won't say any of them bad words," he begged Wingy.

"Why, pops," Wingy protested, "I *swear* I won't say no [obscenity, obscenity, obscenity] swear words!" The roar of laughter from the unseen audience, which had heard every blankety-blank word over the mike, drowned out Venuti's equally unprintable retort.

When the week at the Paramount was over we went on to Atlantic City for another couple of weeks' work at the Steel Pier, and then the band broke up for the summer. I landed a job shortly afterward with Eddie Elkins, who had one of the big bands in New England in the early thirties. We went up to Saratoga at the peak of the August season to play at a club called Reilly's. Eddie Elkins wasn't in Joe Venuti's class. Few men are. I didn't get along with him and he didn't like me. One night while I was on the bandstand a phone call came in from my sister Rose, calling to tell me my father was very sick. I had to fight to get away from Elkins and the boys, who wouldn't believe me, and after hitchhiking rides on trucks all night, I reached home to find that my father had died.

I stayed in Boston most of the next year, since I didn't want to leave my mother all alone after Pa's death. I played with Teddy Roy's band that fall and then we went into the Cocoanut Grove. I used to walk the three miles to the club all that winter wearing only a light topcoat and carrying half a cold chicken in my cornet case, which my mother fixed for my intermission meal each night. One night when Louis Armstrong was in town Teddy Roy invited Louis and me to his hotel room, where we stayed up till dawn listening to classical records. Louis would chuckle about how he wished he had a "hundred of them long-hair cats playing behind *me*!"

King Solomon, one of the big-time gangsters in those days in Boston, owned the Cocoanut Grove. He had several night clubs as well as hotels and other projects in New York, too, but the Cocoanut Grove, for which he hired Sophie Tucker and all the big headliners, was the one that really gave him his kicks. He loved to put on his full-dress suit and greet the customers at the door; he was so delighted to be associated with the distinguished society and business people who came there. King Solomon was riding high until one night while on the rounds of his smaller clubs in the colored section of Boston, he was shot to death in the men's room by a couple of rival gangsters. We were given our notice the next day. The Cocoanut Grove was under his lawyer's name, and when Solomon was killed the lawyer took over. The lawyer died in prison years later while serving a term for criminal negligence in the Cocoanut Grove fire in 1942, in which nearly five hundred people lost their lives trying to escape through the one exit available. Two musician friends of mine died in that fire, Bernie Faisioli, the violinist band leader, and Ecky Watson, a trumpet player, who was one of my best friends. Jack Lesberg was in that band, too, and after he found his way out of the burning building he was in such a daze that he turned around and ran back for his bass.

The loss of Ecky Watson was a tragic one for me. When we were still in our teens, Ecky used to come over to my house at night and rap on my window, saying, "Come on out now, Maxie, you can't just stay home all the time. We've got things to do." I'd sneak out the window and he'd take me to visit his friends in the big, wealthy homes in Boston. Ecky was a favorite of the society crowd, but besides his good looks he was so sweet-natured that everybody loved him. Goodness seemed to radiate from him. It's hard to think of him dying that way.

It was around this time, just before I worked in my first swing band, that I had one more whirl in one of Mezz's jazz bands. After his first adventure with a big band, Mezz was still trying, and he finally landed a booking for a band in the Uptown Low-down Club, formerly Delmonico's, where I had worked for Joe Venuti. Mezz's second big band had, among others, Zutty Singleton, Dickie Wells, Frankie Newton, Sidney DeParis, and me. The two colored trumpet players, Frankie Newton and Sidney DeParis, were both six-footers, but since I was the only one who could read the arrangements, I played first trumpet and sat in the middle. Frankie Newton solved our other problem of unequal height by putting an old automobile seat on my chair so the three of us would come out even on top.

This was a very fine band, and Zutty always tells how Artie Shaw was around there all the time trying to take over the band, but we decided we'd stick with Mezz. We made it an absolute rule, though, that Mezz must not be allowed to play the clarinet. We permitted him to lead the band, even though Zutty would always call out, "Don't *fan* us, Mezz, lead us!" for Mezz had a way of leading that looked as though he were trying to get a fire started. But in spite of everything, we really did swing on Alex Hill's arrangements. Alex didn't use riffs to make us swing. His ideas were closer to the ensemble work of a small band, though of course much simplified, and while Hill's arrangements allowed more space for each man than Fletcher Henderson's arrangements, you'd have to have topnotch jazzmen to make them work. Alex Hill was a young colored pianist of great talent but he was a whiskey man—for a quart of rye or gin he'd stay up all night and write a stack of beautiful arrangements for you—and his death just a few years later was another huge loss to jazz.

The Uptown Lowdown put on a big floor show every night. The red velvet curtains in front of the bandstand would part slowly and dramatically while we swung into "We're in the Money" to open the floor show. One of the acts was a sensational little trio fresh out of San Antonio, with Ernie Caceres on baritone sax, his brother on violin, and another relative on guitar. Hazel Scott was playing intermission piano in the cocktail lounge, and this is the first time I met Hazel and Ernie.

Our theme song, "We're in the Money," was pure wishful thinking. In desperation, the boss, a Mr. Fagin, had a swastika painted in the middle of the dance floor and had newsmen come in to take pictures of it for a publicity stunt. Hitler had just started throwing his weight around in Germany, and the idea was that we had a Negro-and-white band and were proving we didn't believe in that "superior race" baloney, but even Hitler couldn't get customers for us, and after two or three weeks the Uptown Lowdown was down and out. Even then we couldn't get our money, but Mr. Fagin, who was a pretty good guy in spite of his name, paid us off as best he could with bottles of whiskey.

It was a good band, though, and if Mezz had taken it more seriously and didn't have all his other various enterprises going, he would have had a great swing band even before Benny Goodman and Tommy Dorsey and all the others.

Chapter 6

The swing era was launched in 1935 with a two-hour nation-wide radio show on Saturday nights called *Let's Dance*, which started Benny Goodman on his way to becoming the King of Swing. The time was ripe. After six years of depression, the American people themselves were on the upswing again, and a whole new generation of youngsters especially were raring to go. It's hard to realize that jazz had virtually not been heard in the land for six long gloomy years. It was there, but the popular bands of the day weren't playing it. All the public seemed able to take during those somber years was syrupy, soothing music. Up in Harlem, of course, they had been stomping at the Savoy all along to the bands of Chick Webb, Jimmie Lunceford, Cab Calloway, Fletcher Henderson, Lucky Millinder, and Andy Kirk. The white Casa Loma band had managed to hang on, too, and eventually they helped set the mood for the rest of the country with the Riley and Farley band's big hit "The Music Goes Down and Around and It Comes Out Here." But it was the Benny Goodman band that hit the country at the right time with the right sound and the right tempo. The effect was electrifying. Almost overnight the jitterbugs, with their shoulder-length page-boy bobs, their fashionably grimy saddle shoes, and their peg-leg, sharpie zoot suits began pouring out of their homes in every town, city, and hamlet in the nation and streaming into the dance halls to dance to the exciting new sound of swing, and the big band and dance craze built up such momentum that when Benny Goodman appeared at the Paramount Theatre in January, 1937, the kids spontaneously erupted out of their seats to dance in the aisles.

But even more significantly, the big swing bands turned many dancers into listeners, too. Although swing, like jazz, flourished because of a wildly appreciative dancing audience, many who came just to dance the Lindy or the Shag stopped to crowd around the bandstand to listen when the jazz soloists took off on a sizzling improvised chorus. It was swing that finally led the general public, the fans, and the critics to an awareness of the validity of jazz and its place in American life. But it is also significant that swing had been ballyhooed to the public as a "new music." Jazz was called old hat and swing was now the thing, just as in the forties bop was the new thing and jazz was once again out of date.

I was playing a one-nighter at the William Penn Hotel in Pittsburgh in November of 1934 when I first heard Tommy Dorsey's big band. It seemed as if the whole town had turned out to celebrate the Pittsburgh football victory that afternoon and was now jammed into the two adjoining ballrooms, one containing Leo Reisman's band, in which I was playing, and the other Tommy's band.

I had heard Benny Goodman's big new band up in Boston that spring and, as a matter of fact, Tommy had much the same kind of band as Benny's, even down to the Fletcher Henderson arrangements. Fletcher was always trying to get paid for the arrangements he made for Tommy, but he had tough going until Tommy became a success.

The spring before, when Benny Goodman had been in Boston, I had sat in with his band. Benny had asked me to join the band then, but I felt I really wasn't good enough to play in Benny's band—I just had a funny feeling about it. I can't understand it. I was usually so happy to get out of Boston, but at that time I had some good little jobs going and Benny's band, great as it was, just didn't excite me that much that I wanted to drop everything and go on the road with him. But when I heard Tommy's band that night in Pittsburgh, the new, big-band sound hit me for the first time. Although I had been hearing the big colored bands swing for years, I had never heard a white band play that way before.

A few weeks later Tommy came to Boston for an engagement at the Normandy Ballroom, and since he had just had a run-in with Sterling Bose, he was without a jazz trumpet. Bobby Byrnes, who was working for Charlie Schribman then, recommended me, and I sat in with Tommy's band that night.

This was a different kind of music, and it took a little time at first to adjust to playing in the big swing bands. All the years before, we had just played songs as we felt them, but now a whole new era of arranged section playing was starting, and reading the parts and counting the rests was a completely different feeling from the free-swinging improvisation I had been used to. It was a big thing to get used to sitting in a band and playing for a while and then just sitting there waiting for your turn to play again. And this was a different kind of arranged music, which—thanks to Fletcher Henderson, Don Redman, Count Basie, Duke Ellington, and all the other Negro band leaders who had figured it out years ago—enabled the big bands to swing. Formerly the big dance bands would have one section playing at a time, so that the arrangements were really a series of section solos, but with five saxes playing instead of one, and none of them swinging. But now, with one section playing a different rhythm or harmony in counterpoint against another section, and with the riffing of phrases, and by using jazzmen who gave the music a hot, driving tone, the whole band swung.

After a few nights of learning how to apply myself to play in this band I joined Tommy Dorsey in January, 1935, and stayed with him for one unforgettable year.

Working with Tommy Dorsey was like cooking on a hot stove that might explode at any moment—and always did. In the first place, Tommy was very hard to work for because he played very difficult trombone solos. The concentration and control needed to play in that high register was a terrific strain on him, and sometimes Tommy couldn't rise to it and he'd get mad. And in the second place, Tommy was always getting mad. His temperament was so volcanic and his rages so explosive that you could almost smell the sulphur and brimstone. No one was safe. In the heat of battle Tommy had a truly magnificent unconcern for consequences; he took pleasure in the fight for the sheer love of fighting, and as mad as you could get at him, it was hard to stay mad because he got over it so quickly, with no trace of animosity. Both Tommy and his brother Jimmy were natural-born scrappers. When they had their own Dorsey Brothers orchestra they fought around the clock. It was a perpetual Three Stooges slapstick comedy. Tommy would kick off the beat. Jimmy would growl, "For chrissakes, always the same corny tempo!" Tommy would snarl, "Oh, yeah! And you always play those same corny notes!" Jimmy would leap up, snatch Tommy's trombone and bend it in two. Tommy would seize Jimmy's sax and smash it on the floor, and the fight was on. Jimmy now had his own band on Bing Crosby's radio show and Tommy was trying to make it alone.

Tommy's most regular scapegoat in this band was the hapless guitar player, who bore the brunt of Tommy's frustration whenever Tommy made a mistake in his solo. Tommy couldn't even hear the guitar from where he was standing, but when Tommy fluffed a note he'd turn around and scream at the guitarist, blaming it all on him for playing the wrong chords. I often thought the real reason Tommy used to get so furious at this particular guy was that when the bus pulled into a town early enough in the day, this fellow used to run out and get a day job—washing dishes

or working at a garage or delivering orders for a grocery store
—until it was time to go on the bandstand at night. It *was* hard
to like him. The rest of us were so tired we could hardly drag
ourselves around, but this guy apparently never slept, and he
made us all feel as if we were pampering ourselves. He didn't
last too long. But everybody felt the scorch of Tommy's temper;
he played no favorites. The trombone section sat right in front
of Tommy, and one afternoon as the curtain went up on a concert we were playing at Duke University, one of the trombone
players, a new guy who didn't have much experience, thrust his
slide out so far in an excess of anxiety to make good that it slid
off his horn and sailed into the footlights. The poor guy just sat
there looking at Tommy in cold horror. It broke us up, but
Tommy was livid. This poor fellow didn't last long, either.

But as much of a terror as he was on the stand, of all the
band leaders there was no one who was such a great sport off the
stand. Tommy did everything big; he thought big, played big,
fought big, and spent big. He was a great man not only for
parties but for reaching for the check. After giving us hell all
night on the stand he'd take the whole band out for food and
drinks, and even when he was struggling and hard up for dough
he'd blow hundreds of dollars a week buying meals for the
whole band. He was just as generous with his fans. When we'd
play five shows a day at the big theatres, there were always at
least a dozen or more devoted fans who would stay in their seats
from the opening morning show until the last show was over at
midnight. By the afternoon, Tommy, concerned about their
health, would send the bandboy out for trayfuls of chicken
sandwiches and malted milks to be distributed among them.

That first year he had such hard going that he was on the verge
of giving up the band at least once a week. We did one-nighters
from Canada to Texas, traveling around in a dilapidated, anti-
quated school bus with back-breaking wooden seats and no
heater, and on cold nights while rattling over the hills of Pennsylvania and Vermont and New Hampshire we'd make a fire

right on the floor of the bus with newspapers, racing forms, pawn tickets, old letters, laundry lists, and practically anything not nailed down. Those hills! There were many, many times when the bus couldn't make those hills, so we would all climb out, slipping and sliding and cursing the cold, the hills, the bus, and the music business, and we'd push that damned bus up the hill. When the driver would start nodding from fatigue Tommy would take over the wheel himself and we'd rattle along through fog and blizzards and rain and detours to the next one-night stand, three or four hundred miles away. One night in Pennsylvania we were so cold that Tommy stopped the bus at a general store in a little coal-mining town in the Alleghenies where we bought woolen socks, caps with ear muffs, mufflers, and big heavy coat-sweaters, buttoning the sweaters on over our overcoats, and pulling the socks on over our shoes. But bone weary, exhausted, and miserable as I was, I'd think to myself: This is still better than being stuck in Boston playing for those society bands.

The one-nighters were murderous. You'd get through playing a college prom or a dance hall at 1 A.M., grab something to eat before climbing into the bus and riding all night in that frigid torture chamber until anywhere from eight to eleven the next morning, stumble out of the bus into some ratty little hotel, fall like a corpse onto a bed until it was time to get up and rehearse, and then you'd eat, shave, bathe, put on your band uniform and play again until 1 A.M., and then repeat the whole routine day after day, week after week, month after month. If we arrived at a hotel before 6 A.M. we'd have to sit in the lobby until eight o'clock before checking in so we wouldn't have to pay for an extra day. For the first few days you didn't mind the grind, but after a week or so the continuous strain of not being able to stretch out on a bed and grab a solid block of sleep became a torture to your body. You'd get *rigor mortis* from the straight wooden seats and your whole body throbbed all over with the sensation you feel when your foot goes to sleep. And on top of

being numb from cold you were dirty and crummy and itchy;
sometimes we'd carry dirty laundry around for two weeks before
we stayed in one place long enough to get it done. And you'd
begin to ask yourself, if you were still on speaking terms with
yourself, why in the name of sanity you were doing this, but
some wild faith kept you going with the idea that it would all
turn out as the band leader promised you, that if he ever made
it he'd "never forget you guys who are the ones who really made
it for him," and he'd see that each one of you got a nice, big,
fat slice of the bacon when you reached the top. And when the
bandleader made it, you never even got the rind.

Another factor that kept you going was that there were some
wonderful players in those bands, the best jazz players around.
Bud Freeman, Joe Dixon, Dave Tough, and Axel Stordahl, who
played third trumpet and sang with the Pied Pipers as well as
writing arrangements, were with me in that band, and I held on
as long as I did just to get a chance to play with Dave Tough.
No one could play like that in those days, except some of the
great colored drummers like Big Sid Catlett, but it was hard
for a white man to get the chance to play with them, except on
record dates, in those days when segregation was still very strong.

We did one-nighters at colleges and dance halls in New
England and the Middle West from January to late spring, when
we went into the Lincoln Hotel in New York. We also played
the jazz concert put on by Joe Helbock and David Ross at the
Imperial Theatre in New York in 1935. This was a big step toward the jazz concerts that have since become so popular.
There were only a few small jazz groups around then, such as
Stuff Smith's band and Wingy Manone's band, both of whom
had small combos working on Fifty-second Street, and they
were on the bill, but the concert was composed mainly of the
big swing bands, such as Bob Crosby's and Artie Shaw's and
Tommy Dorsey's, in which so many of the jazzmen were then
working. It wasn't like the later jazz concerts, where the individual jazzmen themselves were featured.

Then came more one-nighters down to Atlantic City, a week
in Tybee Beach in Savannah, Georgia, and then on to the Club
Alamo in San Antonio for the month of July, and the Baker
Hotel in Dallas for the next month. While we were at the Club
Alamo we had another job three hundred miles away in Dallas.
Fred Waring had been doing a weekly broadcast for the Ford
Motor Company at the Texas Centennial and when he went on
vacation we substituted for him all that July, doing extra re-
hearsals all week long for the radio show and then getting on a
train early in the morning on the day of the show and riding
three hundred miles in the blistering Texas heat in an un-air-
conditioned train to Dallas, playing the show, and then riding
the three hundred miles back to San Antonio. At the end of the
month Tommy paid us eighty dollars apiece for the month's
work. Dave Tough, who had to take cabs to get his drums to
and from the rehearsal each day, and to and from the train, said
it wasn't that he *minded* the salary, it was just that he couldn't
afford it—it cost him more than that for cab fare. Tommy made
some money out of the radio show, but he needed it and so he
kept it.

But we were young and rugged in those days, and the extra
work spurred us on to extra play so that we could relax. While
we were in Dallas we checked into the country club instead
of staying at a hotel so that we could play eighteen holes of golf
at dawn after we finished working all night. We'd top off the
golf game with some refreshing slices of ice-cold watermelon
soaked in gin before we tumbled groggily into bed. As a solution
to the problem of unwinding from tension it was rather drastic,
but we liked it.

That fall in Philadelphia we shared the bill at the Nixon
Grande Theatre with a colored band called the Sunset Royals.
Their arrangement of "Marie" was so great that I used to stay
around after our show just to hear them play it. After I mentioned it to Paul Weston he called Tommy in to listen. Tommy
got it right away and asked Paul to make an arrangement of it,

which Paul did, incorporating the Sunset Royals' vocal idea, too, and the piece became a regular part of our repertoire, without, of course, a by-your-leave to the Sunset Royals. By this time, though, I'd had enough of the one-night stands, the friction within the band, being cold and tired and breaking my back on those wooden seats—I was fed to the teeth with the whole thing. When we played Hamilton, Ontario, on a snowy night in March, 1936, and then rode all the way back to New York right after the date to play the Roseland Ballroom the following night, it was the last straw. As soon as I saw New York I knew this was the end of being on the road for me. I quit. I'd had a fight with Tommy a week before, and so I quit and he fired me simultaneously. Tommy could get mad in a puff, of course, and I have a quick temper and a big mouth on occasion myself— usually the wrong occasion. Bunny Berigan replaced me, and shortly afterward Tommy recorded "Marie." I always felt it was Bunny's great solo, rather than the commercial idea of the vocals, that made that record such a hit. And then, just when it seemed Tommy couldn't keep the band going another day, Edythe Wright, his vocalist, introduced him to some businessmen who were putting on a radio show for Raleigh cigarettes and Tommy landed the band spot and was on his way to fame and fortune, and I went back home to Boston.

After a few weeks of my health routine of plenty of sleep and long walks and no smoking and drinking, I felt like a human being again, and the rest of the summer of 1936 I worked around New England until September, when Pee Wee wired me about a job at the Famous Door on Fifty-second Street. Pee Wee was working there with Louis Prima, who was going out to California and taking Pee Wee with him, so Pee Wee recommended me for Louis's spot. I was up in Bar Harbor with one of Jackie Marshard's society bands, and since it was the end of the season up there, there was no sweat about coming on to New York to take the job. It was always exciting to get new jobs— especially playing jazz, and especially in New York.

Like most of the other clubs on Fifty-second Street, the Famous Door was on the street floor of a brownstone house and upstairs on the first floor there was a big foyer with built-in leather seats lining the walls, and beyond that were the bathrooms. After playing the first set the first night, I went upstairs to the washroom. A stately young colored girl in a white evening dress sitting alone in a corner of the deserted foyer threw me a half-timid, half-scornful look when I appeared in the doorway.

"What are you doing here all alone?" I asked her, surprised.

When she told me her name was Billie Holiday and that she was working there, too, singing with the Teddy Wilson trio, I remembered that I had seen her up in Harlem a few years before, singing and waiting on tables at the Alhambra Grill, where we used to go to hear Bobby Henderson's fine piano. The fact that I had heard her uptown made us good friends because she was a colored girl downtown in the white section and she felt good knowing I knew about Harlem, and when I heard her sing again I knew why I had remembered her name. She really sang in those days. Her voice *was* the blues, but she could make you feel so happy, too. In her peak years, between 1935 and 1941, her stunning sense of phrasing and tempo were still completely unself-conscious and the unaffected sweet-sadness of her voice could make you ring with joy as well as sorrow. A large, fleshy, but beautifully boned woman with a satin-smooth beige skin, she always possessed an air of hauteur, not only in her manner but in the arch of her brow, the poise of her head, and the dignity of her carriage, but her haughtiness hid a shyness so vast that she spoke in practically a whisper. When she talked to musicians, the subject was usually her mother, to whom she was devoted. There was nothing wild about her in those days; there was nothing showing then but the terrible, proud shyness; and even in her most turbulent, tortured days later on, she was always basically what she had been then—an uncompromising, devastatingly honest kind of girl, and always, in the deepest sense, a lady. Her sobriquet, Lady Day, suited her exactly. Whatever led her to

self-destruction was also there: a bitterness—not simply the
bitterness of her color or life, but the bitterness that often seems
to go with singular talent and that drives a Eugene O'Neill, or a
Bix Beiderbecke, or a John Barrymore or a Charlie Parker to
destroy himself with drink and drugs and excess. If Bix Beiderbecke had been a Negro they would all have seized on that as
the underlying cause of his drinking himself to death.

As a singer Billie had few physical mannerisms. She held her
arms in the position of a runner ready to sprint, scarcely moving
them except occasionally to snap her fingers in a lazy, leisurely
movement. Like Bix, all the hotness and intensity and concentration were inside so that she rode a song with the languid
grace of a native boy riding a surfboard. Billie had the gift of
expressing the perfect mood of a song, happy or sad, rollicking
or blue. The basis of her phrasing was the beat, and she didn't
distort the melody, but the stress and accent and meaning she
gave the words just somehow made the song larger than life-
size. I've always felt that the whole new form sprang complete
in her mind with the first note she sang of any song. The art of
improvising lies in the sense of structure, in the ability to build a
new story out of the bricks and mortar of the original song. Most
so-called or would-be jazzmen can play a thousand ad-lib notes
and not say a thing; not rearrange or conceive of them so that
they tell a new story, with a beginning, middle, and end. Billie
was a master architect.

Billie had just started recording with the great Teddy Wilson,
who had a contract with Brunswick to record pop tunes for the
jukebox market. Teddy would put together bands of the finest
jazzmen: Johnny Hodges, Roy Eldridge, Harry Carney, Buck
Clayton, Ben Webster, Bunny Berigan, Jo Jones, Benny Goodman, and of course, the fabulous Lester Young—and Billie would
sing the vocals for such songs as "Them There Eyes," "All of
Me," "These Foolish Things," "Why Was I Born," "A Fine
Romance," "I Cried for You," "I Can't Get Started," "The
Very Thought of You,"—and once Billie had sung them, they

never sounded right again when other singers did them.

But Billie wasn't known at all yet to the general public and none of the customers at the Famous Door paid much attention to her. Jazz was only barely beginning to catch on and jazz singers weren't in vogue yet. At that time, in the late thirties, the only people who went to night clubs were people with money, mostly society people and celebrities of the sports and show-business worlds, not the general public or the expense-account society, like today. The first Saturday that I worked at the Famous Door, the society people I had played for in Bar Harbor just the weekend before came in and there I was again. Since the ordinary person couldn't afford night-clubbing in those days, and since night clubs were about the only place where you could hear jazz, the public had little chance to learn about it until the swing bands became popular.

I didn't stay at the Famous Door very long because the club didn't want to pay me much. A week after I left, they sent me the train fare to come back, but I wasn't keen about the idea, and the next night when I ran into Bobby Hackett we went to a bar and got drunk and I gave Bobby the money and sent him in my place. But they didn't dig his playing then. Finally, they got Bunny Berigan to come in and he took over the band and did well with it. Eddie Condon and Joe Bushkin were in the band, too, and on Sunday afternoons all the other jazzmen in town would drop in and jam with them. Within a few years, Bobby Hackett, who had started out on the guitar, developed into one of the greatest of the lyrical jazz trumpets, with a special genius for playing a ballad. His expression, tone, and taste are perfection.

Around November of 1936, I was back in New York again, playing at the Onyx Club, in a small band with Jack Jenney on trombone. I also had a job playing in the pit band at the Radio City Music Hall, and at 11 P.M., when I finished the last of the five daily shows at Radio City, I'd rush over to the Onyx and play there till 3 or 4 A.M. For the Christmas stage show at the

Music Hall they had several colored couples do the Lindy, which
was the newest excitement downtown then, and they hired me
to play "One O'Clock Jump" for the dancers. It was very
funny trying to play for these dancers with this huge, concert-
size orchestra that couldn't swing. And that wasn't all that was
funny about the show. The subscribers and regular customers
always turn out for the first new show at Radio City, and when
the old dowagers saw the colored girls being tossed up in the
air during the more imaginative moments of the Lindy, they
raised the roof to the manager, who saw to it that the girls put
on panties after that. I sat next to the lead trumpet, who drank so
much that his colleagues would literally have to guide him to his
seat, but loaded as he was he could play like a son of a gun. In
the course of the show, there was some very difficult circus music,
and sometimes when we came to this part he'd lean over to me
and mumble, "Take it, pal." I'd just stare blankly at him, and
after muttering something highly uncomplimentary about illiterate and undependable jazz musicians, he'd shakily lift his
horn to his numb chops and play it perfectly.

A few months later, around March of 1937, I had another
call from Pee Wee Russell, who was back in New York, to work
at another night club on Fifty-second Street—the Little Club.
In addition to Pee Wee and me we had George Troup on
trombone and Joe Bushkin on piano. George was the first one
besides Tommy Dorsey that I ever heard play the trombone
in the high register that Tommy later became famous for.
When the club had changed hands and its name—it used to be the
original Onyx Club—it had become more of an entertaining night
club, with singers, strippers, comedians, and dancers, and we
played for all the acts. At a rehearsal one afternoon, one of the
dancers handed Pee Wee, who was heading our four-piece band,
a special arrangement for a forty-piece orchestra. It must have
cost the poor girl a couple of hundred dollars to have the arrangement made, but it was almost worth it to see the expression
on Pee Wee—who was trying to play, read, and direct all at

the same time—when we had to sit there and silently count bars in the places where the French horns and flutes and violins were supposed to play. I finally told the poor kid we'd play "Lime-house Blues" and she could make up the dance as we went along.

This job lasted only a couple of weeks, and then I was out of work again. Luckily, Tommy Dorsey, who was in town at the Hotel New Yorker, needed a trumpet player to substitute for Lee Castle, and he asked me to join the band again for this engagement. By this time Tommy had begun to be fairly successful, but I didn't get the kick out of playing with this band that I had with his earlier band. Yank Lawson and Charlie Spivak were doing the New Yorker job, too, and with Yank doing all the jazz trumpet work, which was all arranged around him, there was much less for me to do now. During the New Yorker engagement Tommy had a record date. One of the sides was "The Hawaiian War Chant" on which Yank Lawson played so wonderfully, but Tommy was very nervous and hard to please that day, and after we had completed three sides, he was so disgusted he wanted to knock it off for the day. But Charlie Spivak persuaded him to make one more side so we'd have a whole date out of the session. We made "Boogie Woogie," which was a take-off on Pinetop's "Boogie," recorded back in 1928. Howard Smith was the pianist and arranger. We just slammed it out, in a hurry to get it done with, and as occasionally happens in the music business, the sleeper side of "Boogie Woogie" turned out to be Tommy's biggest seller; at one time it was supposed to be the biggest seller of any record ever made.

Glenn Miller came in one night at the New Yorker and when we finished the set he called me over to his table. "Why are you playing third trumpet in Tommy's band when you could be playing first trumpet in my band?" he wanted to know. I was highly flattered, but I wasn't too tempted. Miller's band was too straight and commercial for my taste, and I decided to turn the offer down.

My luck was still coming in strong, though, for when I finished subbing in Tommy's band it turned out that Benny Goodman needed a substitute for Chris Griffin, who had a sore lip, so I went in with Benny at the Pennsylvania Hotel. Benny was riding high then, with Gene Krupa, Harry James, Ziggy Elman, and all his other great sidemen. Benny liked me and was thinking again of taking me on permanently, but in the meantime Artie Shaw needed a trumpet player, too.

∎

Chapter 7

It was a Sunday, my night off at the Pennsylvania Hotel. I was living at the Markwell Apartments on West Forty-ninth Street at the time, directly across the street from the Plymouth Hotel, where Artie Shaw was staying. Around two o'clock in the afternoon I had dragged myself out of bed for some breakfast, but I was so tired that I had just thrown myself down on the bed again for another nap when Artie's manager came over from the Plymouth Hotel to ask me to help them out by playing a job for Shaw up in Bridgeport that night. I told him I was too beat to make it, and when he came back again a half hour later, I turned him down again. Jazz trumpets were still not plentiful yet and I was the only one they knew who could fill in on short notice, but I explained I was working for Benny and had plans for making good so I could join his band, if only I could get a little sleep. Just as I was dozing off again, he was back knocking at the door, and since there didn't seem to be any way to get rid of this guy, I finally got up, packed my horn, and followed him downstairs into the bus that was waiting across the street, thinking to myself as I wearily climbed over Shaw's fifteen-piece band to the back of the bus, "Well, here I am on the road again."

I had met Artie Shaw at a party at Gladys Mosier's apartment one night around 1929 when I was doing some club dates in New York and Artie was playing in town with Irving Aronson's Commanders. Gladys and Babe Rusin's sister, Sunny, were among the first of the girl pianists around in those days. It wasn't much of a party; nobody had any money and we sat around talking and playing records and drinking corn whiskey from Bumps and Crumps, a bootlegging establishment in one of the old brownstones up in Harlem where for a dollar you could buy a gallon of this homemade fire water. The first drink of the stuff was the worst taste you ever tasted, but after three or four drinks it tasted fine.

As soon as Artie and I began talking about jazz we became buddies, and whenever I was in town after that we'd go up to Harlem together to hear the real thing. A couple of years later, in the early thirties, when Artie was working in the CBS house band and playing some club dates on the side, we were both hired by Leo Reisman to play a coming-out party at the Biltmore. Leo carried on in his special eccentric way all evening, lying down on the bandstand and swinging up his legs and hollering "Yeah!" when things got rolling. This was the closest we ever came to swinging in society bands. During an intermission Artie and I talked about how dreary and banal this kind of music was. Artie had a strong desire to play jazz and of course there was hardly any place to play it then. At the end of the evening we went over to Artie's apartment on Fifty-seventh Street for more talk. Artie was always interested in learning and improving himself—I believe at the time he was taking courses at Columbia University in journalism or writing—and his apartment was loaded with records and books. When I spotted a whole collection of Louis's early recordings in his huge library of symphonic music and jazz records, I was done for, and we sat around till morning playing the records and talking. I told him that someday I'd like to have a band that was a combination of a small jazz band and a string quartet. A jazz band is very similar to a

string quartet, with its fugues and counterpoint and theme development and variations and its voicing; except, of course, that
in a jazz band it's mainly ad lib. And although the instrumenta-
tion is different, the voicing is very similar, only it's the trombone
instead of the cello that plays the fifth of the chord, and the
clarinet the third and the trumpet the melody in place of the
first and second violins.

Later on Artie organized his first band, with Lee Castle on
trumpet and George Wettling on drums, and in 1935 he played
the jazz concert at the Imperial Theatre at which I had played
with Tommy Dorsey's band. Artie's band consisted of two small
bands, one a jazz band and the other a string band, full of violins
and cellos, and he played some original clarinet pieces that were
very good. He had studied composing and he was always very
clever at writing original things. Shaw's band was the hit of the
concert. On the strength of the reviewers' praises he got some
bookings, one of them at the Adolphus Hotel in Dallas, across the
street from the Baker Hotel, where I was working in Tommy's
band.

When Artie's manager talked me into getting on that bus to
Bridgeport, the band had been getting very little work and Shaw
was in a great deal of financial trouble, but I didn't know any
of this at the time, of course. The job at the Bridgeport Ritz
Ballroom was hard going for me, since I didn't know the book
and I was beat, but Artie seemed to like it and he had me ride
back to New York with him in his car so we could talk. Or
rather, he talked and I listened while Artie turned on the old
charm, with his marvelous laugh and his wonderful way of making you feel he was a real friend. When Artie gave you that
special friendship deal, he could get almost anything he wanted
because he could make you feel so good. He reminisced about
the times we had gone up to Harlem and about the time he had
come up to my room on 144th Street, where the Russian opera
singer had kept me awake all day, and how he had been so struck
with my new Schick electric razor. Electric razors had just come

out then, and he had never seen one before.

But I felt I wanted to stay with Benny this time and learn his book and play in his band, so I put Shaw off. When Chris Griffin returned to work a day or so later, Benny said he wanted to talk to me about joining the band. In the meantime, Shaw kept after me. He said he had a few dates that would help him if only I'd come in with him. Somehow he made me feel so good that I became convinced that instead of being just another trumpet player in Benny's band, I'd have the chance to play more with Artie, since he was offering me the lead trumpet spot. And the fellows in his band liked me, and my ego wanted me to be in his band and be liked for playing well, so before I knew it I was in Artie's band.

Artie was looking for someone to give him the one big idea, the big break. I had a fair name then, and I had ideas and was experienced, while most of his men were beginners. It was a very immature band at the start and had no definite style. The players became very great later on—Tony Pastor, Chuck Peterson, Les Robbins, Cliff Leeman, etc.—but at that time they were unseasoned and inexperienced. Their worst trouble was learning to play in tune, and except for Tony Pastor, they didn't know much about jazz or swing. Tony, who had always loved jazz, had always wanted to play in a big band like this, and he was a great factor in the band with his playing and his easy-going, humorous style of singing.

I played two or three nights with Shaw and was still struggling with the book and trying to get the band to play on pitch, since it's up to the lead trumpet to carry the band and give it a tone and set the time. Then, on the fourth day, when we played at the Connecticut State Teachers College, things began to happen. We arrived in New London about nine in the morning, and as soon as I left the bus I had two or three drinks—all I ever needed to knock me out. Then I checked into the hotel and slept like a log till it was time to play for the affair. By then I was fairly familiar with the book; I have to play something new for a couple of days and mull it over, and then I can make it mine. That afternoon when I started to swing those parts, making them sing out, the whole band settled down, as cozily as a kid in a featherbed, smack into the right pitch, and suddenly it was a great new band.

That afternoon made me king with Shaw and the men, and after the job that night Shaw offered me sixty-five dollars a week. His men were getting forty-five dollars. Now I began to rack my brains to think of ways to help Artie get off the ground with his band. I asked Shaw why we didn't work more often than two or three nights a week, and he said his agent couldn't get more bookings for him; when I discovered he had the same agent as Benny Goodman I advised him to change agents at once, since this one couldn't develop Artie in competition with Benny, and he did so. Then the girl singer left the band, and I recommended Billie Holiday as her replacement. If we get Billie, I said, she'll make us. We were playing a date in New York then, and I called up Billie and told her to meet me in the lobby of the Plymouth Hotel at one o'clock. When I introduced her to Artie he hired her on sight, without auditioning her. Billie, all excited, raced home to pack because we were leaving for Boston that afternoon. All the way to Boston I had to keep selling Artie on Billie, though, as he had begun to worry about not having heard her sing. That evening Artie was late showing up at the rehearsal, and since I used to lead when he wasn't there, I started the band on a new arrangement we had to try out for "Yesterdays." I asked Billie to sing the clarinet solo part to fill in for Artie. Billie stood up in front of the mike, listening sort of dreamily while we played the song through once, and on the second time around she came gliding in, in the nick of time, like a lazy ball player starting to lope around the bases but taking his own good time because he knows that ball he just hit is *never* going to stop sailing. While she was singing, Artie walked in, and he just stood there. He couldn't believe she was that good.

As Boston was my home territory, I knew exactly what Artie should do. I told him to see Sy Schribman about playing the

Roseland State Ballroom two nights a week, and about going on
the radio once a week, and above all, I said, we must rehearse all
the time. He did everything, even to playing the blues on the
radio broadcasts. I wanted a half hour of blues, but we finally
compromised on fifteen minutes. It was an unheard-of thing in
those days for a white band to play fifteen minutes of blues. We
worked out some riffs and other things as we went along, and
everybody got a chance to play ad-lib solos on the blues. We
rehearsed day and night, playing dates around New England
through the Schribman office during the week, and playing the
Roseland State Ballroom every Friday and Saturday night, with
a broadcast from there each Friday. The band began to improve.
We'd get on that bus and ride sixty to two hundred miles and
climb on that bandstand and start swinging like mad. We still
didn't draw much of a crowd, but more and more people began
talking about the band, and the broadcasts were slowly making
the band known nationally. The blues sessions especially began
to cause a lot of notice.

Then came the night we played opposite Tommy Dorsey's
band at the Dartmouth prom. Tommy's band was the star attraction, but by this time our band had unity and fire. We didn't have
the fineness and the great pitch of Benny Goodman's band because Benny's band had more experienced men and had been
together a long time, which is what makes a band. But we had a
great swinging band with a wonderful feeling of everybody
wanting to play and, of course, Artie could always swing better
than Tommy Dorsey ever could. As beautifully as Tommy could
play, he was never much of a swing man. And while Tommy's
band had a lot of great soloists and a lot of polish, it didn't have
that exciting, infectious feeling of guys wanting to play.

Tommy opened the prom, starting off with his theme,
"Getting Sentimental Over You." Now, Shaw's theme song,
"Nightmare," was a powerful one with a haunting wildness to it,
and when our turn came we gave it all we had when we opened
up. I had worked hard to make the band into a strong, first-set

band. After we finished the theme, the Dartmouth gym was in
an uproar of cheering. We actually blew Tommy off the stand.
He was a man who was always mad about something, but that
night he was so burned up that he grabbed his horn and stalked
off the stand. Tommy wasn't one to take a losing game; he'd
never trained himself to lose, even though this sort of musical
battle of the underdog band blowing the first band down had
a long tradition behind it.

Later on we had our turn to lose to Bunny Berigan, whose
band was even less known than ours at the time we played
against him. Bunny's band cut us, although it wasn't as obvious
as it was with Dorsey, and not many besides the musicians
realized it. Bunny was a strong player and could weld a band into
a unit, but he had tough breaks. Just when he was coming up fine
and was booked to open the Ritz Carlton Roof in Boston, the
hurricane of 1938 blew the bandstand off the hotel roof and
the job was canceled. That about finished poor Berigan, but at
least it took a hurricane to do it.

It was wonderful being in Artie's band in those days. I was
fascinated with the problem of trying to make something out of
the band, and all wrapped up in playing in it. There was a
double-barreled thrill to playing in the big bands of the thirties.
Though the lack of room to improvise and the pressures toward
conformity were always a big drag after a while, big-band jazz,
or swing, as it was called, had a fascination all its own, with its
excitement and challenge and its tremendous power, and the few
times I had the chance to do it I never felt as good as when I was
playing in front of a big band. I love to play strong like that,
for one thing. It's a good feeling, and having a big live band
right behind you backing you up with those big fat solid chord-
sounds so that you don't have to do it all yourself is a great spur
musically.

In the swing era, though there were nearly a hundred big
bands, there were only four or five great white bands. Of course,
a good deal of the music of the swing-band days was tasteless,

raucous, and unmusical, and, of course, you can't get the truly great hot jazz in a big band that you can in a six- or seven-piece band with great soloists improvising collectively. In the big band, the arranged riffs had to take the place of ad-lib ensemble. But these swing bands were making the evolution from the kind of music before that—from the society bands and "Mickey Mouse" bands of the Wayne King and Sammy Kaye type—to a more sophisticated symphonic conception, but still different, and still in the new jazz tradition, because it swung. The whole idea of the big-band era was actually another offshoot of Louis Armstrong's genius in interpreting a contemporary pop tune into something that swung. When Louis came East in 1924 to join Fletcher Henderson's band, his playing was such a revelation to Don Redman, who was doing Fletcher's arrangements, that Don junked all his previous stuff and developed a whole new conception of arranging for a big band. Everyone—Benny Goodman, Tommy Dorsey, Artie Shaw, Glenn Miller, all the band leaders of the thirties—knew that no one could swing like Louis.

And secondly, Benny Goodman and Shaw and even Tommy Dorsey would alternate the big-band sound with a jazz quintet or sextet made up of jazzmen from within the band, and I have always felt it was the little jazz group within the big swing band that was the secret of the big band's success, even more than the girl singers and the vocal groups and the excitement and power of the big band itself. It was the little ad-lib jazz band that was at the core of the big band and made it swing; it was the jazz in the swing bands that made the swing era, and you were showing off the best in jazz with the little jazz band. The big bands were actually a complete show in themselves, in the old vaudeville tradition, but when the little jazz combo came on stage it gave the audience a change of pace, and above all, the excitement of spontaneous improvisation.

Everything went along fine and dandy the first few months with Shaw's band. Artie was always so nice to me; he'd come over to my house for dinner and be charming and gracious to my mother, and afterward we'd walk in the park and I'd tell him all the tricks of the music game I'd seen and experienced. And my ego blossomed like a rose under Artie's attention and deference. I knew I was a big factor in the band's success and that the other musicians looked up to me and followed me around and did everything I said, and I ate it all up. All of us knew it was a great swinging band with terrific fire, and we were all absorbed in it, with Artie leading us to believe that it was all a part of our thing, too, because we all worked so hard to make it a success.

Billie Holiday loved that band, too. It was a happy band for her. This was the first time a colored vocalist had a full-time, regular job in a white band.

Chick Webb's band, with Ella Fitzgerald singing in it, was working right around the corner from Roseland State Ballroom then, at Lavargi's, and Chick used to drop around occasionally to sit in with us—and what a spark he'd give us. Chick's band was always a great pacemaker for all the swing bands. This little colored drummer was one of the first to use the new high-hat cymbal, which made it possible to hold these big bands together on the beat. The high-hat started out as a single cymbal attached to the lower right side of the bass drum. When the drummer pressed the foot pedal of the bass drum, a little metal hammer would simultaneously strike the cymbal. Then someone had the idea of moving this cymbal to the left side so the drummer could use it to strike the afterbeat. The cymbal was doubled, with the upper and lower parts connected by a spring, and when the drummer pressed the pedal the two cymbals clashed together to mark the afterbeat. In its final evolution, the double cymbal was put on a long metal rod and raised to a position around elbow height, where the drummer could also use his drumsticks or wire brush on it, using it as a substitute for the snare drum. The brilliant hard staccato of the high-hat helped the band swing, whereas the snare drum vibrates so much that the definition of the time is sluggish and blurred.

It's because of the high-hat that Benny Goodman's band was so much better than Fletcher Henderson's old band, and after a while Benny's drummer, Gene Krupa, began to play these staccato riffs on the high-hat right along with the brass section, giving a sharp, exciting definition and swing to the whole band. In the forties Kenny Clarke went another step in developing the bop beat by reserving the bass drum for only special accents and using the top cymbal to keep the steady time. These cymbals, incidentally, were made by Zildian, a Turkish or Armenian firm up in Quincy, Massachusetts, by a process that was a family secret, handed down from father to son.

A jazz drummer is a whole percussion section in one person. While his right foot is striking the bass drum for the beat and his left is working the high-hat pedal for the afterbeat, his left hand is beating out accents on the snare and his right hand is riding the high-hat or one of the big cymbals or tom-toms. He's syncopating like mad. Syncopation, accenting notes normally unaccented, is the basis of jazz and gives it its element of surprise and wit and humor; and sustained syncopation, which builds greater and greater momentum, is what gives jazz its great excitement and its feeling of go, go, go. Since the Africans had no means of making brass instruments or finely wrought string instruments, they concentrated on percussion, on anything they could bang, shake, rattle, or roll, and in using syncopation along with the regular beat, they developed the complex multiple rhythms that is their great musical genius and that was so new to European music. A jazz musician never feels so happy playing as when he's playing with a great drummer. That's about the greatest feeling you can get.

It was this kind of feeling, the feeling of wanting to play, that gave the Artie Shaw band its great punch. The contagion of enthusiasm and inspiration leaps from one musician to catch fire with another, as it did in the case of "Begin the Beguine." One day at rehearsal, when I started to noodle around with the song, Artie told his arranger to copy it that way. When he recorded this arrangement of it later on, it became one of his biggest hits.

Artie was a master psychologist when it came to getting work out of his men. One afternoon when he had the band booked for a dance in Philadelphia, instead of telling us we had to make it, even though he knew we were exhausted, he made a little speech about how far it was and how he felt it was too hard for us, too much to ask of us. Of course we insisted on doing it. Another time, after we had traveled six hundred miles from Boston to Pittsburgh in a snowstorm, only about six people showed up for the dance. Since this was before we had been on the air, we weren't known yet and nobody bothered to come out on a stormy night to hear us, but Artie made a big point of thanking these people and saying how happy he was that at least some-body showed up, inspiring us at the same time, too, by making us feel we were all in this great crusade together.

Then things began to change. The band began to catch on, and I was more and more in favor with the guys, and I got going very strong, enjoying it all to the hilt. And that's when Artie began to change. We began to grate on each other's nerves—things get that way in a band—and I got mad at him and he got mad at me, until finally one day Artie called a meeting of the whole band and said to the guys, "I want you to know this is not Maxie's band; this is *my* band." I was shocked and humiliated to find he was thinking that way about me when all I had been doing was knocking my brains out to make the band a success. I felt Artie had turned on me and wanted to push me out, to dump me now that he had it made, and in my hurt I blindly tried to stop him by doing exactly the wrong thing. Instead of putting things on a businesslike, impersonal plane and working out a contract with Shaw, I went emotional. And it was all further complicated by the fact that I was having my first big woman trouble at this time.

Rhoda and I had known each other since we were kids in Boston. She had always had eyes for me, but I had always been wary of becoming involved for fear I'd get married before I had a chance to do anything with the music. Though Rhoda was married now and had a family, she wasn't happy in her marriage. In her way Rhoda was a wonderful girl, and in her way she was wonderful for me, but as there was no future in it I became so mixed up and so involved that I didn't know where I was; one minute I'd be wild with jealousy and the next minute deeply ashamed of myself for being in such a scandalous mess.

But even my mother couldn't help liking her. My mother had been after me all year to find a nice girl, and she redoubled her efforts when I began getting mixed up with Rhoda. One night in desperation I brought home to dinner a very proper girl whose parents wanted me to go into the family haberdashery business. The next morning my mother said, "You know what, Maxie— you're right. Rhoda is better for you! At least she lets you be you." My mother couldn't stand narrow respectability any more than I could.

As Shaw became colder to me, I turned more and more to Rhoda for sympathy, and that didn't do much to help matters. Twice I felt so depressed about Shaw's changed attitude toward me that I didn't show up for work on time, though I eventually did make it in time to play the second set. And, of course, the worse I acted, the more Shaw really started to change, too. He probably thought, "This guy is going to dump *me* when I need him and he's showing me that he's really not reliable," but I felt Artie was thinking, "I have all this now, and I did it before without him, and I don't need him."

When the band left Boston I stayed behind, too hurt at Artie's attitude to have the heart to keep on with it, and too emotionally involved with Rhoda to be able to break off with her. The radio broadcasts had done their work in building Artie's fame, and when the band opened in St. Louis they were a sensation. I felt very bad about leaving the band, but I was conceited enough to think they couldn't get along without me. I was doomed to disappointment on that score, too. Once you have a band molded, a replacement is always easy. Up-and-coming musicians had been listening to these new big bands and were waiting to replace the men who had pioneered and done the groundwork. Later on, all the big bands changed personnel as fast as the military change generals during a campaign. Each band must have used hundreds of sidemen, though all of them started out with fifteen dedicated guys who believed they were helping a band leader make good and thinking they, too, would make some money out of it, but all they ever got were their weekly salary and union scale for a record date. No royalties from records ever trickled down to the rest of the band. Being a musician in these bands wasn't an easy life, with the mental and physical labor that goes into playing, and it does drag me to think of the band leaders who have made and thrown away millions and never thought of the men who went on the road and slaved to make them rich and then had nothing to show for it but broken lives and broken homes.

So the band went on the road, and it was a great success, and then Artie broke it all up himself, walking out on the band himself a year later. He did what I did, but he waited till he received his first royalties. Artie went off to Acapulco and married Lana Turner, and Tony Pastor took over the band, but neither arrangement lasted very long.

My strongest regret was that I didn't get the chance to see Billie Holiday do her stuff when the band went out on the road, but the reports I heard made me feel good that she was making such a great hit. Physically the grind of one-nighters wore her down, though, and a few months later, when the Shaw band was back in Boston for an engagement, Billie was sick from the rough time she had on the road. I brought her over to the house to meet my mother, who took one look at her and exclaimed, "Why, you look just like my Betty! Come, sit down. Rest," and in two minutes they were so deep in conversation that when I eventually drifted off into another room no one even noticed. My mother sent Billie to a doctor who had her back on her feet in a few days.

Billie had a dual nature—the good, sweet side, and the wild

side. I knew about the wild part of her life, but we never spoke
about it. It was her business and she kept it that way. While Billie
was in Boston, she boarded in a house in an old aristocratic section
that had gradually fallen into neglect and disrepair, and was
slowly being taken over by the poor. Her room was immense,
with beautiful hardwood floors and mellow old oak paneling.
While she was recuperating I stopped by to see her. I brought
along an Orthophone phonograph, one of the finest record
players made in those days—a relic of my Lismore Hotel days
with Eddie Condon. He had been given it as a present by one of
his friends and somehow I had ended up with it. It seemed only
fair to pass it along to Billie.

"*Groovy* gravy!" Billie said happily when I explained about
the phonograph. "Set it right down here"—she pushed aside a
lamp on the rickety little table—"and you set down there"—
she gestured with her elbow at a chair—"and we'll dig some
Prez." Billie had given Lester the title of "President" because
when he played he was top man, and he was the one who had
named her "Lady Day."

The phonograph sounded marvelous in that big room, and I
was more than rewarded by hearing Billie sing along with her
records. Curled up in a lopsided old armchair with her feet
tucked up under her bright-blue woolly robe, her beautifully
shaped head weary against the cushion, she listened to her own
voice with closed eyes, but when Lester's horn took off on its
own, Billie would take off with him. As great as Billie sang a
regular song, to hear her sing along with Lester Young while
he was playing a chorus was something to make your toes curl.
No words; she just scatted along with his tenor sax as though
she were another horn. I listened, knowing all I was hearing, and
it was quite a while before I realized that my mind was echoing
its own accompaniment, right in time with the beat: "God bless
you, girl, God bless you."

Chapter 8

While swing was sweeping the country, the battle of winning an audience for small-band, improvised jazz was just getting up steam. All during the big-band craze, jazzmen had kept on forming small jazz combos and trying to find places to play. Among the musicians who were determined to win a hearing for jazz was my old roommate, Eddie Condon.

In addition to a bulldog tenacity and a devotion to the music that approached dedication, Eddie had another aptitude that was invaluable to the cause of jazz—a positive genius for finding the right persons at the right time and getting them to help in the right way. One of these persons was a young advertising man, Paul Smith, who in the spring of 1938 sponsored Eddie in a series of Friday-afternoon concerts once a month at the Park Lane, a swanky Park Avenue hotel. Although Eddie had nothing against saloons personally—quite the opposite, in fact—he felt that if jazz could be presented in a more dignified setting and given an opportunity to throw off its stigma of raffish low life, it might have a chance.

Eddie gathered together the best of the Negro and white musicians and at each concert they busted the place up. We

enjoyed the concerts as much as anyone else; it was a marvelous
feeling to be playing with jazzmen and not having to hold back.
I remember Willie the Lion Smith feeling so good at these
clambakes that he helped the bartender mix the drinks. However,
many of the regular residents of the Park Lane were railroad
tycoons from the South, and at the sight of white and Negro
musicians drinking and playing together they set up such a
squawk that we moved to the St. Regis, and then to the Belmont
Plaza, and then we ran out of hotels, courage, and money.

In the meantime, Eddie had been working down at Nick's
in Greenwich Village. That June of 1938, Eddie called me to
come to town to play the Princeton alumni reunion with Bud
Freeman, Brad Gowans, Pee Wee Russell, Dave Tough, and
Dave Bowman. After the job we had a long talk about the pos-
sibility of staying together and trying to make a go of it with
our own band.

"I'll get Nick to hire you fellows," Eddie said. "Listen, there
is no bunch of guys around that can get the sound we get. With
Maxie, Pee Wee, Bud, Brad"—he ticked us off one by one with
a deliberate, determined finger—"we could have a hell of an all-
male band. What do you say, fellows?"

Everybody thought it was a good idea except me. That is, I
thought the idea of the band was great, but I was so swamped at
the time with my personal problems that I couldn't commit myself yet to anything. I did stipulate that I'd join only on the
condition that it be a cooperative organization. After the Artie
Shaw experience I was trying to smarten up. This suggestion
met with unanimous approval, and a five-year charter for the
Summa Cum Laude band, as it was christened, was drawn up.

After the Princeton date I went back to Boston. Meanwhile
the fellows kept after me. Condon had Ernie Anderson work
on me, and Ernie kept calling me to come down to New York.
Ernie, an affable, bespectacled young man who worked on a
magazine in the daytime and devoted his evenings to listening to
jazz, found his mission in life when he discovered that gold

mine of unreconstructed characters—Condon, Pee Wee, Bud, *et al*. From then on, aided and encouraged by Eddie, he spent every waking moment devising ways and means to create a popular audience for jazz.

I kept saying no to Ernie's pleas to join the band. Pulled in five directions at once, I did my best to avoid coming to any decision at all. Although I still had it bad for Rhoda, I knew I had to get away from her, and yet I was loath to go in with the Chicago gang. I admired them all so much, and to have them praise my playing was *it*, as far as I was concerned. In fact, that was the whole trouble. Being such a pushover for a pat on the back, I knew that that praise would be my undoing, just as it was with Shaw, and I'd end up being the victim of my own ego again. But on the other hand, with my thirtieth birthday just around the corner, it was time for me to make it on my own now, no matter how tough things got, with no more running back home to Boston whenever I ran into difficulties. And, finally, as it slowly sank into my still bruised pride that the days of being the big star in Shaw's band were over, I realized that the only sensible thing to do was to go to work at Nick's and do my best. When I told my mother I had decided to accept Eddie's offer, we both knew without having to put it into words that I'd never come home again to live. With Rhoda I wasn't so courageous. I just told her I was going to New York for a couple of days. I couldn't admit to myself yet that I was breaking off with her for good. When I came to town Ernie Anderson had me stay at his apartment at the Beaux Arts, and everyone treated me so wonderfully that after a few days I finally made up my mind to stay.

The problem we faced with the Summa Cum Laude band was different from the one that had confronted the Artie Shaw band. In that case the ground had already been broken by Benny Goodman, the public was eager for more, and it was a matter of competition, of whipping an inexperienced band into a personality distinctive and exciting enough to attract attention.

But with the Summa Cum Laude band the general public had not only never heard of us, it couldn't have cared less if it had. People were flocking in droves to the Broadway movie palaces to see the big glamorous swing bands, they were buying their records by the millions, and dancing to their music in dance halls, and as yet few knew or cared about the highly complex music of the small jazz band. Our problem was one of finding a market for a music that was considered to have died a natural death with the passing of the roaring twenties—out of date, out of style, and out of favor. We had to make a comeback for a music that was considered dead before it had even reached maturity.

And where I shone in contrast to the green, unseasoned musicians in Shaw's band, in the Summa Cum Laude band I was among my peers, and each was equal to the whole. Above all, these fellows were a different breed from the swing kings. Now I was with a band composed of dedicated jazz musicians who never wanted to play in a commercial band, even a swing band. Jazz was their deepest, sincerest belief—their whole life—not money, fame, or glory. And though most of us never did get the money, we got plenty of fame within a short time.

Each one in the Summa Cum Laude band had his unique contribution. Eddie Condon, in addition to his swinging guitar, was the great contact man, the hatcher of schemes, the spokesman. Bud Freeman was the dynamo who inspired us with his sparkle, his wit, his immense sensitivity to the melodic and rhythmic mood. Bud is a great, great swinger, and his enthusiasm and bounce as well as his taste and his drive were an invaluable asset to the band. Pee Wee Russell was, hands down, the most unique of us all, because there is no one in the universe with the musical charm, the magic, and the hotness of Pee Wee. Visually he was a sensation, with his long elastic frame and his remarkable, lugubrious face. Pee Wee, part poet, part roustabout, seems to play from his ankles up, and hearing him play is like spending an evening with Mark Twain, O. Henry, and Damon Runyon.

Brad Gowans, a combination of a sweet-natured soul and an extraordinarily talented musician, was a character even back in 1925, when I first heard him play at a dance at the Copley Plaza in Boston. He was an unforgettable sight whizzing around Boston in those days in a racing car he had rebuilt out of an old Ford, his eyes barely visible above the collar of an enormous racoon coat. Brad was always a nut about machinery, and he was forever tinkering about in junk yards, building motorboats, sports cars, power engines, and if he had lived on into the space age he would have come up with an Atlas missile, too. Brad, who was always great in fighting for jazz, not only had a pretty melodic sense and beautiful ideas, he knew how to play ensemble.

The Chicago-style jazz had always been strong on ensemble improvisation. This is the essence of jazz. Many jazzmen who are great soloists cannot cope with the demands of collective improvisation. It was mainly the white musicians who carried on this tradition. With the Negro's strong rhythmic instinct, it was more natural for the colored bands to swing, but their swing was always based primarily on rhythmic riffs—from the run-of-the-mill jump bands up to the great bands of Count Basie and Duke Ellington—rather than on ensemble improvisation.

It was hard going at first trying to hack out a path for ourselves. All of these men were strong individualists, but despite the high-voltage temperaments and the Chicago guys' style of letting loose with caustic, cutting remarks which were hard to take, we somehow or other worked things out as we went along. Bud wasn't too keen on the Dixieland songs, for one thing, and I knew only a few of them. Brad had his hands full trying to get into everyone's head the idea that there had to be some thought and arrangements, however flexible, along with the jamming and the hot solos, and he was always trying to strike a balance between plan and improvisation. Writing arrangements was so natural to Brad that he scarcely realized he was doing it all the time, and when a band leader once asked him if he could read music Brad retorted, "Not enough to hurt my playing."

Brad's arrangements were very loose, with just certain parts worked out and all the rest left free for ad-libbing. Eddie didn't want to lead the band in those days, so Bud fronted us, but the burden of keeping everyone in line fell on Brad, who worked very hard in his nice funny way to try to do it. Brad was the stabilizing force in this band. But in spite of the conflicts and in spite of the problems, we all lived just to play. We all knew the sound we wanted to have, and gradually we evolved into a band that packed a wallop Joe Louis would have envied. And above all, the music was the thing, not our looks or our personalities. When Pee Wee writhed and contorted into fantastic shapes while playing, it was completely unconscious; he wasn't selling Pee Wee, he was all wrapped up in what he was saying.

The Summa Cum Laude band was the forerunner of the whole revival of the Dixieland bands. At that time our style of playing was called Chicago jazz; a few years later they called it Dixieland. When bop came in after the war, we were called Moldy Figs; then we were tolerated with the term Mainstream jazz; and now it's Dixieland again. But, nevertheless, the Summa Cum Laude band wasn't a Dixieland band as the term is used today. Most of the Dixieland bands of today play calendar-art style—using simple, bright colors and broad, thick lines—and they rely heavily on the traditional Dixieland songs, not realizing it's not what you play but how you play it. We played everything, new pop tunes, old standards, and show tunes, as well as blues and rags and stomps and the classic jazz marches and shuffles and shouts and one-steps. After a while it got so that unless we played the Dixieland songs, people thought we weren't playing jazz. They think it's the song that makes it jazz; they never seem to understand that it's the feeling, for when it comes down to explaining what makes a really great jazz band, it's like trying to explain what it is that makes the *Mona Lisa* a masterpiece. You could start by saying that it's the simple things that are the hardest to do. It's hard to play a song simply and beautifully, without tricks or gimmicks, without corn or phoniness of any kind. Before you can improvise sensibly and beautifully on a melody, you have to know how to play the melody right first. You have to have an inborn sense of swing, so that you feel the melodic phrases in terms of the jazz beat. You have to have harmonic sense, good intonation, good taste, and you have to have a sense of order, of structure, of form, so that when you ad-lib a new song out of the original one you can build and keep building up to a new climax, and not just spout out clouds of meaningless phrases and notes. Then there has to be understanding and teamwork among the musicians. They inspire each other and build on each other's ideas. The richness and the excitement comes from the interplay of ideas. They comment on and develop what the man ahead has just said in his solo. And they all have to be able to improvise collectively so that each part makes a beautiful, sensible whole.

The first month with the band was a difficult transition period for me, both musically and emotionally. I had put so much of myself into the Artie Shaw band that I was like an athlete who has overextended himself. Since I knew so few Dixieland songs it was a struggle for me until I learned the whole repertoire. I didn't like to take too many solos at first and I confined myself mainly to ensemble playing in the beginning. That, in fact, was one of the reasons the fellows had wanted me in this band with them. They felt I was the guy who could play that lead with the tone and the time. I had that instinct for making a band, even a seven-piece band like ours, sound rich and full without making my trumpet overbearing. The other musicians had room to play, too; I gave them a chance, leading without dominating, holding them all together during improvised ensemble work and giving them the drive and the beat without being so showy that they were overshadowed and cramped.

"Tin Roof Blues" happened to be one of the few Dixieland songs I knew, and I'd invariably lead the band into it when it was time for the last number of each set. It has since become the custom to use it as the traditional signature for all the bands that play at Nick's.

As the weeks went by I began to pull out of my doldrums. I found a pleasant one-room apartment on Bank Street and kept to a sane routine at first, and after a while I felt so fit physically and so relieved mentally that I used to just sit on the bandstand and laugh. I felt as if a tremendous burden had been lifted off me, and the thought of how seriously I had taken the events of the past couple of years suddenly seemed the height of absurdity. But it used to burn Nick up to see me laugh. He thought I wasn't taking things seriously enough, and Eddie had a little talk with me. That euphoria leveled off after a while, and I began buckling down to learning the songs and putting more thought into my work, and little by little my confidence began to revive.

At first the going wasn't too good, but our luck was in playing for a man like Nick. One of the first night-club owners to take a chance on jazz, Nick Rongetti supported not only the music, letting the men play the way they wanted and never interfering with the band in any way; he fed us and stuck it out with us when business was lousy; there was never a time when a musician down on his luck wouldn't find a warm welcome and a hot meal at Nick's. Business was so bad at first that Nick didn't have the money to lay in a supply of Scotch. Each night, he'd have to wait till about 11 P.M., when he had enough in the cash register to run around the corner to the liquor store and buy a couple of bottles of Scotch.

Then things began picking up. Eddie had talked *Life* magazine into doing a picture story on jazz, and when *Life* finally ran it, along with some plugs for Nick's, people started coming in. Friday- and Saturday-night business started booming, trays of steaks went sizzling by the bandstand every ten minutes, the jitterbugs discovered that dancing to hot jazz was an exciting challenge, and jazz fans who just liked to listen began appearing as if by magic. Hugues Panassie's book on jazz had come out a year or so before and we were suddenly besieged by a strange new breed of fan—the record collector. Pale, intense, studious-looking young men buttonholed us when we were headed for Julius's, the saloon up the street where we relaxed between sets, and plied us with questions about who had played what instrument in some pickup band recorded some twenty years earlier, and the record-collecting craze was on as fans combed attics and Salvation Army warehouses and thrift shops and second-hand stores for suddenly sought-after recordings of race songs and jazz bands made twenty-five years before. They began forming record clubs and exchanging newsletters on jazz and did a brisk business swapping records with each other.

In the meantime, a very significant link in the chain of events that eventually led to the wide acceptance of jazz had begun operating—Milt Gabler, the proprietor of the Commodore Record Shop on Forty-second Street, east of Lexington Avenue. Milt, a round, placid man with a benevolent blue gaze, infinite patience, and a deep heart for jazz, had started a one-man crusade a few years earlier to persuade the big record companies to reissue the out-of-print records of the jazz of the twenties, and then in 1935 he bought the masters himself and reissued them under his own label, U.H.C.A.—United Hot Clubs of America. But just reissuing early jazz records wasn't helping to bring jazz back or to give musicians a living. It had been over four years since any company had made a new jazz record. Milt decided he might as well go whole hog, and he put out his own new records of contemporary hot jazz, under the label of Commodore Records. Later, Milt himself summed up his contribution toward reviving jazz with the apt observation that "Just as New Orleans was the cradle of jazz, Commodore Records was the iron lung."

By January, 1938, when Milt began recording his first Commodore dates, he was also working for the Decca Record Company as an A&R (Artists and Repertoire) man, and on the strength of the Commodore record sales he didn't have much trouble setting up recording dates for us with Decca, too. We

made the *Wolverine* album, of songs made famous by Beiderbecke, on the Decca label, and we also made the four sides,
"Friar's Point Shuffle," "Nobody's Sweetheart," "There'll Be
Some Changes Made," and "Someday, Sweetheart," for the
Decca *Chicago Jazz* album, the first jazz album ever made. Milt
also used the Decca studios to record the two twelve-inch Commodore records of "A Good Man Is Hard to Find." That most
of the Commodore dates turned out so well was due mainly to
Milt's talent for making you feel that the most important thing
in the world was having you play a song the way you felt it,
and he would get you feeling so good and so relaxed that that's
exactly what you did. As Milt expressed it in Gilbert Millstein's
profile of him in *The New Yorker* (March 9 and 16, 1946):

"The thrill I get is not knowing what's going to happen. One
guy hits on something and the others pick it right up and so
they *do* compose while they play. I never can tell when I'm
going to be lifted right out of my seat. That doesn't go with
arranged music. You don't get knocked out. You don't get the
bottom, the drive, the punch, the big, fat, hot note. The musician
has got to have a heart and be able to play pretty things, too,
things that say something different when he takes a solo and
not just what he has heard somewhere else. They have to know
their instruments. Guys that know their instruments don't get
lost, they know how to play the song and improvise on it and
then come back and play around it. Of course, when you get
one of those frantic characters sitting in he'll mess up everything
and throw everybody off. I don't like these screamadeemers on
the horn who have to make faces and play high. That isn't jazz
—a lot of people don't know that. Those guys get out on a limb
and then they can't come back. They get themselves a one-way
ticket to nowhere. Then they miss and it's the worst thing in
the world. He leaves you on the top floor and the whole works
collapses."

Things were happening so fast now with the rush of record
dates and the sudden interest in jazz that I scarcely had any idea

of what it was all about. One of our records from the Columbia *Comes Jazz* album, "Muskrat Ramble," was used as the theme on his disk-jockey show by Ralph Berton, the brother of Vic Berton, who played drums in Bix's Wolverine band. And with the sudden craze for hot-jazz records and the ever-increasing number of jazz fans, we found ourselves celebrities in the highly concentrated, intense world of jazz. I didn't quite know what to make of it all. Here these people were beginning to write about us and talk about our records and look up to us as heroes; compliments and plaudits were showered on us from all sides; and all I knew was that we were just lucky to have a place like Nick's to play in and be making our sixty dollars a week. Maybe if we were making a thousand a week we'd have felt more important, but that sixty dollars a week salary kept our heads down to normal size. We had no idea that people all over the world were beginning to collect our records and idolize us as the stalwart, pure-hearted artists fighting against the commercial music world. All we were concerned about was making our band sound good. But we were creating a new following for jazz and a new respect for it. We were setting a style again of having a band play as the musicians felt the music, and not commercially, as in the big swing bands. We were helping to create a public for jazz, and many of those new fans are now well-known critics and writers and record executives.

And we were also setting new forms of playing songs, as in the Lee Wiley albums, which were years ahead of their time. It was all Johnny DeVries' idea. An advertising artist, and a theatregoer as well as a jazz buff, Johnny was an ardent fan of show tunes, and he was fired with the idea of having Lee record Gershwin songs the way Johnny felt they were meant to be done, in an authentic jazz mood. Show tunes had been recorded a million times but never in the way Johnny had in mind.

Big-band swing was at the peak of its popularity then and the record companies thought it was the worst idea of the year, but Johnny finally found a Mr. Hill of the Liberty Music Shops, who agreed to sponsor the date and turn it out under the Liberty label. We worked out the arrangements one night, and the next day Brad Gowans, George Wettling, Pee Wee, Joe Bushkin, Eddie Condon, and Artie Shapiro and Lee and I went to the studio and made the records. Lee's singing was sheer perfection, and the album sold so well at the Liberty Music Shops that Ernie Anderson was able to sell Rabson's on the idea of doing another one. We worked out a Rodgers and Hart album with Lee next, and later on she did a Harold Arlen album, and a Cole Porter album with Bunny Berigan on trumpet. Lee set the style for years to come with her marvelous phrasing and the haunting timbre of her voice, and later everyone else copied her, as well as the idea of the celeste introductions, and of doing the verse out of tempo and then going into tempo on the chorus. Lee Wiley, who was born and raised in Oklahoma, is part Cherokee, and she says there is an old family saying that "all Cherokees sing." She points to Jack Teagarden and Pee Wee Russell, who are also part Cherokee, as further proof of the saying. Mildred Bailey, too, had American Indian blood, as well as Ernie Caceres, Big Chief Russell Moore, and Cutty Cutshall.

As much as I loved being around with Eddie and Ernie and all the guys, the pace began to tell on me after a while. Eddie was always a great man for parties, and it seemed as though the whole time in the Summa Cum Laude band was one great big party. The other fellows could drink, but, as I've said, after three drinks I was out on my feet and the next day my lip had as much strength as a used rubber band. I met Nancy, who was later to become my wife, during this time, and my personal life had become further complicated by all the turmoil that goes with having a girl. I was caught up in the whirl, but in my heart I felt guilty about the perpetual merry-go-round. All my life I had wanted the chance to play jazz with musicians like these and now that I was doing it I wasn't happy about the kind of living that went with it. I don't know why it so often happens that way—when you're living what should be the greatest moments of your life you are so often confused and miserable instead of happy. Perhaps that is the proof of their greatness. Now that I look back on it I see how wonderful those times were. But in 1938, with each weekend bringing a new crisis in Europe, it would have been surprising if we hadn't felt apprehensive and concerned underneath the excitement of our daily lives.

People were so jittery that when Orson Welles' radio show about Mars invading the United States went on the air, thousands of terrified people in New Jersey hit the road. Kate Smith began ending her radio programs by singing "God Bless America," and I started to stay up till dawn to listen to Hitler's speeches over short wave, as though hearing him first hand would give me some new insight into the madness that was swallowing up Europe. Here in America, despite my name being Max Kaminsky, I was knee-deep in compliments, while in Germany, because of my name and my faith, I would have been in a concentration camp on my way to the gas chamber. Was human dignity a matter of geography?

In any case, I soon had something more immediate to worry about. Around November of 1938, Nick, in a burst of optimism at the upswing in business, brought in Muggsy Spanier's band in addition to ours. Then, after a couple of weeks, he decided there wasn't enough business to warrant having two bands and we were given notice. A week or so later, we went to work in the Brick Club on Forty-seventh Street, a barrelhouse West Side joint—and I mean barrel and house. The Brick Club was also famous for hiring jazz bands. Hot Lips Page had had the band in there before us, with a marvelously flashy drummer named Kid Lips Hackett. Though we were paid only forty dollars a week, we were on the air every night and we hoped we were continuing to build up an audience for the band.

For some reason, this job was hard on our drummers and we had a whole procession of them during the couple of months we were there, including George Wettling and Dave Tough. One night Dave became so zomped he couldn't finish the night, so Don Marino took over. Don was just starting to learn to play then, and after his first set we all turned to him with praise and encouragement.

"Thanks, fellows," he said, "but will you please tell Bud to lay off. He keeps twisting around when he's playing and staring at me as if I'm doing something wrong."

We all turned on Bud then, telling him to lay off the kid and give him a chance. Bud didn't know what we were talking about, and it turned out he wasn't looking at Don at all. There was a mirror beside the drums and every time he took a solo Bud had automatically turned so he could get the full effect of himself in a mirror. Bud, in fact, was part frustrated actor. Over the years he had cultivated a thespian way of speaking that was very impressive. It was so good, in fact, that once when he actually tried out for a Broadway play, reading for the part of a jazz musician, he was turned down because the director thought he sounded too much like an actor!

From the Brick Club we went out to Chicago in the spring of 1939 for a month at the Panther Room at the Hotel Sherman. It was through Lee Wiley that we landed the job, and Lee went out with us to sing in the band. We alternated with Stuff Smith's band, which had Jonah Jones and Cozy Cole; a great band that was vastly underappreciated. "Squirrel" Ashcraft, a Chicago lawyer who had been a jazz fan since his Princeton and Bix Beiderbecke days was famous for his Monday night open-house jam sessions at his Evanston home, and he made our stay memorable with his hospitality. In my book, Squirrel can be rated as one of the top hosts, ever.

For our salary of sixty dollars a week, we did two broadcasts a night, and we also played for the floor show, which included a clown who handed out balloons to the patrons and had them participating in kiddie cart races, and a Spanish dance team for whom we played bullfight music. These were the days when publishers were still going around plugging new songs for the bands to play on the air. Brad would sit up all night writing

medley arrangements of the songs: "April Played the Fiddle,"
"I'll Never Smile Again," "The Wind and the Rain in Your
Hair," and the next night we'd play the medleys mixed in with
the jazz classics. In spite of everything, the band sounded fine
and Lee was singing as only she could, but when the Panther
Room engagement ended there wasn't a soul around offering us
another job. Eddie even resorted to sending a wire to Bing
Crosby, but Crosby's return wire squashed that hope. Los
Angeles was still a hillbilly town and didn't dig, he said.

When we returned to New York Eddie and Pee Wee went
back into Nick's, but I hated to give up without trying the
Schribman formula. When I told Ernie Anderson about Sy
Schribman, Ernie took us up to Boston, where Sy booked us
into some one-nighters in dance halls in New England. Along
with Bud, Brad, and me, we had Lips Page and Al Drootin. We
were spectacularly unsuccessful. The formula didn't work for
us; those kids didn't care whose band they were hearing just as
long as it wasn't ours. Even Ernie had to admit there was still
no popular audience for jazz, but it made him more determined
than ever to give jazz a chance to be heard.

After a few weeks of emptying out dance halls, we slunk back
to New York in August and found ourselves a job at the World's
Fair, alternating with Charlie Barnet's big band in an open-air
dance hall. It was cold and rainy out there in Flushing Meadows
that last month of the 1939 World's Fair as Hitler began to really
blow his stack. When Germany invaded Poland, and England
and France declared war on Germany, that was the end of the
long tragedy of appeasement and the beginning of the terrible
reality of war. It was also the end of the Summa Cum Laude
band, and the beginning of the same old routine of dodging land-
lords, hunting for places to play, and trying not to think of
food. For jazzmen, the years 1939–42 were the depression all
over again.

During that fall of 1939, Milt Gabler started running the
Sunday sessions at Jimmy Ryan's as another way of giving jazz-

men work. You could always count on a five or a ten out of
Milt for the Sunday jam sessions, but besides helping keep the
musicians in bread and beer, these sessions were a kind of oasis
for musician and fan alike. Just as barren as was musical life of
opportunities for playing and hearing jazz, so the sessions at
Ryan's seemed that much richer and greener. There was a moment there, in 1941–42, at the Ryan sessions, when hot jazz
seemed at its purest. Hovering on the edge of public discovery
and known only to a few, it was as yet completely unself-
conscious and untouched by commercialism or publicity.

It's hard to believe that the Fifty-second Street of the thirties,
the forties, and the fifties is completely gone now, gobbled up
by Radio City. Ryan's continued to be an oasis for hot-jazz
fans through the sunset years of Fifty-second Street, when its
kind of music was eclipsed by bop and cool and hard jazz and
its buildings menaced by the wrecker's steel ball. Jimmy Ryan
set another record for constancy by "holding over" one band,
the DeParis Brothers, for over ten years, until the spring of 1962,
when the club was finally razed to clear the site for the new
CBS building. But in the early forties Ryan's was the mecca of
jazz fans on Sunday afternoons. You paid a dollar at the door,
usually to Jack Crystal, who helped run the sessions, and if you
didn't want to drink you could sit in the rows of chairs set up
in the center of the floor and listen without anything to distract
you except the bobbing head of the cat in front of you. The club
was small, the atmosphere intimate, and the audience listened
hard. The feeling was that musicians and fans alike lived just
for Sundays, and that Jimmy Ryan himself, genial, debonair
ex-hoofer turned night-club owner, was having as big a ball as
everyone else. The fans, who included specimens of all the
varieties—the earnest jazz purist; the jivey hep cat; the intense
intellectual; extroverts from the advertising world; Broadway
types; sentimental drunks; dedicated drinkers; plain people; and
plain characters—were all members of the same fraternity. One
devoted fan was memorable for his absence. He was a Bronx

baker, and most every Sunday at four he was a captive to his trade, stoking up his ovens for his Monday-morning bread. But his friends made notes of every set at Ryan's and gave him a blow-by-blow verbal playback the next day. Another fan was a dentist, who stood next to the drums at every session, and the sight of his blissful face was as much a part of the sessions as the music. The Ryan's regulars were the most sincere and discriminating group of fans I ever played for anywhere, and you could hear a swizzlestick drop as they listened to musicians like: Jess Stacy, Joe Sullivan, Dave Tough, Kansas Fields, Big Sid Catlett, Bill Coleman, Joe Thomas, Emmett Berry, Red Allen, Rod Cless, Jay C. Higginbotham, Sammy Price, Pee Wee Russell, Vic Dickenson, Bud Freeman, Zutty Singleton, Billy Butterfield, Brad Gowans, Frank Orchard, Muggsy Spanier, Ernie Caceres, Bobby Hackett, Sid Weiss, Mel Powell, Sidney Bechet, Lips Page, Dick Cary, Albert Nicholas, Cliff Jackson, Kaiser Marshall, Wild Bill Davison, Vernon Brown, George Wettling, Joe Bushkin, Marty Marsala, Sandy Williams, Benny Morton, Roy Eldridge, Jack Bland, Miff Mole, Charlie Shavers, Don Fry, Artie Shapiro, Edmond Hall, Danny Alvin, Gene Schroeder, Jack Lesberg, Don Byas, Joe Grausso, Bob Haggart, Lou McGarity, Wilbur and Sidney DeParis, Barney Bigard, Buck Clayton, Bob Casey, Al Morgan, Johnny Windhurst, Mezz Mezzrow, Art Hodes, Pops Foster, Pete Johnson, Albert Ammons, Lester Young, Johnny Simmons, Earl Hines, Meade Lux Lewis, Deane Kincaide, Eddie Heywood, Ray Conniff, Tony Parenti, Gene Sedric, Panama Francis, Hank D'Amico, Al Hall.

The sets fell into a pattern of a white band alternating with a colored group, although they were often both slightly mixed, and it became the tradition to have both groups jam together after the last set on the roof-raising "Bugle Call Rag." Nobody played "The Saints" then. At Ryan's the music was the thing, and when a musician was building a solo you never heard a sound from the audience. You could *feel* them listening.

But eventually Ryan's, too, felt the pinch of war and the

quality inevitably deteriorated. Musicians were being drafted
every day, the fans were scattered far and wide, and a different
type of audience took over—4-F, jivey characters in zoot suits
to match the frantic screaming tenor saxes which were the
precursors of bop.

In the middle of 1940, the Maginot Line collapsed and the
British were nearly wiped out at Dunkirk. Here, isolation and
intervention were burning issues—and the scarcity of jobs was
bugging jazzmen. There was Ryan's and some other places for
gigs, but no steady work. Though I recorded a good deal during
this time, no royalties for any of the records ever came my way,
and I never even had the sense to think about it. So many
musicians are poor businessmen; Fats Waller, for instance, used
to sell his marvelous songs for fifty dollars apiece when he was
broke, which was often. I didn't mind washing out the same
pair of socks every night, but when I was reduced to putting
cardboard in my shoes I decided it was time to resort to the
one thing I had always resorted to—going back to work in a
commercial band. Being a con man was never my style; I was
never one for bumming free meals and free lodgings, and when
there was no work as a jazzman I tried to find any kind of work,
even though it involved doing routine playing as well as swallowing my pride. Having nothing to eat and nothing to wear is a
great aid to swallowing. I went to work in Tony Pastor's band
at the Hotel Lincoln for a few months, and then the first half
of 1941 was another big struggle again.

Finally, gulping down a particularly painful lump of pride, I
called up Artie Shaw. Shaw was very cordial on the phone, and
he even invited me over for dinner at his apartment that night
on Central Park South. He had just made some very successful
records with a big band in California—"Dancing in the Dark"
and "Stardust"—and had come East that August to organize
another, bigger band with thirty men. We talked about music
and books, as usual, and about his ideas for his new band.

"If I were getting a big swing band together, I'd get Lips
Page," I said, ready as ever with the advice.

"Who," Artie asked, "is Lips Page?"

"Well, you might say he is only the greatest trumpet after Louis," I said softly. So Shaw hired Lips for his new band, along with me and Dave Tough.

A thirty-piece band was unusually big even for those days of big bands. There had been no band of this size since Paul Whiteman's in the late thirties. A couple of weeks later, we started to rehearse the band and I started eating again. We had four trumpets, with Lee Castle and Steve Lipkin besides Lips and myself. Georgie Auld was in this band, and Jack Jenney, Johnny Guarnieri, and Mike Bryan, as well as many wonderful string musicians whose names I can't remember now. Lips fitted in perfectly, playing and entertaining beautifully with songs like "Blues in the Night" and "Take Off Your Shoes, Baby, You Keep Running Through My Mind," and Artie was delighted with him. I played a little lead, but not much. Lips and I shared the jazz work, but I felt I was just sitting back and taking it easy compared to the earlier Shaw band when no one could play.

We went on the road up to New England again, and Artie was bigger than ever. People followed his bus and swarmed in to collect autographs whenever it stopped. Though I eventually began to go crazy in this band, too, because after a while I couldn't just sit there and play that same stuff night after night, I was so thankful to be able to buy some shirts and underwear and shoes and a suit that I was determined to stay as long as I could this time. We were all paid wonderful salaries for those days, in fact, my kingly $175 a week was the most money I had ever made up to then, and I had the sense to know I ought to hang on to it no matter how dull it was.

Lips never forgot that I was responsible for his getting the job with Shaw. Forever after, I was Buddy to Lips, and years later, whenever we ran into each other he would relate the story to everyone within earshot. "I was never so happy in my life," he'd say, his eyes shining at the memory, "and this is the man who got it for me." Besides that, he liked my playing, too. Like Glenn Miller, he was always saying I was the best lead trumpet man, but I always felt Lips was the most underrated of the jazz greats. Born in Dallas, Texas, Lips had come to New York in 1936 with Count Basie's band, along with Lester Young, Buck Clayton, Don Byas, and Jo Jones, and to me he *had* it; no one else could break it up like Lips. His drive was tremendous, and he could play chorus after chorus without ever repeating himself. They have said that about other musicians, but Lips was the only one I have heard who could actually do it. In Lips' good days he could do thirty or more choruses, each one different. In his last years, when he'd come down to Condon's club and sit in and play to Ralph Sutton's intermission piano, Lips was so great that the customers used to come up to the stand and thrust fistfuls of dollar bills at him. Lips gave them so much that they felt applause wasn't enough for him and they showered him with money. It was quite a sight to see Lips play while his hand that held the trumpet bristled with greenbacks.

Lips broke up audiences even in the most segregated sections of the deep South. One night after the show, a cracker came up to the bandstand and said he thought Lips played so great that he wanted to meet him. After shaking Lips' hand, the Southerner said, ". . . and Ah want you to know this is the first time Ah ever shook the hand of a colored man." Lips flashed one of his wide, happy grins and said in his wonderfully pleasing way, "Well, buddy, it didn't hurt, now, did it?"

Though Lips was only forty-six when he died in 1954, he sure had a good time. To him every day was a ball, and a big one, and he lived more in his brief life than a thousand other people put together. I tried to keep up with Lips one night after work when we were on the road. Lips had that knack of lighting up a room with so much joy and life that everywhere he went, everyone felt they couldn't do enough for him. The bellboy in the little beat-up hotel where Lips was staying kept the whiskey coming in fast and plentiful supply while Lips and I swapped stories about bands, music, and musicians. At ten o'clock the next morning, I conked out cold in the middle of

one of Lips' stories, but Lips told me later that he and the bellboy finished the last of the liquor and then Lips had a huge
breakfast at noon before he turned in. This was a mild night,
but mild or wild, there weren't many who could keep up with
Lips.

We were playing a Sunday-afternoon show at a theatre in
Providence on December 7, 1941, when the manager interrupted
the performance to announce that the Japanese had bombed
Pearl Harbor. A few weeks later we were doing a record date
at Victor when Artie's manager handed him his letter of greet-
ings from Uncle Sam. The band was immediately given its
notice.

"Well," I said to Dave Tough as we packed our instruments,
"that's the way it goes. The minute we get a chance to make a
little money they have to go and have a war. See you around
the Automat, pal." I had no idea that Dave and Artie and I
would be seeing a lot more of each other within a year.

As the New Year of 1942 was rung in on a world up to its
eyeballs in war, Eddie Condon and Ernie Anderson started to
launch the jazz concerts at Town Hall. And it was the war itself
that was the decisive factor in bringing about recognition for
jazz.

The only hours that Town Hall had available for rental were
the dinner hours of five thirty to seven thirty, and the manager
was so surprised at anyone wanting to rent at this "dead" time
that he gave Eddie the hall for a hundred dollars. At the first
concert, on February 21, 1942, only thirty people or so showed
up, but nothing could discourage Ernie Anderson. He had all
the faith in the world in jazz and in the concerts. Although the
box-office receipts were so poor that half the time we weren't
paid for playing the concerts, the fans were as loyal and enthusiastic as Eddie and Ernie, and they kept coming back, and
each time a few more came with them. Condon, who has a
reputation for clever repartee in private life, turned into a
quaking leaf on the Town Hall stage, and he limited his scarcely

audible remarks to a muttered, "I don't think this next number will bother you people at all." I guess we all felt it was a mammoth undertaking, trying to get jazz across in the austere atmosphere of the concert stage. Many years later, when I played Town Hall again, I was amazed to see how small it was; in my memory it had loomed as immense as Madison Square Garden. And we ourselves presented a rather strange sight in contrast to the polished, show-biz appearance of the big swing bands with their slick uniforms and glittering music stands. We just walked out on the bare stage, dressed in business suits, gathered round in a semicircle, and blew. There were no stands and no music; just a chair for Eddie, and the American flag in the back of the stage.

After each concert we'd reassemble at Eddie's apartment and hold a post-mortem and we'd tell ourselves to give up, but Ernie Anderson would always say, "Let's try just once more." We'd sit around far into the night, racking our brains trying to think of a big idea for publicity.

"I know people would come if only they knew about the concerts," Ernie would growl, as he opened a second bottle of Scotch.

"Maybe one of us could do something scandalous and get it in all the papers and that would bring publicity . . ." one of us would suggest dreamily.

"Just *one* favorable review," Ernie would mutter, as he paced up and down the room. "Just one good sentence—hell, just one good *adjective*—and I'll blow it up all over town!"

The summer of 1942, while the concerts were suspended for the season, Eddie Condon and I worked in Joe Marsala's band in the Log Cabin up in Armonk, New York. This was the beginning of the end of the big-band era, for with the musicians being called up right and left in the draft, we had a new replacement practically every night. We were on the air nightly, too, but the broadcasts were nothing to look forward to because it was actually just a pickup band each time.

That summer was the low point in the war for the United States. The Japanese had overrun the Philippines after Mac-Arthur's last-ditch stand on Corregidor, and they were turning their eyes toward Australia. At home we were being introduced to rationing, and the problem of getting enough gasoline for the nightly drive up to Armonk became another headache. The factories began operating night and day, and as morale at home as well as for our men overseas began to become a concern, music began to play its part—not only the songs, like "The White Cliffs of Dover," "The Last Time I Saw Paris," "When the Lights Go On Again All Over the World," but the uplift of the jazz beat began at last to find a response in the public's consciousness.

When we resumed the concerts that fall, the impossible miracle finally happened. The Monday after our first Saturday concert of the season, we opened the New York *Herald Tribune* to find that Virgil Thomson had reviewed the concert more favorably than Ernie Anderson could have wished in his wildest dream. The succeeding concert was such a sellout that the mounted police was called to help keep order. And, of course, that was the one concert that Ernie missed, having been called to California the day before. That night down at Condon's, where we assembled for the usual bull session, I was so thrilled and excited at the miracle of our success that I burst into tears.

We had the right format for these concerts. We had sat around and talked about it by the hour and we had worked it all out, from the opening set by a jazz band with a fireball number, followed by a great pianist, Joe Sullivan, Teddy Wilson, James P. Johnson, or Jess Stacy, and then a quartet composed of Bobby Hackett, or Benny Morton, or Barney Bigard, with piano and drums and bass, and then a singer like Lee Wiley or Billie Holiday, and then another set with the band, and then the final jam session. Most important to the success of these concerts, in addition to the quality of the performers and the pacing of the numbers, was Eddie's handling of the jam sessions that closed each concert. He never allowed these all-out sessions, which would number about twenty musicians, to degenerate into wild riffing contests, with order and meaning sacrificed for the merely sensational. The people who put on the thousands of jazz concerts and festivals that followed in the next twenty years rarely understood that jazz needs to be presented by musicians who know the music and can organize it and keep it under control. These Town Hall concerts were the first regular series of jazz concerts ever given. They ran for years, and they were an enormous factor in making jazz known and available to everyone.

Chapter 9

Artie Shaw came to New York in the late summer of 1942 to form his Navy band, and when I told him I had received my draft papers, he asked me to join his band. Although Artie and I had had plenty of battles ourselves, going into his Navy band seemed to me a better idea than going into the Army. I was nearly thirty-four, and I preferred doing something I knew to going into the Army and never having a chance to play any more. Artie, who was now Chief Petty Officer Shaw, arranged it all, and a few weeks later I received a letter from the Navy Department with instructions to report to 90 Church Street for assignment to the Artie Shaw Navy band as musician first class.

I showed up at the recruiting center the next forenoon, expecting to have the whole procedure over with in half an hour. Three hours later, I was standing on a long line, and when I ended up, stripped for a physical, on another line an hour after that, I was still trying to get someone to look at my letter.

"Later, chief," the medical officer growled when I offered him the letter. He was cranky with fatigue, and after he had finished with his examination, he leaned back in his chair and rubbed his forehead wearily for a minute before informing me that I was too short to join the Navy. "Not to mention a few

other little deterrents, such as a hernia and an ulcer," he added
dryly.

"All I had in mind was blowing the trumpet," I said. "Look,
I've been trying all day to get someone to read this letter. It's all
explained in here," and once more I held it out to him. The
medical officer folded the letter carefully when he finished reading it, put it back in the envelope, and handed it to me.

"We'll pretend we never saw this letter and you just go home,
okay?" he said gently.

"I don't see why I can't blow as well in the Navy with those
handicaps as I have for years as a civilian," I said hotly. The
head doctor, whom I demanded to see next, gave me the same
kind but firm advice, and I finally got the idea that the Navy
didn't think I was much of a prize. I put on my clothes, shoved
the letter in my pocket, and went home.

A week or two later, I received another letter from the Navy
Department instructing me to report immediately to 90 Church
Street. I felt they didn't deserve it, but I decided to give them
one more chance at me, so early the next morning, a Saturday, I
took the subway down to Church Street again. I had a job that
night, and I wanted to be sure I would make it on time.

"Stand over there," a flint-faced chief barked when I showed
him the letter. I joined a group of guys standing sheepishly in
one corner of the room, and after I had waited around for a
couple of hours, my name was finally called out, along with
four or five others, and we were sworn in and ordered to report
to the receiving center at Pier 92 on West Fifty-second Street.
Pier 92 didn't sound so good, but the Fifty-second Street part
of it was reassuring. Up at Pier 92, another chief, seated at a
desk behind a wire cage, checked our names against his list as
we came in, and told us to sit down. We sat down on a wooden
settee in a corner of the office, and we could have been invisible
for all the notice anyone took of us for the next four hours,
until I finally waylaid a lieutenant and explained that I had to
go to work that night.

"Buddy," the lieutenant said, fixing me with a cold blue eye, "you're not going anyplace tonight. You're in the Navy now. Sit down."

Even these simple, explicit words didn't sink into my one-track musician's mind. The world might be blowing up but all I knew was that I was supposed to be doing some blowing that night myself. When six o'clock came and I found myself holding a tin plate and standing in line for chow, I still couldn't believe I might not make my job. I had no idea yet that this was the start of a long career of standing in line, but it took just one whiff of the Navy beans and baloney to make me realize I had to duck out of that mess hall fast. I hadn't eaten since breakfast and now I felt as if I never wanted to eat again.

Several hours later, a sailor handed me a limp pillow and a gray blanket and told me to go upstairs and bunk. By this time they had had lights out and I was forced to feel my way along in the dark. After waking up several hundred guys, I realized that this embarkation center was actually a huge camp, and when I finally found an unoccupied cot way up in the fifth tier of bunks, another chilling thought struck me. "My God," I said to myself as the unavoidable fact finally hit home. "I *am* in the Navy!"

In a few minutes I began talking to the guy next to me. "What goes on here?" I asked. "I feel like I've been shanghaied." It didn't seem possible that several thousand men could be herded together and stacked up in tiers like that, right under the unsuspecting noses of New Yorkers, and my own nose, which was even more finicky than my stomach, couldn't believe there could be an odor like this.

My neighbor, a sympathetic type who seemed to be an old hand at all this, tried to calm me down a little. He told me that if I sneaked downstairs I might be able to get to a phone, so I crawled back over the same three hundred guys and called the fellows to say I couldn't make the job—something they had begun to suspect by now. "And, say," I added as an afterthought,

"I might not be seeing you guys for a while. It looks like they mean business here."

All day Sunday I sat around waiting and brooding, but even after they had set me on a detail of cleaning the latrines I was finally able to convince myself that I was George Washington, and what with Hitler and the Japs and all that crap going on, this was something I should do for my country. In spite of the confusion and the fact that I had discovered I was the only one out of the two thousand men there who had no boot training, no uniform, and no equipment, I decided just to wait and see what happened next.

Monday finally came, and things began to make a little more sense when the other musicians, who had been out over the weekend on seventy-two-hour passes, showed up and I discovered that I'd been sent to Pier 92 for the simple reason that this was where Artie's band was assigned—although none of us knew yet, of course, that we were set to go out on a tour of the Pacific. Soon I saw Claude Thornhill and John Best and some of the other guys I knew, and met the ones I didn't know, such as Conrad Gozzo, Rocky Calucci, Frank Beach, Sam Donohue, and Tasso Harris. Some were from the Newport base, where Artie had been stationed. Since the Navy had had a band already set up for him there, he had to take some of those men, but he needed musicians who could swing to have the kind of band he wanted for his tour, which is how he was able to get me and Dave Tough in the Navy.

For during the time I'd been trying to enlist, Artie had been arranging for Dave to come into the band, too. Dave showed up that Monday morning in good shape, sober and serious, and he gave me confidence, especially when I discovered he had gone through a similar experience getting into the Navy. Dave was not only about the same height I was, he looked like an emaciated imp. His wife, Casey, had fed him spaghetti night and day for two weeks in an attempt to put some weight on him, but Artie had taken the added precaution of accompanying him to the induction center to make sure he was accepted. When Dave stripped for his physical, the medical officer took one unbelieving look at him, and turning to Artie, he said incredulously, "Do you really need this man in your band?"

"This is the world's greatest drummer," Artie snapped.

"Then get him the hell out of here before somebody sees him," the officer snapped back. "This guy is not only an impossible physical specimen, he violates every basic requirement for size, weight, height, and health," he snarled as he stamped his approval on Dave's papers.

We were at Pier 92 for about three weeks until our twenty-piece band, which was officially designated Navy Band #501, was finally organized. We'd rise at 5:30 A.M., my normal bedtime, and march out on the pier to play "Stars and Stripes Forever," "Under the Double Eagle Flag," "Anchors Aweigh," and "The Washington Post March" while the poor gobs went through their exercises and marched around in the chilly October air. Dave wasn't strong enough to carry a drum or even the big cymbals, so they gave him a peck horn. It was very funny to see him wrestling with this unfamiliar instrument and trying to get some kind of tone out of it. In fact, we were a horrible excuse for a military band, in spite of the good musicians. Rehearsing didn't help much, and after we finished whatever gruesome details they put us to, we'd just sit around the rest of the day and practice the fine art of griping. On weekends I'd grab a seventy-two-hour pass and rush over to play at the Town Hall concerts on Saturday and at the Ryan's sessions on Sunday.

I made a quick visit home on one of these weekends. There was a sudden cold snap that Saturday, with the temperature dropping down to freezing, and my mother was concerned about the short length of my pea jacket. That afternoon she caught sight of an admiral stepping briskly down the street in his long blue greatcoat. "Here," she said, thrusting some bills in my hand. "Take this and buy yourself a nice warm coat like that sailor is wearing."

Soon after that, one night in November the whole band was herded into an open truck and driven to Penn Station.

"Take a good, long look," Dave said softly as the driver turned down Broadway. Even in the wartime dimout the Great White Way looked great to us.

"I still feel I've been shanghaied," I said.

We were on our way to Honolulu, but all we knew was that the train was taking us to San Francisco, where we were stationed at the Navy barracks on Treasure Island. Artie was married to Betty Kern at the time, and she and her father, Jerome Kern, came out to the Coast and stayed at the Mark Hopkins until the band left for Hawaii.

A couple of weeks later, we boarded the *Lurline*, a Matson Line cruise ship which had been converted into a troop ship. The first day at sea, while I was standing on the chow line, the ship's purser passed by and at the sight of me he stopped short and exclaimed in shocked tones, "Max Kaminsky! What in hell are you doing here?" I thought I was doing something wrong, as usual, but it turned out that he was a jazz fan, and when I finished explaining about being in Shaw's band he said brusquely, "Come with me," and he led me off to the galley. The Chinese chef turned out to be a neighbor of mine from Thirty-third Street and Third Avenue, where I had been living, and from then on nothing was too good for me. When I had finished the last crumb of the lemon meringue pie, the purser, Mr. Goodman, said, "You bring the rest of the boys in the band down here to eat, too, from now on." I used to ask Mr. Goodman for a bag of fruit, and I'd stand in front of my cabin and call out, "Fresh apples, peaches, oranges, anyone?" and hand them out to the crew right and left. I felt so sorry for the crew, having to eat that miserable regulation chow all the time, that I wanted to give them a treat, too.

We arrived in Honolulu on Christmas Day of 1942. Long rows of tables and benches were set up near the pier, piled high with turkey and all the trimmings, but the five-millimeter guns they had shot off as a salute when we docked had so stunned me that I was goggle-eyed with shock all through the meal and I could have been eating shredded coconut husks for all that anything registered.

We were stationed in Honolulu for nearly five months, and in no time at all it got to seem like five years. The sameness of the languid climate and the regular daily rainstorms began to pall after a few weeks. I never could get used to that one-climate deal. We shared our quarters with another Navy band, a regulation outfit, so that altogether there were about forty men in our barracks. All the bunks were set up in one section of the dun-colored frame building and the rest of the space was set aside for ping-pong tables and a rehearsal room. The fact that both bands were scheduled to practice at the same time did nothing to enhance our opinion of the Navy way of doing things.

Our barracks in Aiea, a little village outside Honolulu, was in the middle of a mosquito-infested swamp, formerly the site of a pineapple plantation. We spent most of our time cleaning the mud out of the barracks, and whenever it dried out enough to stop being mud, it turned into a fine coral powder which covered everything with dust and caused a chronic irritation in our throats. I bought several bottles of terpin hydrate codeine for my cough. It had a little kick to it, and whenever the whole Navy thing got too much for me, I'd duck into my bunk and take a couple of extra swigs to calm my nerves. If it weren't for terpin hydrate codeine, I don't know how I'd have got through the war.

Artie had a room at the Halekulani Hotel and Claude Thornhill lived in a friend's apartment in Honolulu. I had an offer from a fan from Nick's, now an officer stationed in Honolulu, to stay at his apartment, but I was told that for me it was against regulations, and although that was untrue, I, like a schmuck, believed it. They kept us plenty busy, in any case, which was good. On Monday, Wednesday, and Friday afternoons we played at The Breakers, a club for enlisted men on Waikiki

Beach, and at night we played at the Pearl Harbor Officers' Club and at officers' parties and dances, and gave concerts at the different camps all around the Islands.

Except for Claude Thornhill, Dave Tough, John Best, and me, most of the musicians in the band were young kids, and they'd take off like a shot for Honolulu every chance they had. It wasn't long before they had a lot of romances going—one of them even got married—and naturally a lot of friction started. It's hell on a civilian to be plucked out of his ordinary life and put into military service and sent to a far country, but a musician has a hard time even in civilian life because so much is required emotionally to play that when he stops he is a madman, and those kids hadn't much experience yet in learning how to handle themselves.

Eventually I worked out a routine of getting up at six in the morning, and after breakfast bumming my way to the recreation hall in Pearl Harbor to pick up the mail instead of waiting all day for it to be delivered. (The road to Pearl Harbor, about a half-hour walk from Aiea, wound past the bay where the battleship *Arizona*, with 1,100 dead men still aboard, lay on its side on the blue waters.) The fellows in the band called me The Mailman, but it was something to do and at least it got me out of those barracks in the morning. The rest of my free time I spent writing letters and reading. Living in a barracks with forty men was no ball, and when Artie occasionally invited me to have breakfast with him at the Halekulani I looked forward to the comparative privacy as much as to the ham and eggs, which were a big treat after the Navy chow.

After a few weeks I met a Marine, John Straeter, cousin of Ted Straeter, who was a jazz fan and knew about me. He was in charge of the officers' mess in the nearby Marine barracks and every couple of weeks on a Sunday night, which was our night off, he would come by in his jeep and leave bottles of whiskey and Cokes for me, and the four or five of us who stayed in the barracks instead of charging into Honolulu would have our own private little bash.

On one of the holidays in February, there were so many parties being held at different officers' homes that the band had to be split up into little groups. Claude Thornhill, Dave Tough, one of the sax players, and I were sent to play at a party which Admiral Nimitz was attending, and once the Admiral, who was a piano buff, got an earful of Claude playing things like *Rhapsody in Blue* and some of the classical pieces, he dropped anchor next to the piano for the rest of the night. He had Claude, who is a very interesting and entertaining fellow, over to his house every chance he could after that, and Claude told me later that Nimitz said he thought a great artist like Claude shouldn't be in military service.

"I told him I didn't mind doing my bit just like everyone else," Claude said, "but that I felt I could do a bigger job if I could be in charge of a band of my own." Artie's personality was still getting people's back up, but he was having his own troubles, too, adjusting to the military life and all the Navy red tape and regulations, and he was a natural target, in his crisp white chief's uniform, for the bored Navy wives, who all trained their guns on him at every dance we played.

One night in May, we received our orders to board the battleship *North Carolina*, which was part of a task force headed for the South Pacific. When we sailed the next morning, Claude was at the dock to wave good-bye to us. Admiral Nimitz had arranged for his transfer from Artie's band and assigned him to form his own band to play on the islands around Hawaii.

"Well, we just play the wrong instrument, that's all," Dave finally said, as we glumly watched the shoreline fade into the horizon.

I had another surprise in store for me that afternoon when the medics discovered from my records that I hadn't gone through boot training and didn't have any of the required shots for overseas duty. To make up for lost time, they gave me the whole series at once. I tottered back to my cabin and made a somewhat wavy beeline for my bunk, which was, as usual, on the fifth tier. I never could carry all my gear by myself and had to hire sailors to lug it on board for me, and by the time we got it on the ship the only cot left was one of the top ones. Just gazing up at my bunk made me so dizzy that I wheeled around and fairly crawled back into the sick bay. "Oh, well, a lot of guys die every day around here," was the greeting I received down there, and it so unnerved me that I turned around once more and headed back for my quarters and somehow managed to climb up to my bunk, where I lay like a zombie for two days.

The band was assigned to damage control, which meant that when we were under fire we were stationed in the damage-control room to lock all equipment, shut off the fans, and seal off each compartment in case of a hit. Off the control room was the gun storeroom, out of which they hoisted up the big cannons. The first time I heard them shoot those sixteen-inch gun salvos, the shock was so appalling that I sprawled on my face. I didn't think I could ever live through it again. But I did. I never knew what the shooting was all about, though, since the minute the alarm sounded we all headed for our battle station in the control room, where we couldn't tell what was going on, and I never cared to inquire.

Since we didn't have any other duties beside damage control, I used to hang around the pilots and watch them steer the ship. I became friends with one of the bosun's mates, and when we were near the Equator I asked him if I could steer the ship. When he told me we were crossing the Equator I instinctively tightened my grip on the wheel and said, "Yeah, man, I just felt the bump!" They all laughed, and I was only kidding, but the odd thing is, years later I read there really is a bump.

Our new station was in Nouméa, the capital of the French-owned island of New Caledonia. After the fall of France in 1940, most of the French colonial empire went along with the Vichy government, but the Frenchmen in New Caledonia got mad, and one day they came pouring down from the hills into Nouméa, kicked out the pro-Vichy governor, and took over the island for de Gaulle.

This little coastal town had no facilities for the thousands upon thousands of American troops that descended on it in 1942, and its food and water supplies were severely rationed. We were allowed one milk can of drinking water a day and every second day we were allotted a bucket of water for washing, which we kept under our cots. Empty gasoline cans, in which we boiled our dirty clothes, made very adequate laundry tubs. Our barracks, on the outskirts of Nouméa, were in the midst of a wire-enclosed encampment where they kept all the Navy jeeps and trucks, and although technically Artie bunked with us, he lived in one of the local officials' home. Along with short water rations we were given lectures by Artie about being on guard against food poisoning and dysentery, since the refrigeration facilities were so poor that the Navy couldn't guarantee that the chow it fed its men wasn't tainted. After a couple of meals of bad meat, we decided that it wasn't worth the gamble, since it all tasted so terrible anyway, and we took matters into our own hands. As musicians with a long experience of being on the road, most of us were used to foraging for ourselves. One of the men wangled several cases of tuna fish from some undisclosed source, and each day one of us would get a pass to go into town to buy a half-dozen loaves of fresh-baked French bread, and between candy bars and the food we were served when we played at officers' parties, we made out all right. That French bread especially tasted delicious.

All the buildings in Nouméa were built on stilts as a safeguard against termites. The town itself was tiny and primitive, although many of the planters' homes were quite grand. None of the stores, which kept typical tropical hours, opening from ten to twelve and again from three to five, had electricity, and we searched in vain for a restaurant. Our big thrill there was getting a shower for fifty cents once a week at the public baths. We were so filthy from living out of a bucket of water that although the shower nozzle barely dripped, we thought it was great. On Sundays we'd watch the natives stream down from the hills in their best finery

to promenade in barefoot dignity around the little park in the
center of town. But the most unforgettable sight in Nouméa
was the hill in back of town, dazzling white in the tropic glare
with the hundreds and hundreds of crosses marking the graves
of Allied soldiers and sailors and airmen who died in the battle
of the Coral Sea.

The one problem we couldn't lick was the mosquitoes, which
were so tiny they came right through our netting. I woke one
morning to find that a whole battalion of them had been busy
all night drilling a hole in my knee, and within hours I was down
with dengue fever, a form of malaria. There was no sick bay
here so I just huddled in my cot, dosing myself with Empirin
whenever I was conscious. A few days later, when the delirium
and fever had worn off, I woke up to find Eddie Condon's wandering brother, Pat, sitting on my bunk. Thinking I was still
delirious, I shut my eyes again and let out a terrible groan. That
sensation of waking to find yourself observed was not unusual
in the tropics, I was to discover, but it was more likely to be a
spider as big as your fist eying you from its web in a corner of
the netting. It took Pat Condon quite a little while to convince
me he was real. Pat was in the Merchant Marines, and when his
boat put in at Nouméa and he heard Shaw's band was there, he
came ashore to look me up. I was so pleased to see him that I
crawled out of bed and played with the band at a camp show
that night, and the next day I was able to go back to my regular
routine.

Every morning we would pile our instruments into one truck
and climb into another truck to be driven down to the pier.
Motor launches were waiting there to take us out to the destroyers and battleships anchored in the harbor, where we'd give
concerts for the men. We also played at all the different camps
around the island for the Marines and Seabees and Army troops.

When we had played for the troops in Honolulu we were
always warmly received, but the men in the South Pacific theatre
were so starved for bands from home that they went wild at the

mere sight of us. One night while we were playing at one of the camps in the jungle, it started to rain, but the men refused to let us go. We were set up in a hollow in a clearing in the hills, and the men rigged a canopy over us and we played on while those poor soaked GI's sitting out in the open yelled for more every time we paused to wipe off our instruments. Once when we played for a Marine camp, the men were so fired with enthusiasm that they insisted we stay on while they whipped up some refreshments for us. "We don't have much, but we'll fix you up fine with a millionaire's salad," one of the Marines said to us with a happy grin. He was carrying an ax, and within minutes they had chopped down a coconut-palm tree. From the top of the tree they extracted the inner core, a yellowish-white tube two or three feet long and about six inches thick, which they sliced into a bowl and dressed with oil and vinegar. An expensive little dish, costing the life of a tree, but it did have a delicious taste, somewhere between a nut and celery.

The second night after we arrived in New Caledonia, we were taken out to the aircraft carrier *Saratoga* to give a concert. Since it was night, the men were gathered on the lower deck, and our entrance alone sent them off into an uproar. We set up the bandstand on the huge aircraft elevator and began playing our theme song, "Nightmare," as we descended slowly into the midst of the wildly cheering men. It was like being back in the Paramount Theatre again, except that the bandstand there used to rise slowly from the pit, while on the *Saratoga* it descended into the audience. As I sat there looking out at these thousands and thousands of sailors and feeling the waves of homesickness flow out of them at the sound of the familiar songs, I began to fill up so much that when I stood up to take my solo on the "St. Louis Blues," I blew like a madman. On hearing me let loose, Dave started to swing the beat, and when I picked up my plunger and started to growl, those three thousand men went stark, raving crazy. Even the fellows in the band were shaken. They thought it was a one-shot thing, but I decided that from then on I'd try to break it up for

the men everywhere we went and try to play the way I knew
they felt inside. The next couple of times I couldn't do it, but
after a while I got the feel of it and could get it going at will.

And the men seemed to feel what I meant. Sometimes my horn
would get to them when nothing else worked. Once, at a base
hospital on one of the islands, the entertainers knocked themselves out trying to get a response from the men, but when I
started to growl something happened and those broken men came
to life again and banged their crutches and beat the arms of their
wheel chairs, or just yelled and shouted themselves hoarse if they
were too smashed up or too weak to applaud.

They sent us out by plane to play at camps near the fighting
zones, and the going became rougher for us now. One time when
we straggled off the plane after one of these hitches, a tired-
looking young pilot who was waiting to take the plane up again
gave us a surprised look and said, "Gee, you guys still living?"
We weren't too sure ourselves. We were sent for a while to
Espíritu Santo, one of the islands in the New Hebrides chain,
and we were even less sure there. Then they sent us to Guadalcanal, where the question became purely academic. We always
seemed to be in foxholes. They set up tents for us, but when that
alarm went off—zoom! we were back in those foxholes so fast
we moved like one man. By now my trumpet had acquired a
greenish tinge, which I couldn't rub off, and our sheet music was
so mildewed, fly-specked, and dog-eared that it was as limp as
pulp.

While we were on Espíritu Santo, a cruiser was torpedoed
nearby and the surviving men brought ashore to our base. The
next night they rigged up a screen outside on the side of a hill
and ran off the movie *Arsenic and Old Lace*. Whenever I see a
revival of that movie, I remember what a great antidote it was
for the horrors these sailors had just gone through, and how
moving it was to see the look of shock gradually replaced by the
healing forgetfulness of laughter. I met some wonderful men in
those Godforsaken islands, and some old friends, too. One day
when we were on the dock waiting for the motor launch to take

us out to a destroyer, I met a friend of mine from home, George
Poor. Contrary to his name, George Poor was a wealthy guy
who had a yacht back home and had been messing around with
boats all his life up in Marblehead, Massachusetts. When the war
came he went into the Navy and was assigned to a sub chaser as
a junior officer. The tiny sub chaser, not more than one hundred
feet long, sailed the seven thousand miles from San Francisco to
New Caledonia without escort. Since the executive officer was
from Iowa and knew more about cows than he did about ships,
George was a life-saver to him. When they limped into Nouméa
they were in sad shape, with their bulkheads all smashed by the
rough seas, but somehow George had got them there in one piece.
The crew, composed almost entirely of colored guys, was crazy
about George, who also played trumpet in their little band. He
was not only handy on a ship, but he was so great for morale
that after they landed in Nouméa his executive officer reported
to Navy headquarters and formally requested them to make
George executive officer of the ship in his place.

When we arrived on Guadalcanal, though the worst of that
bloody struggle was over, it was still a hotbed of strife, with air
raids every night from the Jap bases on Rabaul and Bougainville.
Two days before we arrived, there had been a devastating straf-
ing of Lunga Point by a ninety-plane Japanese fleet, and the
tents in which we were quartered were so riddled by bullets they
looked like mosquito netting. Needless to say, all our concerts
were given in the daytime, and we competed with the chattering
of monkeys, the screeching of parrots, and the whistles of the
bright-colored little parakeets, which were as common as our
sparrows. But when the sirens blew to alert us for Condition Red
—the warning that enemy planes were approaching—the jungle
would become suddenly still, and not even a leaf seemed to stir in
the hushed silence until you began to hear the hum of the planes
and the scream of bombs and then the nightmare began again.

One night at eight o'clock, we were sitting around in our tents
in the dark waiting for the air attacks, which came regularly two
or three times a night, when one of the men came running in, on

the verge of hysteria, to report that a Jap sniper had been spotted around the camp. Our nerves were strung so taut with strain and fatigue that in a few seconds the whole camp was in a turmoil, with guards posted every three feet, and someone yelling for guns to be issued to everyone, which meant us, and volunteers creeping out into the jungle to track down the sniper. When no sniper was uncovered, an investigation was set under way to find out how the rumor had started. Someone had seen what he thought was a Jap skulking past the commander's wooden hut; the culprit was finally traced down and revealed to be Dave Tough. Poor Dave looked odd enough in ordinary civvies but to the war-weary troops on Guadalcanal, Dave in khaki fatigues was a sight to make the blood run cold.

After we had been on Guadalcanal for a couple of weeks, we were alerted one night around eleven o'clock to get ready to leave. We packed in the pitch dark and lugged our gear out to the road, where a truck was waiting. The fellows already in the truck were on tenterhooks to get going before the next air raid started.

"Come on, on the double, you guys, or we'll miss the plane," Artie snapped as Dave came panting up to dump his gear into the truck. The driver gunned the motor and the truck lurched forward as he released the brake.

"Hold it!" Dave yelled. "I've got to go back for the drums. Someone give me a hand with them!"

The driver pulled to a reluctant halt, and aside from some heavy swearing there wasn't a sound to be heard from any of the fellows. "O.K.," I said, swinging back down over the side of the truck. "Just give us two minutes, Artie." While Dave and I stumbled down the dark, pock-marked road, I was wondering how the hell we two shrimps were going to get those drums to the truck in one trip. It would take the combined strength of both of us to handle the bass drum alone. As we rounded the bend of the road, the idea came to us simultaneously to cut through the woods to make faster time, and as we turned word-

lessly to plunge headlong into the jungle, we nearly broke our
necks crashing into a large, immovable metal object.

"I'll be a son of a bitch," Dave croaked in a stunned voice as
he regained his feet. "It's a *wheelbarrow!*"

How that wheelbarrow got there I'll never know but we didn't
stop to wonder. All we knew was that it was an out-and-out
miracle, and we managed to heave the drums into it and trundle
it back to the truck before the jittery driver began pressing down
on the accelerator again.

In addition to the air raids, malaria, and nervous hysteria, there
were other hazards on these South Pacific islands, as I discovered
one day when I decided to go out and look for the shells and
cat's eyes all the servicemen used to collect to send home. One of
the sailors on Espíritu Santo, I think it was, told me he knew a
beach where I could pick up these shells by the pailful, and one
morning he came by in his truck and drove me out to a remote
section of the beach. Parking his truck in the shade of some palm
trees, my friend pulled his cap down over his eyes and settled
back for a snooze while I set off down the rough footpath for
the beach. After a few minutes' walk I spied a party of natives
wending their way toward me. If they hadn't seen me at the same
instant that I spotted them, I would have been nothing but a
speck on the horizon a second later, but now there was nothing
I could do except keep walking toward them as calmly as I could.
They had the wild, frizzy hairdo of the black-skinned Mela-
nesians, their nostrils, lips, and ears were pierced with slivers of
white bone, and they bristled with so many spears that they
looked like a bunch of porcupines. But as they approached, I saw,
with just as sudden a shock, that not only were the poor devils
bedraggled and filthy, most of them were suffering from ele-
phantiasis, dragging themselves along on their swollen, trunklike
legs. When the ragged, diseased little band halted a few feet
from me, their darting eyes looking everywhere but directly at
me, I stepped forward with a big, compassionate American smile
to offer them cigarettes and coins. That broke the ice, and in a

few minutes we were all puffing up a storm. They had no interest in paper money, but they were fascinated with my cigarette lighter. By way of further introduction, I took out my ID
card and showed them my picture and then pointed to myself.
Their faces split into wide grins, showing their blackened, betel-
nut-stained teeth. This amiability so encouraged me that I pointed
out to the bay where several destroyers and a battleship were
riding at anchor, and explained to them that these all belonged
to the U.S.A.—"Friends" I repeated over and over. They
couldn't understand a word I was saying, of course, but I had
the impression they thought *I* owned all those ships. To clear up
the confusion, I sang a whole chorus of "I Can't Give You Anything but Love, Baby," ending up with a few jig steps and a
buck-and-wing. The song and dance really broke them up. They
laughed and jabbered at each other, nodding at me and then at
each other. I figured they thought I was some kind of harmless
nut, and in a few minutes they straggled away down the path,
still nodding and grinning their black-toothed grins. A little
farther on, I passed a grass hut, and, in pantomime, asked the little
boy who was playing in the tall scraggly grass beside it who those
fellows were. He pointed after them, nodding solemnly, and then
drew his little brown hand slowly across his throat—the native
sign for headhunters.

After I had recovered from the idea of having entertained
headhunters, I filled my hat and pockets with shells and headed
back toward the truck. On the way back, I took a look inside a
huge rotting tree stump. The mottled gray snake curled up inside
it must have been twenty feet long. I covered the quarter mile
back to the truck in less than ten seconds, vowing to myself to
stick to the guided tours from now on.

But I had another surprise in Auckland, New Zealand, a couple
of weeks after our second tour of the steaming swamps of Guadalcanal. One afternoon, while walking through the sleepy little
town, which was not more than a dozen houses long, I heard a
sound which made me freeze in my tracks. After I convinced
myself I wasn't having hallucinations and that it was actually a

Billie Holiday recording of "I Cried for You," coming full blast from a little store about twenty feet ahead, on my right, I sprang into action. A young Chinese man stepped out from the room in back of the shop as I came charging in, my ears flapping like a hound dog. "How in hell did you ever hear of Billie Holiday in this nowhere place?" I demanded. When I calmed down, he explained he had friends in England who shipped him jazz records, and it turned out he even had some of mine. He was thrilled about the Artie Shaw band being in town, and the rest of my stay in Auckland I spent most of my time off visiting him, occasionally bringing along one or two of the other fellows in the band. It was a great treat to hear his records, and I'll never forget the wonderful Chinese meal he cooked for me one day.

It was also in Auckland that one of the worst indignities of war befell me—fleas. It was bad enough during the day, but at night it was agony, and my body was in shreds from the scratching. I never minded the malaria attacks as much as the flea invasion. The medics put me in an iron bathtub and doused me with hot water mixed with some solution and I hung all my clothes out in the sun, but nothing discouraged my uninvited guests until two weeks later when we were sent to another island and I found somebody who had a can of Flit. I stripped down to my skin and had one of the guys spray me, and then I sprayed all my clothes, and that finally did the trick.

From New Zealand we were sent out again to Vella Lavella and some of the other islands in the Solomons and then over the Coral Sea to Australia. From Wellington we went to Melbourne, where the Navy had taken over a small old hotel. This was the first time in eleven months that I had a room all to myself and a real bathroom. I never budged out of that hotel room unless I had to.

In the remotest jungle camps and on the most out-of-the-way islands, we kept running across officers who were jazz fans and who knew Dave and me and knew how unnatural this rugged outdoor life was for us. "Wait till you get to Sydney," they'd say. "You go straight to Sam Lee's club; it's the nearest thing to home you'll find on this side of the world." We must have jotted down the address of Sam Lee's club thirty or forty times between us.

The minute we landed in Sydney, Dave, Conrad Gozzo, and I went out on the town and off on a bat. After we had spent all our money, we hailed a cab and then spent the next twenty minutes trying to decide where to tell the driver to take us. We didn't want to go back to the hotel, but we couldn't think of where to go without any money. While we were debating, the cab driver was doing a slow burn. We had just come from the jungles and all we had to wear were our hot, dirty wool sailor suits and we were so beat and so loaded that we weren't a sight to inspire confidence in anyone, least of all a cab driver. Dave, who was usually the one we had to take care of when he was drunk, suddenly rose to the occasion. "Now, just a minute, my good man," he said in great dignity. Pulling out his wallet, he looked through it with shaky hands until he found a grimy card. "Drive to the officers' club in King's Row," he said with a lordly flourish of his hand.

"You'll never get in there," the driver said, casting a contemptuous look at our bedraggled condition. When we arrived at the door, Dave turned and said to the driver, "Maybe you had better wait a minute." We followed Dave up the steps while he rang the bell.

"Shove off, you coves," was the doorman's greeting after one look at us. But Sam Lee himself happened to be passing the door, and he came over to see what the commotion was about. When Dave introduced himself, Sam Lee couldn't believe it, and we couldn't believe what happened next. In a few minutes we were eating steaks and signing autographs and lapping up Scotch. Sam Lee was a New York theatrical agent who had gone on a tour of Asia some years before the war as manager of a vaudeville team, and when he ended up in Australia he decided to stay on and open his own club. We had no money for the rest of our stay in Sydney, but we didn't need any. That night and all the other nights we were Sam's guests.

In Sydney we were quartered in another little hotel taken over by the Navy. There was always a lot of resentment against the band on the part of the other Navy men and our lot was not an easy one whenever we were quartered with them. Our position was always ambiguous, anyway. We were in the Navy as regular sailors, and not in Special Services, but we hadn't even gone through boot training, and in the eyes of the regular servicemen we weren't one of them, which was true, and they thought we received extra privileges, such as extra pay, which was not true.

At the hotel in Sydney, the sailors used to come in loaded every night and raise the roof, and then blame us. One day the whole band was ordered to appear in the captain's office. It seems that some toilet seats had been wrecked and the blame laid on us. The captain gave us hell, while we all stood there like a bunch of shamefaced school kids. I guess each one of us was waiting for the other to say something. When I saw that no one was going to speak up in our defense, I began to get mad. Pulling myself up to my full height, I stepped forward and addressed the furious captain.

"Sir," I said. "I want you to understand we're musicians. We've traveled all our lives and we've played in the best places and in the worst places, but if there is one thing we've learned, it's how to behave ourselves. We get loaded, but we're not ignorant hillbillies. Many of us have had a whole life before we came into the Navy, and we respect ourselves too much to pull any fool stunt like that. It's not our habit to go around breaking toilet seats. And if we ever did anything we shouldn't," I added in a final burst of indignation, "we'd own up to it like men and not try to lay the blame on someone else."

The captain studied me silently for a long moment after I'd finished and then he said abruptly, "I believe you. Charge dismissed."

Although it was a life-saver to get back to civilization again, by the time we had reached Australia we were suffering so badly from shell shock and were so worn out and weary that one by one we started to get sick. I could hardly play and I began having nightmares and would wake up screaming night after night. The whole band started to fall apart, and after a final trip to New Zealand, they sent us back to Brisbane to be reassigned to the United States for rehabilitation.

Homeward bound on board a Liberty Merchant ship, which sailed alone to San Francisco in the Jap-infested waters without an escort, Dave and I were assigned to watches on the twenty-millimeter gun turrets. It took the combined strength of both of us to lift the bombs and to cock the huge guns. They're lucky we didn't blow up the ship just trying to load the guns. To keep our spirits up, I used to bring my trumpet out on the long night watches and after opening the intercom system to the other turrets, I'd put in a mute and play for all the guys, very softly, all during the watch.

After the medical examination at San Francisco, the doctors reported that Dave and I were in very bad shape and they recommended immediate discharge for us as well as for a couple of other guys in the band. They sent us back to New York by train in December, 1943. During my thirty-day furlough, Nancy and I were married, but it seemed I wasn't in New York more than ten minutes before Milt Gabler had set up a series of recording dates, one of which was for a twelve-inch "Basin Street Blues," with Jack Teagarden, who was in town, too. After taking one look at my brine-encrusted horn, Milt ran out and bought me a gleaming new golden Selmer trumpet as a home-coming present.

In January, Dave and I were sent to a base in Long Beach, Long Island, and then down to the Navy School of Music in Washington. They didn't know what to do with us. Nobody seemed to have received the doctors' reports from San Francisco, and Artie was too busy getting his own discharge in San Francisco to bother about us. By that time I was sent to sick bay at the Bethesda Naval Hospital, where I was finally discharged in March of 1944.

A week after I was back in town *The New Yorker* sent a reporter to interview me. The following is the little piece they

Louis Armstrong

Jack Bradley

Tommy Dorsey Band, 1935: *back row*. l to r trumpets, Joe Bauer, Steve Lipkin, Max Kaminsky, drum, Dave Tough, guitar, Carmen Mastren; bass, Gene Traxler, *second row:* trombones, Les Jenkins, Walter Mercurio, Tommy Dorsey, saxes, Joe Dixon, Fred Stoltz, Bud Freeman, Clyde Rounds; *front row:* Axel Stordahl, Edythe Wright, Jack Leonard; piano, Dick Jones

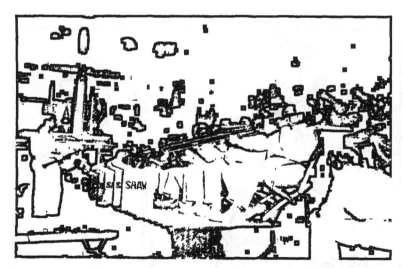

The Artie Shaw Navy Band No. 501 entertaining aboard the U S.S *Curtis,* seaplane tender, off Espiritu Santo, July 1943. Max Kaminsky is the trumpet man at upper right.

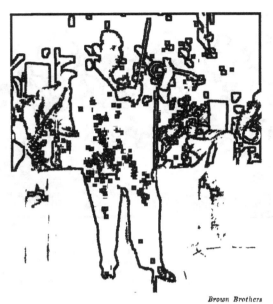

Joe Venuti

Big Sid Catlett

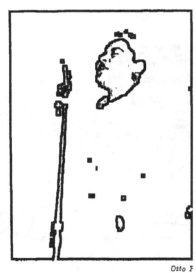

Billie Holiday

Otto Hess

Brad Gowans   Max Kaminsky   Dave Tough

Otto Hess

The Summa Cum Laude Band at the Brick Club, 1940. l. to r. Pete Peterson, bass, Morey Feld, drums, Brad Gowans, trombone, Dave Bowman, piano, Pee Wee Russell, clarinet, Max Kaminsky, trumpet, Eddie Condon, guitar, Bud Freeman, the leader . . . missing!

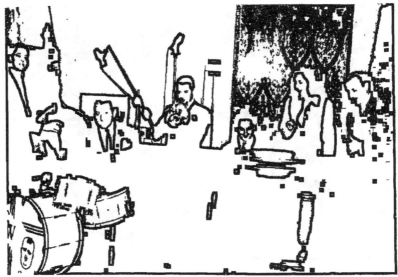

Otto Hess

Recording the Lee Wiley "George Gershwin" album: l. to r.· Artie Shapiro, George Wettling, Max Kaminsky, Joe Bushkin, Lee Wiley, Bud Freeman

Otto Hess

Jam session at the Belmont Plaza Hotel, 1938 Hot Lips Page, Max Kaminsky, Bobby Hackett, Brad Gowans in rear

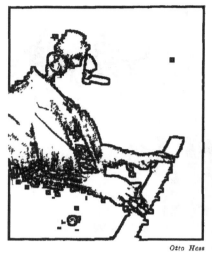

James P Johnson

Otto Hess

Thomas "Fats" Waller

Otto H

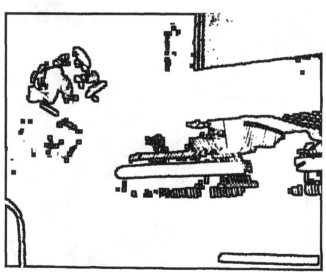

Willie "The Lion" Smith

Otto Hess

State Department tour of the Far East, 1958-1959. l to r Stan Puls, Jack
Teagarden, Ronnie Greb, Jerry Fuller, Max Kaminsky, Don Ewell

Max Kaminsky playing for the rubber workers in Malaya on Far East tour

Jack Bradley

Louis Armstrong recording session, 1960 l. to r Louis Armstrong, Dizzy Gillespie, Gene Krupa, Max Kaminsky

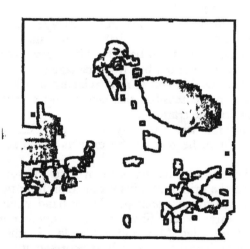

College Jazz Session, 1956, Max Kaminsky, Pee Wee Russell

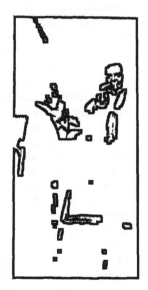

Max Kaminsky and Jackie Gleason, CBS, 1962

wrote up in "The Talk of the Town" in their December 25, 1943, issue:

Musician 2/C

We've just talked with a member of the Navy swing outfit—led by CPO Artie Shaw—which returned recently from a year-long tour of our Pacific bases—Max Kaminsky, listed by the Navy as Kaminsky, Mus 2/c, but known to habitués of Nick's and other such hot-jazz shrines as one of the best hot-trumpet players in the world. Max is a slender, dark fellow, exactly five feet tall. A year ago last October he was playing with Joe Marsala's band at a roadhouse in Armonk when he heard that Artie Shaw, for whom he had previously worked, was recruiting musicians for a tour of some sort.

"I was pretty sure I couldn't pass an ordinary physical and this seemed about the least I could do," he told us. "I called up Artie and said, 'What's this I hear?'

" 'Maxie,' he said, 'how would you look in the Navy?' And that is how I am where I am today, an unrehabilitated man."

The entire band was recently ordered back to this country for hospitalization, rest, and rehabilitation, but Max managed to talk his way out of going to a hospital and is now relaxing in what he obviously considers a more sensible manner, living at the Piccadilly Hotel and playing the trumpet.

He played at Town Hall last Saturday in one of Eddie Condon's jazz concerts. Soon, he told us, he expects to be re-called to active duty.

Immediately after Max enlisted, he was sent over to Pier 92, the receiving centre, "on the grinder." This means marching up and down the docks in an ordinary oom-pah Navy band while recruits listen. In about three weeks Shaw had got together a twenty-piece outfit that included Max and a couple of other men from the old Shaw civilian band as well as representatives of such distinguished outfits as Benny Goodman's, Charlie Spivak's, Bob Chester's, and Tommy Dorsey's. They were sent to San Francisco and after a brief shakedown period of rehearsal in an old warehouse were shipped out on an itinerary that in-

cluded Hawaii, New Caledonia, the New Hebrides, the
Solomons, New Zealand and Australia. Max told us that they
traveled on every kind of fighting vessel but a submarine. "I
think they had that in mind once but the bass wouldn't slide in,
or something," he said. They also made some of the sleeper jumps
in Navy planes. When they traveled by plane they were airsick
and when they went by water they were seasick. On the big
ships Max was assigned a battle station, one time helping man the
damage control room, another time manning a twenty millimetre
gun with Dave Tough, formerly Benny Goodman's drummer.
"Nearly fired it one morning, too," he said. "Probably just as well
we didn't."

On arriving at a Navy base, the band would go to the hospital
and entertain the wounded first. Then they'd tour the harbor in
a launch, clambering up to the deck of each ship with their
instruments, giving a concert, and clambering back into the
launch. "There was a time I heard Dave Tough say he wished
he learned piccolo instead of the drums," Max told us. "He said,
'I bet I would have been the happiest piccolo player in the
world.'"

After entertaining the ships' crews, the band would visit all
the camps in the vicinity, playing in the open air and jumping for
slit trenches whenever air raid warnings came. At these concerts
they sometimes had an audience of natives as well as soldiers.
When the natives started jumping up and down as if it were
Saturday morning at the Paramount Theatre the boys knew they
were in the groove. "We played for crowds all the way up to
50,000," Max said. "That was at some cricket track in Australia.
Our smallest audience was 1500. But wait," he added, "while
I tell you about playing on the Saratoga. You know at the
Paramount the band comes slowly up out of the pit playing the
theme song? Well, on the Saratoga they built us a stand topside
and they built it square on top of the piece of deck that gets
lowered with planes on it. We sat there and began to play and
they pushed a button and the stand went down into the ship, and
all the boys were sitting waiting down there with their eyes
out on stems. If I ever have such an exciting moment in my life
again, I bet I'll lose my mind from the excitement."*

* Reprinted by permission. Copyright 1943 The New Yorker Magazine, Inc.

Chapter 10

For the first two or three months after my discharge from the Navy I had no desire to work or to see anybody or even to touch the trumpet, and I scarcely ever left the apartment. At night I had trouble falling asleep, and then I'd inevitably dream I was choking and that I had to keep pulling wads of black cotton and black cloth out of my mouth. It was all mixed up in my mind with the bombings. The malaria attacks hung on for several years after the war, and the scaly sore on my leg never did heal, but the nightmares of those first six or seven months were the worst.

Then one afternoon in April, I stopped in at Brentano's to pick up some books, and things started happening again. Bill O'Gorman, who worked for Brentano's, was an old fan of mine, and as soon as he spotted me he came over to talk to me.

"I've got an idea for you, Max," he said when he found out I wasn't working. "A little club in the Village. It would be a perfect spot for you."

I said I didn't think I was in any kind of shape yet to go out and work but he insisted I at least look into this setup. He took down my phone number, and a week later he called me up and

persuaded me to come down to this club, the Pied Piper, on
Barrow Street in Greenwich Village, and talk to the bosses.

The Pied Piper, a spacious, well-proportioned room, used to
be a saloon called La Boheme. The former owner had fallen into
the practice of taking all the money out of the jukebox and
keeping it himself, until he finally arrived at a point where he
owed the jukebox concessionaires so much money that he gave
them the club in exchange for the money he owed, and now these
three men, the owners of a jukebox business in Brooklyn, and
acquaintances of Mr. O'Gorman, found themselves in the night-
club business. They changed the name to the Pied Piper, stocked
the jukebox with a pile of new records, and waited for the
money to roll in. I sat down with two of these discouraged new
bosses that Saturday night, and even on a Saturday night during
the war when the Village was boiling with servicemen there
wasn't a soul in the place, not even one lone, drunken sailor.

"Look," one of the partners said to me. "We're stuck with this
joint and we don't know anything about running a club. All we
know about is installing the jukebox. Right, Joe?" Joe nodded
glumly, and turned to me. "So why don't you take it over and
see what you can do with it?" he said.

These guys knew nothing about jazz or me, but since Mr.
O'Gorman had recommended me, they were sold on me already,
and they were so sincere and goodhearted in their way that I
decided to give it a try. Up to now I had had no desire to go back
to work, but the idea of having my own little band was the
incentive I needed to try to get back to some kind of normal
living again. In fact, I was so inspired by the whole thing that I
started rounding up a band that same night. Rod Cless was available, so I hired him for the clarinet spot, and Frank Orchard on
valve trombone, and when I called up James P. Johnson and
Willie the Lion Smith and found out they were interested, I
really began to get excited. The pay was very little. All I could
get out of the owners was $55 a week for each man, including
myself, but they threw in a free meal every night for the mu-

sicians and all the whiskey they wanted, so I didn't have too much trouble getting men. I managed to talk the bosses into investing in a Steinway baby grand, and I took James P. up to Fifty-seventh Street and turned him loose in the store until he found one that talked back in the right tone of voice. With James P. Johnson and the Lion and a baby grand, how could we go wrong? We opened up about two weeks later, and nothing could have been righter.

With the war opening a path a mile wide for jazz, this was the turning point. Our troops all over the world were clamoring for jazz bands, jazz records, and jazz broadcasts, and eventually even the top brass were becoming aware of the morale value of jazz. In fact, the following year, 1945, the War Department announced that the Commodore records were first on every soldier radio hit parade, and while I was in the Navy the fellow in charge of the PX at Pearl Harbor had told me that my Commodore recordings of "Ballin' the Jack" and "I Ain't Gonna Give Nobody None of My Jellyroll" were in especially great demand.

Besides Nick's, the only other jazz club in the Village then, half a block away from the Pied Piper, was Café Society Downtown, but the latter, with its regular night-club acts, was more of a show place than a jazz club. They did, nevertheless, present great jazz artists; I'll never forget the time they had Billie Holiday and the three great boogie-woogie pianists—Meade Lux Lewis, Albert Ammons, and Pete Johnson—and the blues shouter Joe Turner, all on the same bill.

In any case, I had no conscious idea of the burgeoning interest in jazz when I opened at the Pied Piper. I just felt that somehow if I felt like going back to small-band jazz, other people must be wanting it, too, and this seemed a good opportunity to put together a little band I could enjoy with some well-seasoned musicians who liked to play.

Ernie Anderson arranged for me to appear on disk-jockey programs to spread the word about the Pied Piper; *The New*

Yorker magazine gave the club a fine write-up; the newspaper columnists gave it enthusiastic plugs; and the place caught on practically overnight. Tim Costello brought the Vanderbilts down, Duke Ellington used to drop in to hear his good friend James P. Johnson, and it wasn't long before the club became a regular musicians' hangout, with all the jazzmen who were still in the service sitting in whenever they were in town, so that instead of six musicians on the stand there was likely to be a dozen or more. Frankie Newton sat in so regularly that I finally persuaded the bosses to hire him, too.

It was at this time, on one of the disk-jockey programs that used to plug the Pied Piper, that Arnold Stang made his wonderful remark about my name. When Fred Robbins, the disk jockey, interrupted his interview with Stang to announce that he was about to play one of my records, he turned to Stang and said, "You've heard of Max Kaminsky, haven't you?"

"Max Kaminsky!" the quick-witted Stang retorted. "Why I knew him before he changed his name!"

I've been using that remark ever since when people ask me why I haven't changed my name—a question I am constantly asked. "But I have changed it," I say. "You should have heard what it was before!"

Except for the usual tourist traps, and the regular weekend invasion of carousing servicemen and curious sightseers, the Village was a quiet, homey place during the forties. While it had always had its bohemians, the atmosphere during the war years was unfrantic and neighborly; there were no beatniks yet, no freaks or boppers or bearded folk singers. The children of the local Italian population played hopscotch and stick ball in the streets, and Washington Square Park was full of babies and mothers and respectable, old-fashioned bums and unfancy dogs. The atmosphere at the Pied Piper was equally unfancy and informal. We had no air-conditioning, and between sets on sweltering summer nights the customers would pick up their drinks and grope their way through the smoky haze to the sidewalk, where they'd gather in little groups on the nearby steps and try to breathe while they listened to the intermission pianists—who were one of the most enjoyable things about the Pied Piper. James P. was officially the intermission pianist and Willie had the band spot, but we had no rigid rules and they switched jobs whenever they were in the mood.

James P. Johnson, a stocky man with powerful shoulders and great big ham hands, could produce some of the most delicate musical sounds I ever heard. He was about fifty then, and his royalties on songs such as "Charleston" and "If I Could Be With You" provided him with a steady income, but I managed to persuade him to come out and work again. A very modest and reserved man, he was usually serious and concentrated when he played, but when he got really going on the piano he'd have the whole building vibrating. He enjoyed the Pied Piper hugely, especially the fact that he could have all the whiskey he wanted. Sometimes when we'd go on an outside job, James P. would bring along his son to watch over him and see that he didn't get too mellow, but it always ended up with our having to take care of both junior and senior Johnsons.

I never tired of trying to let James P. know how much I appreciated him. He not only had such a beautiful way of playing, he had the right way of playing, with nothing corny about it. Besides being a great piano man in his own right and an accompanist without equal for such singers as Bessie Smith, Ethel Waters, Chippie Hill, and Maggie Jones, he was also the composer of piano jazz classics like "Carolina Shout" and "Snowy Morning Blues," as well as of large-scale serious compositions. Johnson spent six years writing his jazz-conceived concertos and choral pieces and symphonies, but as naturally discouraged and deeply hurt as he felt about his works being unplayed and unrecognized, he didn't carry on about it.

That yearning of a comedian to play Hamlet, and vice versa, seems to be a part of human nature. Both James P. and Thomas "Fats" Waller, like George Gershwin, yearned to be recognized for their "serious" musical side as well as for their so-called light music. The desire to find acceptance as a "serious," classical-type musician is more than ever prevalent today. The only difference between musicians like Fats and James P., and many modern musicians—who take a little commonplace riff and orchestrate it for a French horn and oboe and call themselves jazz "composers" and howl about how they're starved for recognition—is that Fats and James P. had talent. Nobody wants to be called a mere "song writer" any more. Fats Waller was noted for being one of the fastest and most prolific writers there ever was; he turned out numbers like "Ain't Misbehavin' " and "Honeysuckle Rose" in less than an hour.

"A pianist without a left hand is a very weak pianist," Fats has said, and it was James P. who taught Fats how to use his left hand, for Waller had started out with classical training. Count Basie, Art Tatum, and Duke Ellington were also greatly influenced by Johnson and Waller, and later Thelonious Monk, the master of modern jazz piano, got it from the Duke. When James P. was really swinging, nobody could catch him. I'll never forget one record date when he plunked a quart of gin down on the piano, sat down, and began swinging so great that he and the piano and the bottle of gin were all bouncing like one creature. Johnson was a different story from the pianists of today who just get going with block harmonies. James P. would produce a hundred different changes in ideas and expression and images, a far cry from the monotonous kind of roly-poly, repetitive, continuous playing they do today. The boppers began to use the bass fiddle to take the place of the pianist's rhythmic left hand, and so the modern pianists use the left hand just to establish the chord changes. Lately, however, the old, full piano style has begun to return to fashion.

Fats has also said, "A pianist should be rich with sound—he should never let the richness get out of the piano, and he should cover distance; he should really play those open chords of tenths and elevenths." And like Fats Waller, with whom John-

son helped create the Harlem stride piano style, which broad-
ened the scope of ragtime, James P. could make you laugh and
feel good. That was the spirit then—not to be so smart or clever,
just to get feeling good. The two men were lifelong friends; they
bought houses next door to each other out in St. Albans, Long
Island, with Clarence Williams on the other side and Hank Duncan a couple of doors farther down.

Willie the Lion was like a lamb around James P., for as great
as the Lion is and as self-assured as he always acted about himself, he accorded Johnson the highest respect because James P.
was the master piano man. And the latter in his turn respected
the Lion's talent as a composer of contemporary piano pieces,
such as "Finger Busters." Willie was one of the first to play the
so-called modern chords. He knew all about the modern European symphonic composers and he was using the whole-tone
system himself thirty-five years ago when he wrote impressionist
pieces like "Morning Air." Way back in the twenties he'd sit
down at the piano and while roughing out some dissonant chords
he'd call out, "Yeah! I'm getting the message from Delius loud
and clear this evening!" and then he'd go to work and beat the
dissonances into behaving with good sense and a good sound and
swing. When Fats took Willie to Carnegie Hall to hear Horo-
witz, Willie said, "He's great—but he doesn't *swing!*" Duke
Ellington thought so highly of Willie that he composed a piece
in his honor, "Portrait of the Lion," and Beiderbecke used to
head for Harlem whenever he was in town especially to hear the
Lion play the new modern chords, which we all knew about then.
After the early ragtime era it was these Harlem stride pianists
who started to do other than the expected by using different
inversions and inventing new patterns by use of the modern
harmonic changes.

In any case, everyone seemed to enjoy the Pied Piper, and
working there gave me a great chance to forget about all my
ailments. I began to sleep better as the dreams eased off a little,
though I would still jump three feet or automatically hit the

pavement whenever I heard a backfire. During the six or seven months I was there, I made several records with my band and James P., and I began to feel better about my playing, too.

We even almost made the movies, for during this time they were filming the screen version of *The Lost Weekend*, and they wanted to use the Pied Piper for the scene where Ray Milland steals a woman's pocketbook in a nightclub to get money for his whiskey. The whole movie crew came down and blocked off Barrow Street and shot the scene in the club with the band playing in the background, but then the third Pied Piper boss, who was a very difficult man, loused it up by demanding all kinds of money and rights on the scene and it all fell through.

And then, finally, there came a big turn of events. I had never, as usual, had the sense to sign any kind of contract or make any business deal with the owners to get myself anything if I got the place going. All I did was agree to bring in the band, and I was just paid scale for my ideas about the food and entertainment and for my services, and once the two bosses sold out to the third partner, everything proceeded to go wrong. They sold out to him because they couldn't get along with him, and I was stuck with him because he was the kind of guy no one could get along with. Then I hired a certain musician who began to have eyes for my job as the place became more and more successful. He started feeding a line to this boss about how he could do even better than I had done, and a month later I was out of a job. This musician took over, and a couple of months after that, in March, 1945, the Pied Piper went out of business altogether and closed its doors.

On December 4, 1944, my last night at the Pied Piper, I stayed around after closing time to take down my pictures from the entrance and gather up my stuff, and then I went over to the bar and had a drink. When Rod Cless clapped a shaky hand on my shoulder and mumbled good night, I asked him to sit down and have a last one on the house. He declined, and after I realized how drunk he was I asked him if I could walk him home.

He lived right around the corner on West Fourth Street. But he said no, and when the bartender offered to accompany him, he refused him, too. Although Rod was a heavy drinker, he was always so polite and pleasant that it was hard to tell how drunk he was, and being the nice guy he was, he didn't want to put anybody out by having them see him home. I walked to the corner with him, but when he kept insisting he was all right I went back to the club. Rod's apartment was up three or four flights. On the way upstairs he lost his balance and toppled backward over the railing. He died four days later in St. Vincent's Hospital. I guess I spent hundreds of wakeful nights saying, "If only . . ."

I was very sorry to lose the Pied Piper, but it had pulled me out of my slump, and I was ready for the old normal battlegrounds again. In January of 1945, Art Hodes asked me to come in with him at the Village Vanguard, where we worked as a trio for the next nine months, with Art on piano and Freddie Moore on drums. Max Gordon, the owner of the Vanguard, was always a very agreeable man to work for and while I missed playing in a full band, I liked everything else about the job. The Vanguard was deep in its folk-singer period then, with artists like Leadbelly, Richard Dyer-Bennett, Josh White, Burl Ives, Susan Reed, and Pete Seeger, but it also had singers like Chippie Hill and comedians like Irwin Corey, a very funny guy. One night when one of the acts didn't show up and Max Gordon asked me to go out on the floor and entertain, I played and sang a couple of choruses of "When the Saints Go Marching In," choosing it simply because it was so short. It went over well enough so that I kept on playing and singing it in different places, but I had no idea that it would snowball some ten years later into the theme song of the Dixieland bands.

Early in February, the government, in an effort to conserve fuel, imposed a midnight curfew on all bars, cabarets, and theatres, so for the next few months until May, when the order was rescinded, we worked only three hours a night. I had always had a yen to play the guitar, and having just bought a cheap one in a hock shop around this time, I began to mess around with it every night when I came home from work. After I had gone through a couple of elementary practice books, I inquired at one of the guitar stores on Forty-eighth Street, the Spanish Music Center, about a teacher. They recommended Miguel Angel. I couldn't have found a better teacher for me if I had looked for years. Mike, a soft-spoken Mexican slave driver, got hold of a Tatay guitar for me and put me to work in earnest on classical studies. A music-loving mouse who lived in my house used to appear each night at the first plucking of a guitar string and he'd hang around companionably all night until dawn while I perfected calluses on my fingers and strained my back learning the fingerboard. I studied with Mike for about six months until I went up to Boston. What with one thing and another, it was sixteen years before I resumed my studies. I went right back to Mike Angel again, and he started me all over again from the beginning with a new system he had perfected during my sixteen-year layoff.

In October of 1945, I went up to Boston with Brad Gowans and Pee Wee Russell to work at the Copley Terrace. The club hadn't been doing much business so the boss, Al Boris, decided to take a chance on putting in a jazz band. We were on the air every night, so that people knew we were there and could hear what we could do, and business began to pick up. Soon the place was doing so well that when Eddie Condon called up from New York to ask Pee Wee and Brad and me to come into his night club, which was opening that December, I told him I couldn't come. Brad decided to accept Eddie's offer, but Pee Wee stayed on with me in Boston.

All the years I had lived and worked in my home town I had been trying to get someone to open up a jazz club, and now that it finally seemed to be the time, I decided to take a fling at it myself. What made it at all possible was that I was being paid three hundred dollars a week at the Copley Terrace, the largest

salary I had ever received. I put aside two hundred dollars each
week, and by March or so of 1946, when the Copley Terrace engagement ended, I had saved up three thousand dollars. I hunted
around until I found a place that fitted my purse, a little base-
ment room in the cellar of a beat-up hotel on Huntington Avenue. It was so filthy that it took a couple of weeks to clean it up,
and while the scrubbing and fumigating was going on, I ran
around buying a piano and fixtures and seeing people about publicity and trying to arrange for licenses to operate it. When the
place was finally aired out, I gave the walls a couple of coats of
whitewash and hung out a sign that read MAXIE's, and when I
was all ready to open, I discovered I had somehow spent all my
money without being able to get a license to sell even Coca-Cola
or a hot dog, let alone liquor. All I had was a cabaret license, and
all I could provide was music, chairs, and ashtrays. I opened
anyway, with a six-piece band which included Pee Wee, and in
this little hole in the wall with no bar, no food, no tables, no
decorations, and no dancing, where the customers had to sit in
rows on wooden folding chairs and couldn't even order a glass of
water, we took in fifteen hundred dollars in admissions at a dollar
a head, in two weeks, during which time I quickly found out
that I would never learn how to run a night club. I might be able
to take care of the band and ideas for the food and entertainment, but despite all my years of experience in the music business, I was not the man to take care of the graft and the rackets
and the liquor and the politics and the police payoffs, and I
never would be. It was all pretty ridiculous the way I tried to
do it, on half a shoestring, and no backing or pull, but I did at
least have the satisfaction of knowing that my music and my
timing was right. After I paid off all my debts, I folded up my
empty wallet and stole back to New York. A couple of months
later, when Eddie Condon again offered me a job in his new
night club at $125 a week, I was glad to go back to work as a
plain musician.

Eddie's attractive club on West Third Street in Greenwich

Village, tucked behind one of the New York University buildings, was a far cry from my humble venture into business. With
Eddie's many friends and wide connections he was able to
arrange for financial backing, to lease a large club in a good
location with marvelous acoustics and a well-stocked bar, and to
obtain a liquor and cabaret license. It was still very difficult to
find any whiskey in 1945, but with his magic way of talking
Ernie Anderson persuaded the King's Ransom people to supply
the Scotch, without having to put up a king's ransom; Ernie
also hired Russell Patterson to decorate the club, and he arranged
for the nightly broadcasts from the club and for all the publicity
in the newspapers and magazines. Through Ernie Anderson's
efforts during the preceding four years in sponsoring and pro-
moting the Condon Town Hall concerts, and the overseas broadcasts and concert bookings in cities and colleges throughout the
country, the name Eddie Condon had become synonymous with
jazz, and people came from all over to see him in person.

When I went into the club, the band was composed of Dave
Tough, Freddie Ohms, Joe Dixon, Jack Lesberg, and Gene
Schroeder. It was a fine band, and later on, when Pee Wee
Russell came in with us, and then when Bud Freeman joined the
gang, too, it seemed like old times. James P. Johnson played
intermission piano for a couple of months, and later Joe Sullivan
took that spot over again. Brad Gowans was missing, but Freddie
Ohms, a young trombonist who was a newcomer to the music,
was a jazz natural.

Eighteen years had gone by since I had first met these men in
Chicago. The whole world had blown apart and been pasted
together again since then, but through all the hard times, the
frustrated hopes, the busted beginnings and the bitter ends, the
thousands of miles we'd traveled and the thousands of songs
we'd played, and despite all the changes and flux in the prevailing
musical tastes, we'd hung on, just trying to play that thing. We
were no longer star-struck, half-baked kids, full of clinkers and
ideals. To be playing together now was something we had

earned, and to us it sounded and felt so good that at times we
seemed to overflow, building up to such a momentum that we
would rise above the beat for a split half second, like a swing that
has swung too high. I've heard us do that on a couple of records;
it makes you feel like you have to grab hold of something to
steady yourself. We felt we had finally made it, and we looked
forward to settling down at last and staying at Eddie's for years
and years. But the past eighteen years had been only the prologue.
The worst was yet to come.

Although I had been aware that during the war years the
interest in jazz had been swelling like a balloon, I had no idea
how fast and furiously it was puffing up until it finally burst
right in our faces. By the end of the war, the interest in jazz
was so widespread, and in musical circles so intense, that the
middle and late forties became an era of incredible nonsense
about jazz. The monthly Eddie Condon Town Hall concerts
attracted such huge audiences that now they had to be held in
Carnegie Hall; in 1943, Duke Ellington had started giving
annual concerts at Carnegie Hall, jazz programs were included
in the Carnegie Hall Pop Concerts, and a mammoth jazz concert
was even held at the Metropolitan Opera House in 1944. The
jazz V-discs and the weekly WCBS jazz broadcasts, emceed by
Eddie Condon, which were short-waved to our servicemen all
over the world, attracted hordes of new converts, who in turn
were filled with the evangelists' zeal to spread the good word
about jazz. Aficionados had begun publishing little jazz magazines
by the dozens, jazz and fan clubs sprang up all over the country,
and jazz concerts were being held every five minutes. Recording
companies sprouted up like mushrooms, and national magazines
such as *Esquire*, as well as the trade publications like *Down Beat*
and *Metronome*, which ten years earlier had ignored jazz, began
sponsoring annual jazz popularity polls, usually climaxed by a
jazz concert, a nationwide broadcast, and recordings of the "all-
star" band of the winners, which brought together some strange
mixtures of style and vintage. For years we had gone hungry

fighting for recognition for jazz, and now it was all much too much of a good thing.

Inevitably with all this quantity, the quality began to suffer. It takes more than just the gathering together of a group of musicians to produce a jazz concert. Just because jazzmen don't require written scores and painstaking rehearsal and special settings to play their music doesn't mean a jazz concert doesn't need careful, knowing, professional presentation, like any performing art or entertainment. The very simplicity of the jazz concert setup made it a natural for the promoters and fast-buck boys who swarmed in on it like a pack of wolves. But they had no idea of what jazz *did* need. The kind of jazz we played had a functional base. When we had started to play jazz years before, we had played to provide the music for dancing. Before our time jazz had been played in marching bands, in street parades, at picnics, funerals, weddings. Before that, jazz had been evolved from blues and work songs, in the cotton fields, on the levees and riverboats, on the railroads, and above all, it had taken form in the churches, in the gospel singing. All this was in the music. It came out of the raw stuff of life. It was a take-off-your-shoes-and-get-with-it music. The direct, down-to-earth communication of these feelings was its appeal, but the trick of preserving the spontaneous character of jazz without having it degenerate into a raucous, senseless, tasteless mishmash isn't easy. A jazz concert needs the knowing discipline of a pro just as much as a symphony orchestra needs a conductor, or an army needs a general.

But while it was bad enough having the opportunists swoop down like vultures to exploit the newly discovered commercial possibilities of jazz, the worst of it was that the very people who professed to love jazz the most became its greatest menace. Jazz, like Dr. Frankenstein, had all unwittingly created a monster in its own image—the jazz addict—who, in becoming all hopped up about the social significance of jazz and its significance as an art form, very nearly snuffed the life out of it. For now jazz no longer belonged to the musician and the dancers; it was taken over lock, stock, and barrel by the fans, the addicts, the record collectors, the amateur critics, the recording companies, the promoters, the night-club owners, the A&R men, the lecturers and writers. These were the people who now decided what was jazz and what wasn't, who dictated how it should be played and on what instruments, and specified who could or could not play "real" jazz.

By the time I went into Eddie's in the fall of 1946, things had gone far and happened fast. A couple of years earlier, record collectors had become so carried away with the excitement of finding out about jazz that they had tracked down some of the venerable New Orleans jazzmen. Heywood Broun's son, among many others, trekked down to New Orleans to record the music of the early practitioners of jazz, and eventually most of the early New Orleans musicians, such as Mutt Carey, Kid Ory, Bunk Johnson, George Lewis, and Jelly Roll Morton, some of whom had been working at other lines of employment for years, were brought out of obscurity. At least they had a chance to enjoy some recognition, but it was cruel in a way to take these men, some of whom had been away from their horns for fifteen years, and all of a sudden to drag them into the limelight and expect them to live up to the claims that had been built up around them when they were in their prime. They were hailed as the only rightful heirs to the jazz throne, and after being taken to New York and Chicago and Los Angeles, where they were eulogized and lionized and recorded and put on concert stages for a brief season or two, they were tossed aside for a newer kick. Meanwhile, in their wake a whole school of amateur critics arose to preach a sort of Negro mystique, which claimed that unless you were a Negro with preferably a New Orleans pedigree, you couldn't possibly play jazz. Young white musicians out on the West Coast were inspired to form bands that were, note for note and instrument for instrument—down to replacing the bass and the guitar with the tuba and the banjo—exact replicas of the early New Orleans bands. Lu Watters was one of the first, with his Yerba Buena band, and later two of his sidemen, Turk Murphy and Bob Scobey, formed similar bands.

All this had been snowballing for two or three years before Eddie opened his club, and it began to come to a head after we had been there only a month or two. We did the unforgivable thing in the eyes of jazz addicts and collectors and critics: not content with playing only the Dixieland and New Orleans tunes, we played standards and pop and show tunes, as we had always done before anyone knew about jazz, and the more we widened our repertoire and experimented with new things, the more the self-appointed guardians of jazz complained. It was really funny when you think about it. For years these people had been hailing Pee Wee and Bud Freeman and Dave Tough and me as great jazzmen, and now when we had really been through the mill all these years with the music, they decided we didn't play "authentic" jazz. And when we played things like "Savoy" and "A-Train" and "How High the Moon," they became actively violent, and to a man the New Orleans revivalists began sounding off about how we didn't play "genuine" jazz.

And then, on top of all this, bop began to appear on the scene. This would have been okay, too, for the pioneer boppers were at least sincere in trying to work something out with those modern chords we'd been hearing for twenty years. But the critics and fans and writers had no sense of proportion, and just as the revivalists declared there was no genuine jazz except New Orleans jazz, the modernists proclaimed that bop was now the only thing and anyone who didn't play the new bop style was a living fossil. "Moldy fig" was the exact term. Big bands such as the Stan Kenton and Woody Herman groups, which adapted jazz to modern classical music and called it "progressive jazz," began making a splash in the commercial field. Together with bop, they made Big Business out of the word "jazz"—an even more commercial business out of it than the big swing bands did.

During the early forties while we had been blowing hot at the Sunday sessions at Ryan's, bop had been incubating at Minton's up in Harlem on Monday nights. The boppers were going through the phase of rejecting everything they had grown up with, but before they had a chance to develop a little taste in their thinking and their music, the critics and jazz writers began climbing on the band wagon, and by the early fifties the output of "modern" jazz records, spurred by the invention of the LP, had reached a phenomenal level. Anyone who made a weird sound or played an out-of-tune little lick could call himself a genius and the critics were too ignorant and afraid to laugh them back into some kind of reality. It really was unfair to the new young "modern" musicians, for they became overnight sensations before they had a chance to mature musically. And so from hot music it became hate music. Like the fairy story about the emperor's clothes, no one dared to say the king was naked, and pretty soon the only form of jazz you heard on the radio was bop, and later there was "cool" and then "hard" jazz. No one had a chance to hear any other kind of jazz. In the fifties a whole new generation of young people grew up knowing nothing about real jazz, and among them were the new musicians and new critics.

I always felt that the so-called modern school was cutting itself loose from the earth roots of jazz. The more they intellectualized it and worked out every new, purposefully discordant note and phrase ahead of time and polished and shaped it, the further they were taking it from jazz and the closer they were bringing it to classical music—and worse than that, to conformity. In abandoning the diatonic scale, with its compromises and its "minorities," by which I mean the two semitone notes in each major scale, and by tending more and more toward the twelve-tone system, in which all notes are equal, they are not bringing about the "equality" they want in life—they are only obeying the overpowering impulse of these times toward conformity. Minority does not mean inferiority, it means difference, and it is the differences that make a democracy, not conformity and sameness. *Vive la différence!*

For I believe that jazz is something truly new in music. You keep hearing how composers of serious music—from Debussy to Ravel to Stravinsky to Copland—were at first enthralled with jazz and then discarded it as too shallow a field for deep plowing. Although I feel they didn't really understand it, in a way I feel they were right. Small-band improvised jazz belongs in the same special category as Italian grand opera, the Viennese operetta, and American musical comedy. These three forms are considered to be the only musical entertainments that are also perfected art forms, and I think jazz should be added to them. Jazz is a highly personal music. Its appeal is in its spontaneity. That's what keeps it ever fresh, ever new. That's the excitement of it and the challenge, and that's what makes it so hard to play. A jazzman has to prove to himself every day that he can play jazz. Not many musicians have the qualities of mind and heart that it takes.

Modern jazz represents the contemporary state of mind, and wants to play it cool, both life and jazz, because of an insecurity that the older generation of jazzmen did not feel. We were the pioneers, rebelling against the Victorian-European music, as the writers of the twenties did in literature. We were ridiculed and called barbarians, too, as the boppers were in the forties, but in spite of the hardships of the twenties and thirties and forties, we were full of fight and hope. But the poor new generation was hit with the atomic age and all that it implies of doom before they were dry behind the ears. They haven't done any living yet, and they want to live, so they play it cool. They've taken the spunk out of the beat by loosening it, and they've taken the beauty out of the tone because they are afraid to believe in beauty, to commit themselves to it.

To get back to the fracas at Condon's, the know-it-all amateur critics began writing vituperative articles in *Down Beat* and the other jazz publications, attacking our band, complaining that the songs we were playing were downright heresy, that Gene Schroeder wasn't good because he wouldn't fit in with Bunk Johnson or Kid Ory, that Freddie Ohms was new to jazz and didn't like to play it, and that Dave Tough looked like he needed a blood transfusion. Freddie Ohms and I were replaced on January 30, 1947, with George Brunis and Wild Bill Davison, and then Dave Tough and Jack Lesberg quit because they refused to work with Brunis and Davison, who were referred to by Dave in an "equal time" interview in *Down Beat* as, respectively, "a clown and a musical gauleiter." Feelings, as one can see, ran high, bitter, and personal. Bud Freeman went to work in South America, while Freddie Ohms went into Nick's, Jack Lesberg went with Leonard Bernstein. Pee Wee and Gene Schroeder stayed on with the new band, as of course did Eddie Condon. Dave Tough went back to Woody Herman's band, joining up with the modernists.

In the meantime, in the midst of all this upheaval, I suffered another loss, a personal one. A couple of weeks before I left Eddie's, I had a call from my sister Rose that my mother was in the hospital. All the way up to Boston on the train the next morning I tried to talk myself into believing it was a false alarm, and I was still hopeful when I spoke to the doctor before going in to see her. After all, her own mother had lived to be a hundred and twenty-five, and Mom had her heart set on cutting her.

"Well, she's nearly ninety, and when you get that old your machinery is bound to wear out," was the matter-of-fact, Yankee way the doctor put it. I knew then that she was dying, but the sight of her thin, withered face was a shock, and her hand felt like tissue paper.

"I'm going to go see Pee Wee now, Ma," I said when I was leaving. She smiled then, and that was the last of it. She had always been fond of Pee Wee Russell, and she knew that I was telling her it was good-bye. She knew it was my life to have to go and play. She had been so proud of my playing, and she had loved to hear the crowds applaud when I played in Boston's Symphony Hall. "Don't mourn for the dead, take care of the living," she had so often said to me. "And when I die, I want you to go out and see a movie." I flew back from Boston that afternoon, but I didn't go to a movie. I got deliberately and thoroughly plastered, and then I had to soak under the shower till I was sober enough to go to work. I kept remembering how I used to play Louis Armstrong records around the house night and day when I was home in the thirties and how my mother was convinced it was I who was on trumpet. Nothing could shake her conviction. "That's Maxie, but he doesn't want to tell me because he's so modest," she'd say knowingly to Rose, and then turning to me she'd say, "You needn't be ashamed. In fact, it's very good!" Everywhere I go, all over the world, I still meet musicians who ask about my mother.

In March, 1947, I went into Jimmy Ryan's with Art Hodes and Danny Alvin for a few weeks, and then a month later, when Jack Teagarden came to town, I went to work with him for several months in a six-piece band at the Famous Door on Fifty-second Street, which also had Big Sid Catlett's band, with Thelonious Monk on piano, on the same bill. We had Peanuts Hucko on clarinet, Jack Lesberg on bass, Morey Feld on drums, and Sanford Gold on piano, and the band sounded so good that when Sid Catlett's band was through playing, he'd stay and play along with our band, too. Jack Teagarden was even more tireless than Big Sid. The minute our band finished a set, Jack would take his horn and go across the street to Ryan's or the Three Deuces and sit in with those bands. The manager tore his hair out by handfuls. "You're supposed to be appearing at the Famous Door exclusively!" he'd scream. "Just being neighborly," Jack would drawl in his calm, unruffled way. We enjoyed the manager's discomfort, but we had our own troubles, too. Jack always had such a wonderful big heart for everybody that in the course of walking down Broadway during the day he'd hire every musician he'd meet. When night came, it would wind up with our having six or eight extra players milling around on the stand, and we'd have to explain that they were welcome to sit in but there was no money for paying them. We had a hard enough time as it was getting our seventy-five dollars a week from the bosses.

Mezz Mezzrow was across the street in Ryan's then, and Dave Tough was at the Three Deuces with Bill Harris and Flip Phillips, while Dizzy Gillespie and Charlie Parker had one of their first bop bands down the street at the Spotlite. Dizzy was having his own troubles, too, since there weren't too many listeners for his music yet. He was setting the new style by playing sixteenth and thirty-second notes in dazzling high registers, carrying on the style of Roy Eldridge. His daring use of progressive chord changes and fast, intricate intervals soon made him the leader in the school of modern trumpets.

We also had a daily half-hour radio job at WMGM while we were at the Famous Door. The radio job was hard because we had to use the studio drummer and piano player and they weren't used to swinging, but on the other hand we used to get paid regularly at WMGM and we all needed the money, especially me, for a couple of months later, on October 22, 1947, my first son, Sam, was born, a month after my thirty-ninth birthday. The housing shortage was still acute then and it wasn't easy managing with an infant in our one-room apartment on West Twentieth Street, but having Sam made it all great, anyway.

In spite of the mounting campaign of hostility from the new bop cultists, the late forties were a sort of golden time for jazz, with plenty of all kinds of jazz to be heard all over town. Not only were the hot jazzmen and boppers playing in clubs next door to each other, they were likely to be playing in the same club. Though Fifty-second Street's sun was setting, it gave off a warm, mellow glow in its declining years. This street had once harbored comfortable brownstone houses occupied by well-to-do families with children and dogs, maids and cooks, and back yards with trees and gardens. In the Prohibition era, the club owners began buying some of these respectable houses and opening their speakeasies on the ground floor. After repeal, when the clubs became legitimate, more and more began sprouting up. By the time Rockefeller Center was built, most of the families had moved away and the remaining private houses became rooming houses, where you could rent a spacious, high-ceilinged room for five dollars a week even up to the early forties.

The heyday of Fifty-second Street was from the mid-thirties to the mid-forties, when it was known all over the world as Swing Street. After that it began to deteriorate, with girlie clubs springing up like weeds and office buildings encroaching on all sides. But in the late forties there were still wonderful sounds to be heard, with the clubs presenting musicians like Henry "Red" Allen, J. C. Higginbotham, Art Tatum, Stuff Smith, George Brunis, Sidney Bechet, Buster Bailey, Sidney and Wilbur DeParis, Dizzy Gillespie, Trummy Young, Johnny Guarnieri, Rex Stewart, Roy Eldridge, Ben Webster, Charlie Shavers, Bobby Hackett, Buck Clayton, Charlie Parker, and Coleman Hawkins —the great "Hawk," who had pioneered in the playing of the tenor sax, is a poet, not only in his command of his horn and in his big, warm tone, but in his bottomless well of rich ideas, his intelligence, and his taste. The wonderful Pearl Bailey, a mere slip of a girl then, was just starting as a singer, and Reilly's bar, across the street from Ryan's, was still the musicians' home-away-from-home, between sets or between jobs. Over at the Aquarium you could hear Louis Armstrong, Count Basie, Lionel Hampton, or Gene Krupa, while Nick's in the Village was likely to have Miff Mole, Marty Marsala, Muggsy Spanier, Ernie Caceres, Billy Butterfield; the Café Societies Uptown and Downtown would have Edmond Hall or Vic Dickenson, Cliff Jackson, Pete Johnson, J. C. Heard; and the Vanguard and Eddie Condon's were going strong. Those were still happy, swinging days.

Chapter 11

The summer of 1948 found me in a panic. Except for Friday-night jam sessions at the Stuyvesant Casino and Central Plaza and occasional gigs, I had been out of work for several months, and with no sign of work in sight I was desperate to find a way to get my family out of our stifling one-room apartment and into the country for a few weeks. By the end of July, with the rent coming due and no money in the bank, I finally reached for the telephone one morning and called Jackie Marshard. Jackie was brief, businesslike, and to the point.

"If you can get hold of fifty dollars and fly up to Boston today, I'll see what I can work out for you," he said crisply. "Bring your trumpet and a tux."

Though I was weak with gratitude that Jackie hadn't brushed me off, having to walk into his office that Friday afternoon in August was one of the hardest things I ever had to do. And when we were face to face, it was all I could do not to turn on my heel and walk out.

"Money is everything," Jackie had said to me twenty-five years before. Since that time, Jackie had made his million dollars, and

I had made my reputation as a jazzman, and now here I was coming to him for help.

"It's a long time since the days of the Shawmut Syncopaters, eh, Maxie!" Jackie said, shaking hands jovially. As he lowered his expensively tailored frame into his leather swivel chair, his eyes flicked over me, taking such deadly inventory that I felt I was back at 90 Church Street, trying to enlist in the Navy. "Well, here he is, the jazz hot-shot," I could hear him think. "Hmmmm, not very impressive, a little half-pint, crowding forty, beat, scared, and broke."

As for Jackie, though he was the same age as I, he not only looked as fit and handsome as ever, he seemed actually to glow with prosperity and well-being. His booking office, which he had opened some dozen years earlier in partnership with Lou Bonick, another orchestra leader, was doing so well in the society-band field that Jackie had branched out into other lucrative ventures, such as managing Vaughn Monroe's band, which he had built into a national success. After he and Lou discussed the ordering of some posters for a dance at which Vaughn Monroe was appearing, Jackie turned his full attention to me, while I put forward my case for jazz, explaining that Dixieland, as I was now resigned to calling it, had a great chance of catching on with the public, and that now was the crucial time, while the public interest in jazz was still high.

While Jackie wasn't completely sold, his business instincts were intrigued. "I'll tell you what we'll do, Maxie," he said. "Lou and I will put you on the payroll at seventy-five dollars a week until we see what happens and how you make out. In the meantime, I'll put you to work right away." He took a quick look at his wafer-thin gold wrist watch. "I'm flying up to Bar Harbor right now and I'll take you with me and have you sit in with the band at the country-club dance tonight. How's that?"

"You'll never be sorry, Jackie," I said gruffly. I had to resort to a couple of quick blasts into my handkerchief at the thought that here was help from a real friend. I didn't have to be ashamed now of having had to come to him. Jackie had made his, and now he was going to help me. And this time I'll make it, I swore to myself.

"O.K., Max, it's all settled, then," Jackie said, snapping on his Panama. "Let's go."

In the cab Jackie unburdened himself for a while about high society and his disillusionment with the lives led by the extremely wealthy. The gist of it was that while he took an obvious pleasure in being able to talk so knowingly and familiarly about highly placed people, now that he had made a mint of money himself he found he wasn't getting the satisfaction he had expected, and he revealed that he was, in fact, turning more and more to religion as his business affairs grew more and more successful.

I turned a quizzical look on him at these words. "And to think that the time we met I wanted you thrown out of the shul because you were so disrespectful," I said, grinning.

After reminiscing for a while about the old days in Dorchester, we got down to business again, and Jackie asked me if what I was trying to do with jazz music could be done in Boston. "I never could see why not," I said, and I told him about my shoestring night club and how fifteen hundred people had flocked into that dreary little cellar in two weeks. "Boston people always have to go to New York for their fun; it's time they admitted they were human, too, and had some places of their own in Boston," I said.

Jackie was so cheered at this picture that he asked me how I was fixed for money at the moment. When I said I had a few dollars on me, he pulled out his wallet. "This will repay you for your plane fare," he said, handing me fifty bucks. Again I had trouble with that lump in my throat.

Once Jackie's little four-seater plane was airborne, I began to relax. I had learned to love flying, and my spirits lifted as the plane nosed higher into the clean blue of the sky, until I overheard Jackie's guest congratulating him on the birth of his second son two weeks earlier, and then my worries about getting my family out of the hot city came pressing down on me again. "But

I still say money isn't everything," my mind kept insisting stub-
bornly, and underneath my thankfulness was that same old
rankling jealousy as I noticed Jackie watching my face to see
my reactions to being on a plane, and I thought with sulky satisfaction of all the flying I had done in the Pacific and how Jackie
had no idea I had flown as much as or more than he with all his
private planes.

Mr. Small, at whose house Jackie always stayed at Bar Harbor,
met us with a car, and after I was settled in my room, I went
downstairs to the big kitchen, where the musicians and the pilot
and Jackie were gathered.

"Come on, Maxie, live it up," Jackie said, handing me a glass
half filled with Scotch.

I was so intent on playing well that night that I refused at first,
but Jackie insisted.

"This is living!" he said, lifting his own highball in a toast.
This was another new facet of Jackie, for in all the years I had
known him he had never smoked or drunk. Turning to the pilot
then, Jackie said, "See this little bastard," waving his glass at
me. "He put me in this business. If it wasn't for him and his
lousy Shawmut Syncopaters, I'd never have all this."

"You would've made it no matter what business you went
into, Jackie," I said. "You have the flair for making money."

"Yeah, but you have to be lucky, too, and maybe I wouldn't
have been so lucky or looked so good in some other business," he
said, mugging.

The dance that night at the country club was a disappointment
to me, all keyed up as I was to knock them dead. The season at
Bar Harbor is just getting under way at the beginning of August
and the club was almost deserted, with only three or four couples
showing up. There was no chance to show Jackie how people
responded to jazz, but when Jackie and I walked back to Mr.
Small's boardinghouse in the quiet of the summer night, I tried
again to get across to him the tremendous interest in jazz.

"We'll see," was all he said. "Listen, tomorrow you go back
to Boston and see my brother Harry. Tell him to take you out

on the job he's playing tomorrow night. It's a big private debutante party down on the Cape, and you'll have a better chance to make something out of it. Tell Harry what you need in the way of money and he'll take care of you."

I flew back to Boston the next afternoon and from the airport I went straight to Jackie's office, where I washed and changed back to my tuxedo again. I piled into the car with the rest of the musicians, many of whom I knew from the days in the thirties when I had played jobs with the Marshards. The party that night at Marion, out on the Cape, was a different matter from the dance the night before. After we had played for a couple of hours, that wonderful comedian Frank Fontaine entertained and then Harry took the mike and gave a little spiel about jazz, repeating the things I had told him, but not really knowing what it was all about.

"We have a man in our orchestra tonight who has made a big name in jazz," Harry concluded. "Ladies and gentlemen, may I introduce Max Kaminsky," and at the mention of my name, the house came down. I don't know who was more surprised, me or Harry. I had expected some of these society kids to have heard of me but I hadn't foreseen such total and instantaneous acclaim, and I just sat there for a second, staring back open-mouthed at open-mouthed Harry.

"This is what I was trying to explain to Jackie," I said excitedly to him after the dance was over. "Did you hear those kids! I'm telling you, Harry, a jazz band, properly presented, could make a great thing of it now!"

"Yeah, maybe so," Harry said. "We'll see."

I didn't hear from Jackie all the following week, and the seventy-five-dollar check didn't arrive, either. I was sitting around the following Sunday morning debating whether to give Jackie a ring or to forget the whole thing when the telephone rang. It was Louis Rosenthal, my old buddy from Boston.

"Maxie, listen—did you see the papers? I couldn't *believe* it, but it's in the papers."

"What's the matter, Rosey?" I said. "Calm down."

"It's Jackie. He was killed. He crashed his car into a tree last night."

I sat there stunned for a few minutes after I had hung up the phone, and then a thought trickled slowly into my mind. How envious are you now? a chilled inner voice asked. Swearing, I seized the phone book and looked up the number of the *Daily News*. Like Louis Rosenthal, I couldn't believe it either, even after the *News* confirmed it.

"Maybe if I get the Boston papers . . ." I muttered.

At the Times Square newsstand, I bundled the Boston papers under my arm and walked across the street to the drugstore and sat down on a stool and ordered coffee before I opened the papers. It was true, all right, even down to a photograph of the smashed car on the front page. Thirty-nine years old, and he had made a few million. "His reflexes were never very good," I muttered to the newspaper, not realizing I was talking out loud.

"What was that, mister?" the counterman asked.

"Nothing," I mumbled. I gathered up the newspapers and flipped a coin on the counter and left.

"A driver of men," my thoughts continued as I walked down Broadway, "but he was lousy when it came to driving a car, or playing a drum, or just playing. He had worked hard, and had just started to live and drink and enjoy life, enjoy his money, and here I had come to the point of giving up all I cared about so I could do something for my family. No, money isn't everything, but this is a hell of a way to win an argument," I thought.

They buried Jackie on my birthday, September 7th.

A few weeks later, Harry called me to come to Boston to play some more jobs and see if I'd go over as well as I did the first time. When I continued to get ovations and break up the place, I began to feel then that if Jackie had lived he would have backed me in a jazz band. Jackie loved to create business and success, and had he been managing the business end of things, he would have made me, but that wasn't to be. His brother Harry had no interest in anything but continuing with the business as Jackie had set it up, and he just used me as a sideman, with a special little act of my own.

So for the next twelve years I did the society-band circuit three times a year.

The society-band business is one of the looniest of all the loony fields in the music business. The granddaddy of all the society-band leaders is Meyer Davis, with some sixty orchestras in his bull pen, all booked solid as far as fifteen years in advance. Ruby Newman is another veteran, along with Emil Coleman, Lester Lanin, Ben Cutler, Jimmy Lanin, Harry Marshard, and others. It's a murderously competitive field, but once a band leader is established in the society circuit, he's likely to be set for life. The band leaders become part of the whole sentimental tradition of the family and the social group, and it takes a certain personality to go along with all this—or maybe it's an uncertain personality, like the bandleader who, when asked by a dowager if he was Jewish, smoothly answered, "Not necessarily, madam," without his baton losing a beat. Different leaders are trying to break through the Diamond Curtain all the time, and occasionally society will try out jazz bands like Turk Murphy's and Ralph Sutton's, but on the whole they stick to the established leaders whom they know well.

There is a story famous in music circles about the band leader who was getting some heavy competition from an up-and-coming young leader, whom we'll call Bobby Brown. One night when the established band leader was driving to an engagement with a busload of musicians, they ran into such a heavy snowstorm that eventually they bogged down in a drift about two miles from the place where they were to play. When it was obvious even to the hysterical band leader that they were hopelessly stuck, he let out a wail that drowned out the gale outside. "That Bobby Brown will stop at *nothing*!" he howled, shaking his fist at the raging storm.

There is no beat like the society beat. For seven or eight hours, the society bands will grind out some five hundred songs like an

unending chain of link sausages, all at the exact same lively, brisk
tempo, which is so marked that you have to be stone deaf, or
stoned, not to follow it. The band leader's one fear is that the
party will fizzle out from under him, and there is no one who
cares more deeply about keeping things jumping than the leader
himself.

The two major debutante seasons are December and June,
with a third minor season in September, before school starts.
Nowadays the musicians are generally flown from date to date,
but until just a few years ago, the men used to pile into cars at
eight o'clock in the morning after finishing one party and drive
four or five hundred miles to another city, arriving in time to
catch an hour's rest before playing all night at another party.

The arrangements for all these goings-on are usually put into
the hands of a specialist, the professional social secretary, who
will charge up to $1,500 for taking over all the preparations:
clearing the date, booking the band, sending the invitations, and
arranging for the caterers and decorations. The cost of the food,
drink, and flowers can be anywhere from $2,500 to $10,000, and
the social secretary's commission from the florists, liquor dealers,
musicians, and decorators is reckoned as high as 20 per cent of the
total cost. In the days before income tax, it was nothing to spend
$20,000 and $30,000 on a debut, and in the thirties the coming-
out parties of heiresses like Barbara Hutton, Doris Duke, and
Brenda Frazier cost between $50,000 and $75,000. Before that,
the peak was reached in 1928-29, when $75,000 to $100,000 were
sometimes spent on debuts. Nowadays the proceeds of the cotillions and debutante balls are donated to charity.

The dancing will seldom start before ten or eleven o'clock, but
the band leader will insist that the entire band be there before
seven-thirty on the excuse that usually around eight there'll be a
call for cocktail music, when the leader will appoint a three-
piece group, called strolling musicians, to play while the rest of
the band sits and waits, herded into some corner where the butler
considers it safe to leave such barbarians. Most of the servants

consider us with the cold eye of a small-town cop viewing a
caravan of gypsies, and many outsnob their masters, but some are
considerate and courteous and will help you find some food in
the ten-minute supper break, around 1 A.M. This doesn't mean
the orchestra stops playing for even ten minutes, though. We eat
in shifts. It's best to go with the first shift, when the leader
goes, because the leader allows himself a leisurely twenty minutes
or half hour for his meal and you get a chance to eat without
choking to death, but the men on the second shift will barely
have got the first forkful to their mouth when the leader will
come rushing up screaming that the party is dying on its feet
and to stop goofing off. Sometimes the caterers will miscalculate
and by the time the musicians are ready to eat, there's nothing
left beside the dried hors d'oeuvres and some soggy caviar. It's
tough when this happens at a private home miles out in the
country where there is no chance of ducking out to a hamburger
joint for food, so on the next job you pad your pockets with
chocolate bars, and of course it will turn out to be a place where
the caterer used to play alto sax in a college band and he'll load
your plate with so much food you can't lift it.

Most society bands are pickup bands, put together for each
date and composed of men accustomed to the society circuit,
who know all the songs and are used to playing them at the
society tempo. One night during our dinner intermission, one of
the guests came over to tell me and the saxophone player how
wonderful the band sounded, and he marveled at how we could
play without sheet music, flowing from one song into another
without a hitch. He ended up asking wonderingly, "How long
have you fellows been together?" The saxophone player con-
sulted his wrist watch and said, "Since nine o'clock."

The June and September private coming-out parties are
usually held outdoors under huge red-and-white-striped tents.
Thousands of pink roses or white chrysanthemums will be twined
around the posts and banked behind the bandstand, or a jungle
scene might be simulated with tons of gardenias and orchids and

potted palms, or it might be done up in a Parisian sidewalk café *décor*. One family in the Midwest who spends each summer in Nantucket had replicas of its windmills and lighthouses painted on canvas props. At another party, the entire band had to dress in kilts. How the Scots keep warm in them I'll never know. The first thing the musician's eye focuses on amidst all this splendor is the bandstand, to see if there are any drapes or hangings behind it for protection against the wind, an unexpected drop in temperature, or a sudden thunderstorm. Lately, caterers have begun to supply plastic sheets which can be dropped down from the canopy to keep out the weather, but musicians have launched debutantes into society while wearing overcoats on top of their tuxedos or playing while rain dripped down their collars and dribbled into their instruments.

I guess it's hazards like these that account for the heavy drinking among society-band musicians. Of all the dedicated drinkers I have known—and I have known some of the most inspired— the men in society bands make jazzmen look like sissies when it comes to whiskey. I have never seen men drink so much and still play a job all night long, without missing a beat. Some band leaders protest virtuously that "my men never smoke or drink," when a tray of drinks is sent up to them, and the men kindly try not to destroy this happy illusion.

One of the most awe-inspiring drinkers I ever knew was Bill Dooley, a drummer who was one of the main attractions in the Harry Marshard band. A great big fat guy with a limitless capacity, Bill was a great entertainer, and underneath a W. C. Fields exterior and a wryly witty mind beat an immensely kind, cheerful heart full of fun and nonsense. He was the one who held the band together. As soon as the band checked into a hotel, Dooley would be on the telephone, and within a half hour all the musicians would be sprawled comfortably around his room, playing pinochle, studying tip sheets on the horses, and arguing amiably about baseball while room service wheeled in endless wagons of Scotch and ice and brandy and platters of steak and pots of coffee. I remember one time when a musician happened to confess to a weakness for whipped cream, Dooley reached for the phone and ordered five dollars' worth of whipped cream for him. Dooley had a whole repertoire of songs that were always a big hit, and he was a wonderful opener for me, paving the way for my performance. Bill died in 1959; even his big heart finally gave out from all the years of pumping away and driving all day and playing all night.

The cotillions and the debutante balls, where the season's crop of debs is presented to society in one shot, aren't as hard to play as the private coming-out parties, and since the former are always held indoors at a hotel or country club, the musicians are assured of shelter and food. But the parties in private homes are the most interesting. I always felt that one of the reasons musicians put up with the back-breaking work is simply for the thrill of glimpsing the fabulous homes and lives of the rich. They get their kicks from driving up to a palatial stone mansion, about a city block long, set amid velvety lawns sweeping down to the lake or bay. The walls in the 130-room house will be hung with French tapestries acres wide, or paneled in oak or floored in dazzling Italian marble, or there will be galleries hung with paintings collected from all over the world and filled with so many priceless works of art that a state trooper will be stationed in each room to guard them. But at the end of a three-week tour of the society circuit, the musicians are surfeited with the sight of so much luxury, so much rich food, and so many jewels, so much perfection and so much wealth. They are polluted with whiskey, their nerves are jangling from lack of sleep, their skin is gritty and gray from too much smoking and stained with travel weariness, and they're fed up with everything. The only thing they agree on now is that they hate the leader.

Actually, most society band leaders are marvelously funny, frantic fellows, operating a highly specialized, complex business under tremendous pressure. It's a wonder they keep their sanity. The inconsistency of their behavior with the society swells and

with their own men, though, is always good for a laugh among
the musicians. One of the leaders was on a kick once about how
he was going to write a book about bandstand etiquette for the
musicians' edification. He was harping on this for three days, and
then the next day at a lawn party at a posh country club, one
of the colored attendants, a dignified old fellow, came over and
tugged politely at the leader's jacket just as he was about to give
the down beat. The leader turned angrily and snapped, "What
the blankety blankety hell do *you* want!" The entire band
whooped and hooted at this flagrant hypocrisy and one of the
musicians hollered, "On what page will *that* remark be in your
etiquette book?"

One heart-warming memory I have of a society party happened back in the thirties, and involves Fats Waller, who was in
Boston for a theatre engagement. Jackie Marshard had called me
to ask if I could get Fats to appear at a society charity ball that
night. I told Jackie the first thing to do was to send a case of
vintage wines to Fats at the theatre, and that I would do the rest.
I had an early gig that night and when I showed up at Fats'
dressing room after his last show and explained about the wine,
Fats was receptive to anything—as he usually was, anyway.

"Why, sure, man," Fats said jovially. "Just a couple more sips
of this *fine* wine, and I'll be glad to do my bit."

When Fats was introduced at the affair, he waited till the
applause died down. "Thank you one and all," he said, with an
airy wave of his hand, "and now I want to introduce that great
trumpet man Max Kaminsky!" He gave me a nudge with his
powerful arm. "On your feet, boy," he muttered. Before I could
protest that *he* was the one invited to play there, not me, he had
me up at the piano with him. That was Fats' way; he was always
making somebody else great.

I guess the most foolish thing I did was to fall into society
work each season, since these were the crucial years when I might
have been able to do something, but when December rolled
around, with Christmas looming on the horizon, the prospect of

making fifteen hundred dollars for three weeks' work was hard to resist, and it would be the same way when the June society season came around, with the need for money to get my family out of the city closing in. In April, 1951, when my second son Matthew—the spit 'n' image of me—was born, I depended more than ever on the sure thing of the society work, and I was very grateful for it. Home conditions at least were improved now, for we had been living for the past couple of years in a sunny top-floor apartment, right next door to our old one-room apartment on West Twentieth Street. We stayed there for six years, until 1955, when we moved to a little house in Westport, Connecticut, where the boys had plenty of room to play baseball and swim in the Sound. My sons got a great kick out of my playing the trumpet, but as little as they were they seemed to sense the difficulties with it all. Once when he was around five years old, Sam came over to me when I was trying out a new mute and said seriously, "I don't care how good you are on the trumpet, Dad— I like you anyway."

Chapter 12

The next seven or eight years, from 1949 to 1957, followed the same general pattern; the scramble for work all year, in between the two or three weeks of society work every season that I could count on to tide me over.

Most of the jobs I had during this time were uptown in the Broadway area. Except for Nick's, Eddie Condon's, and the Central Plaza, the Village had gone cool with bop, beatniks, and Zen, and the only place that was still swinging was Broadway. Fifty-second Street was still holding on by its fingernails, but except for Jimmy Ryan's, where I had a trio for three months in the winter of 1948–49, and one or two other spots, there was very little hot music to be found there any more. The boppers and progressives were established in the few clubs left which hadn't deteriorated into girlie shows. A couple of big Broadway places opened up and flourished for a couple of years, such as Bop City and the Royal Roost, which presented a mixed grab bag of entertainment with popular singers, progressive bands, boppers, and traditional jazz bands. In the meantime, some of the smaller Broadway clubs began trying out jazz, and it turned out that I had the first jazz band in the Metropole and Birdland, and the last band in Billy Rose's Diamond Horseshoe, where we played the last two weeks before it closed.

The original Metropole was on the corner of Forty-eighth Street and Seventh Avenue, where the California restaurant is now. When the Metropole decided to bring in entertainment, they began with gay–nineties–type singers, and finally worked up to jazz in 1949. When they started off on their new jazz policy, they kept on a couple of the old-time singers to alternate with my band, just in case we didn't go over, but the Metropole was perfect for jazz. We caught on right away, and on Friday and Saturday nights the people were ten or twelve deep all around the great circular bar, which was so huge that we had to keep shifting around after each number to face a different part of the audience. The next year, the Metropole sold that corner building to the Maisel restaurant chain and moved to its present site next door. The new Metropole was narrower and didn't have the wide street frontage or the great circular bar, but nevertheless it continued to be extremely successful.

I was hired for the opening of the new Metropole, too. We busted into "South Rampart Street Parade" for our opening number to give the place a rousing send-off, and we hadn't played half a chorus before one of the bosses yelled out, "It's too Goddamned *loud*!" We faltered to a ragged halt, and there was a big controversy until finally Mr. Harriman, another of the bosses, said soothingly, "Maybe you'd better put in a mute, Max." Shortly afterward, the owners ran into some complications and closed the place down for eighteen months. When they reopened, they went back to the gay nineties policy for a while, and then the partner who had complained about jazz being too loud sold out, and Mr. Harriman called me up and asked me to come back. I was tied up with something else then, though, so Mr. Harriman went to an agent, who brought jazz back there with all the big names he could find, and in no time at all the Metropole became the loudest and most successful jazz emporium in town. It's a great place to work because it has something of the real old-time unconfined atmosphere of jazz. The people can just walk in and have a couple of drinks at the bar right in front of the band without bothering about tables, but though the atmosphere is casual, they come there to listen, and it's a good feeling to play to customers who come for the music and not just to be seen.

Just around this time, December, 1949, Birdland opened its long red doors, and although it became the mecca of the boppers, I blew the first note in there. Billy Shaw, the agent in charge of organizing the opening show, was a fan of mine, and he booked my band for the opening "International Jazz Festival," which included a wide array of talent: the bands of Lester Young, Charlie Parker, Stan Getz, Hot Lips Page, and Lennie Tristano, as well as a singer who was just starting out, Harry Belafonte. A couple of years later when Belafonte took off his tie, unbuttoned his shirt, and went calypso, suddenly everyone could hear him, but at that time he dressed conventionally and sang straight and nobody noticed him at all. Well, he had lots of company at Birdland, because nobody particularly heard us, either. The only time we made much impression was when George Wettling accidentally knocked over the three sets of drums on the bandstand, and since it was New Year's Day, even that didn't make much of an impression on anyone except the boss, who blew his top. I also had Dick Hyman, who later ran the Arthur Godfrey show, on piano, Sol Yaged on clarinet, Irving Lang on bass, and Munn Ware, one of the finest jazz trombonists around.

Feelings between the boppers and the traditional jazzmen were strained, to put it gently. Lips Page was very unhappy there because all the other musicians were trying to play the new style and they didn't mind showing their disdain for Lips' style. He'd complain to me about how he was being treated, but I kept telling him not to think that if a guy plays a whole-tone scale or an exotic interval this is the end of the world. The music they're trying to play has been around since the beginning of time; the shepherds in the wilds of Persia and Afghanistan are still playing it today.

But some of it did sound so bad. I remember the first time I heard one particularly "far-out" band at Birdland; it had such an upsetting effect on my nervous system that it actually made me feel nauseous. But Charlie Parker, who was rated the great genius of all that music, liked my band better than anything else he heard there. We had nothing else in common; I couldn't drink the way he did and I didn't know his friends and never went out with him on any parties, but musically we became good friends. He and Lester Young were the only two musicians down there who would go out of their way to speak to me, and they always made a point of coming over to the table and talking about something musical. No matter how much the boppers want to claim Lester Young and say he started the "cool" school early in the thirties with his dry tone and unfrantic rhythmical approach, Lester was always a hot jazzman. They do the same with Lester as with Beiderbecke; the critics try to claim that the seeds of the modern school lay in them in such a way as to negate everything else they stood for. There was so much bitterness on the part of most of the new bop players toward the older musicians in those days that it was shameful, and they were just as mean and ornery to poor Lips, and to Louis, too.

But Charlie Parker's music never bothered me the way some of the other music did, with its bad tone and taste and intonation. For as far as the "modern" chords are concerned, I'd been listening to them in the classical music ever since the late twenties—in fact, I'd been hearing that kind of atonal melody in the Torah singing ever since I was a child, and when I first started to improvise on the trumpet as a kid, I used to go off into those atonal intervals that I had heard in the temple chants simply because they were so familiar to me and so easy to do. I hadn't enough discipline and control as yet to improvise on pitch and to know how to build a solo. But Charlie Parker's music didn't seem to me so completely out of tune as so many of the others', nor did it have complete disregard for any sane relationship with a song. Parker's playing had at least some authority to it, as well as first-rate intelligence and artistic expression, and Parker could really

swing, whereas so many of his imitators and followers never had
it and couldn't get it. Parker knew; he could hear those sounds
right, and he could fuse them into some order and form. The next
time I met Charlie Parker we played together, and I found myself enjoying it very much. It was on a television show for CBS.
Parker had his own band, with Miles Davis and Max Roach,
while the studio put together a little combo of house musicians
for me to play with. At the end of the program, we all jammed
together on the blues, and while Parker still played his style, it
fitted in beautifully with what I was doing.

As salty and contemptuous as the young bop musicians were
toward the older generation of jazzmen, I don't blame them as
much as I do the critics and promoters, who were the really
vicious and ignorant ones. The so-called critics wanted to be "in"
on the birth of a new genius, since they'd missed Beiderbecke
and Louis Armstrong when they were starting out, and they
were trying to make this *their* thing.

A perfect example of how insidious it all was is the case of
Dave Tough. Dave had had all the admiration and glory for
years until modern jazz became popular, and then he couldn't
stand not being the best, or, rather, not being called the best.
He fell for the new musicians who came in to play the music
of the boppers. Dave had gone through a life of happy jazz and
swing music, but with the new music being made into a new
cult, he couldn't realize that this music was just youth trying
to make a living and that it had nothing to do with Dave's
greatness. If he had given it time, he would have heard the
barrenness of so much of it, and how a great deal of it was only
exchanging old clichés for new clichés. In time it would all
pass, no matter how much certain people might herald the musicians Dave worried about. These musicians had the forces of
business people to back them, and the audience, knowing nothing
about music, fell for this and admired the bad-taste musicians.
Few people know the difference between the good and the bad.
I couldn't talk to Dave in those days of 1947, though, for I too

was in an unknowing spin and I had to wait to be able to see and reason it out. The first step I took was not to die just because I wasn't in favor with certain cults of musicians and critics. Of course, I never was the widely popular man Dave was, with his *Down Beat* awards year after year as best drummer, so it was easier for me to take the ups and downs. Dave was always the best, and to lose that must have hurt him much more than I would ever know, just as the awful things they said about Louis at this time must have hurt him—calling him "Uncle Tom" because they said he didn't act "dignified" enough for them. Dignity was their new password, their god, while many were carrying on in ways that had nothing to do with dignity. It's all very pathetic. And, of course, in music there is always a time when one is hurt, but it does make me feel bad to think that so many of the great ones—Dave Tough, Lips Page, Brad Gowans, Freddie Ohms, James P. Johnson, Fats Waller, Frankie Newton —died at a time when their music was being ridiculed.

But despite all the hard feelings caused by the attitude of the new jazzmen, the modernists did, of course, widen the scope of jazz. They extended the use of passing notes, which Bix had explained to me back in 1926, to include passing chords, and their experiments in more complex multiple rhythms are fine, though it seems at times they are putting the tension into the melody and taking it out of the beat. Since the forties, the modernists have been learning some taste, and they're not so slavish in their imitation of the barren clichés of bop.

There has to be change, but sometimes when they talk about removing the old restrictions in jazz, I feel like the people in the new housing developments. They were moved out of the old, restricting slums and put in clean, new, modern buildings, and then it was discovered that some of the old so-called limitations were vital to their happiness.

And one thing I do feel bad about is what has happened to dance music since modern jazz. Modern jazz came about at a time when there was still the wartime tax on dancing in clubs, and since you couldn't dance to it anyway, the kids eventually turned to rock 'n' roll. In spite of its poor taste, rock 'n' roll at least had kept those earthy blues chords and rock-bottom beat, and the kids took to it at once. Young people need dancing, and since no one was doing anything about giving them a music to dance to, they found their own, such as it is. But in the thirties when the kids danced to the big swing bands they had been dancing to a music that was in far better taste than what the kids nowadays are hearing in the rock 'n' roll bands. In short, I feel that the kids of the fifties and sixties have been gypped by not having a chance to have a good swinging music in good taste to dance to.

If things were hectic at Birdland, the next place I worked, the Aquarium, was even wilder. Now a swanky Spanish restaurant, El Liborio, the Aquarium was then a low-down sailor joint in the Hotel Somerset. I didn't mind the low-downness of it, for after the freeze at Birdland it felt good to have somebody, even rowdy drunken sailors, enjoy themselves and the music, but at times it did get pretty frantic. But the riot we had there one night wasn't caused by the music. It seems that practically the entire crew of a battleship had come down with V.D. from fraternizing with the girls they had picked up at the Aquarium. The minute their ship hit port again, the crew came storming in with one idea in mind, to wreck the joint. When the bottles and chairs began to fly through the air, I turned to the cigarette girl, Jean, who had been after me for weeks to give her a chance to sing. "Now is the time," I said, helping her up on the stand. She was delighted; a little thing like a riot didn't bother her, and we went into "Sweet Sue" and "Ida" and all the calming kind of music we could think of while we waited for the riot squad to arrive.

I worked at another dive, on West Forty-fifth Street, that was just as weird. It always smelled of stale beer and cheap perfume, and of the disinfectant they used to kill the smell, and the customers' interest in jazz was only perfunctory. The boss, a brash

Broadway type with several clubs in the area, used to make the rounds every night to check the take. One night one of the customers took sick, and when they couldn't revive him they sent for an ambulance. Just as the body was being carried out the door on a stretcher, the boss breezed in, and he bustled right past the stretcher without flicking an eye at it—in fact, I had the impression he absent-mindedly flicked his cigar ashes on it in passing.

But this boss wasn't as bad as the gangster who liked my music so much he wanted to set me up in a night club he owned in the Village. The club was a good size and shape and was in a marvelous location for a jazz spot, and I was hot about the idea until I found myself sitting at a table in this club with four or five hard-eyed mobsters in wide-brimmed hats, striped suits, and wild ties, all of them puffing on vile-smelling cigars except the big boss himself, who didn't drink or smoke, but who exuded such coldness that at the mere sight of him my enthusiasm ran right out of the bottom of my shoes. I had just enough presence of mind to keep my hands out of sight so no one would see how they were shaking.

"Well, what do you think?" one of the pin-striped types prodded.

"Well—I'll have to talk to my lawyer first," I countered. I had no lawyer, but I sure was going to get one fast.

The boss spoke up then. "You sound yellow," he rasped.

All eyes snapped on me. "Well, it's just that I'd like to bring my lawyer down here to talk to you guys and then we can figure it all out. I'm not much of a businessman myself," I said placatingly.

The boss took a different tack. "You haven't any confidence in us," he said in aggrieved tones. But I was unmoved and kept insisting on the lawyer until they agreed.

The next day I called up Al Miller, a lawyer who had years of experience in the theatrical field. Al Miller is just about my height, and the two of us together wouldn't have impressed a rabbit, but Al knew how to handle himself in a situation like this. He talked while we all listened, and he sounded great, and he and the big boss went into the back room and talked some more. When they came out, Al shook hands with the boss and we all took cordial leave of one another.

Outside, Al took my elbow and propelled me up the street until we reached the corner, then he hissed in my ear, "My advice to you is this—*run for your life!*" He signaled a cab and hopped in, and that was the end of that deal.

Then there was the time a promoter came to me with a proposition for opening a club in the room underneath the Phoenix Theatre on Second Avenue. This room had been the 181 Club, the most notorious fag joint in the Village. It had finally lost its liquor license, and this guy, whom I'll call Gus, got in touch with me. "Here's what we'll do," he said. "This room will make a great club for you. We'll make it a three-way partnership. You bring in the band and I'll run the place, and this pal of mine, an ex-cop, will get the license for the club."

I knew Gus was as crooked as a dog's hind leg, but he liked me and knew that all I cared about was having a band and that I didn't want a part in any deals except taking care of the music end, so I said, "O.K., you handle the business part and I'll bring in the band." The ex-policeman put in his application for a license, and in the meantime we opened up and for two weeks we played for an audience that was served only soft drinks. The A.B.C. investigated the license application, and when the ex-cop couldn't prove to their satisfaction that the money for the license was his own, they turned him down and the whole deal fell through. It wasn't until a few months later, when I picked up the newspaper and read that Gus had been found murdered in the back seat of his car, that I realized what I would have been getting mixed up in if the deal had gone through.

The middle-class propriety of Childs restaurant in the Paramount Building, where we opened on March 17, 1952, was a welcome respite from the honky-tonks and gangsters. I seldom make auditions, because I have enough trouble after I'm hired from the complications that arise with the bosses and from my own personality, but for this job it was mandatory that I audition, and since I was out of work I agreed to it. I put a band together, rehearsed it one afternoon, and took them down to Childs to audition for a group of austere-looking business people who were in charge of the corporation. The second I saw them I knew that if they heard any jazz they would scream. I did want this job very badly so I immediately put in a mute and had Ray Diehl do the same on his trombone, and we stole softly into "Tea for Two." The men still had the expression of people who expected something else, but who were so far being tolerant. I went into another song I was sure they knew, and then, remembering that the band would be opening on St. Patrick's Day, I turned around and played "My Wild Irish Rose" and "Danny Boy." The agent came over then and said, "They want some jazz." So I played jazz, and they thought it was great, but if I had played it first they wouldn't have liked it. Too loud, they would have said.

I met Bobby Brenner of MCA through the job at Childs. He came down there one night when we happened to be blowing up a storm and became very excited about my playing and my band. When I left Childs in the fall, we had several meetings and Bobby eventually came up with the idea of a tour of the colleges. I hired Jimmy Crawford, Eddie Barefield, Ray Diehl, Dick Cary, and various bass players and went out on the road that fall and again the following spring, playing at colleges and halls in New England, Pennsylvania, New York, and New Jersey. Some were quite successful and some didn't draw so well. It was a good idea and if it could have been kept going, it would have been very successful. During that time, Dave Brubeck started out on the same kind of tour. He was just starting to become popular and famous then—he had made the cover of *Time* magazine that fall—and he did well on his tours.

One night we filled in at an upstate college for another trumpet player's band, which couldn't keep the engagement. This frat party was to start at midnight, and we drove there from another date some hundred miles away. The affair was being held in the back yard of the frat house. When we arrived fifteen minutes late, the student committee angrily demanded to know where the other band was. They hadn't even been notified about the change, and they were naturally burned up, but we had driven there in a mad rush to help out and we didn't feel so good about our reception, either.

By this time the students were all loaded. The girls and fellows were pushing each other into the pond—I forgot to mention there was a large pond in the yard, filled with water lilies—and the kids were swimming around in their clothes, and it was all getting frantic and out of hand. We climbed up on the shaky little wooden bandstand the kids had built next to the pond and started to play. The kids were making so much noise you could hardly hear the band, so after three or four numbers we just stopped. The committee came over again and started yelling at us again for not being the other band, and they said they wouldn't pay us, but finally they ordered us to play again. In the meantime, the kids were getting so drunk that they started splashing water all over us and squirting beer at each other and us. Realizing that it would take the merest breath to start them toppling the bandstand and us into the pool, we finally had the sense to stop. "Grab your stuff, boys, and run!" I called to the men. Pee Wee Russell couldn't make it up the side of the muddy hill, but we managed somehow to pull him up to safety. I don't think the kids even realized we had left. Early spring, when the students go wild with panty raids and such, is no time to play a college; fall and winter are the safest times to venture on campus. The whole outcome of this was that the union fined me forty dollars for playing a job without having a signed contract for it, and the trumpet player who had been hired originally, and taken an advance of $140 for the job, kept it, and he didn't appear to defend us. We had not been paid at all, of course.

After two or three other unfortunate experiences of this sort during the tour, I finally gave it up as a helluva way to make a living. Of course, there were other places where the kids were respectful and enjoyed it all. Sometimes I felt safer in the most low-down dive than on a college campus, but at many of the concerts the reception was so great and the date such a sellout that I could see this could be successful if it could be held together on both ends.

Another time we went down to play a single date at the University of North Carolina at Chapel Hill, and here we had a different kind of trouble. We drove down directly after a date in Pennsylvania. We had finished the job there at 1 A.M. and figured we'd drive till about six in the morning and then stop at a hotel and catch some sleep before going on. But by this time we were down South, and no hotel or motel would take us in since I had a couple of colored musicians with me—Eddie Barefield and Keg Purnell. In one place in Virginia I asked a motel keeper, "Do you have six beds for us?" and he said, "Yes, indeed, come right in," but when I told him I had two colored guys with me, he said, "Get the hell out of here before they string us all up."

So this became very, very bad. Finally Eddie said, "Listen, man, just drive to the place we're supposed to go." So we drove all the way to Chapel Hill. As we went through the city, we asked where the colored section was, and I let Eddie and Keg out there before driving on to a white hotel. Later that day when I picked up Eddie and Keg, they told me they had found a wonderful place where they had fine food and whiskey and had a great time. Since we were stuck in a stuffy old hotel, we were the ones who felt left out.

At the concert we had played here the year before there had been no tension about our having a mixed band, but this time the cracker janitor and the local help in the gym began giving us terrible looks. We played on, and after the concert some of the kids invited us to the fraternity house. They fed us wonderfully, but I began feeling nervous when I overheard some remarks about how unusual it was to have colored guys in the frat house, and I thought I had better get us all out of there. I hustled everyone into the car, and just as we were pulling away from the curb I saw in my rear window a state police car pull up at the frat house. We drove nonstop all the way back to New York, U.S.A. We did try stopping once outside of Baltimore for food. At first the proprietor agreed to let Eddie and Keg eat in the kitchen, but he changed his mind, and I got mad and started to recite the Gettysburg Address. Eddie and Keg grabbed me so I wouldn't start anything I couldn't finish. When we were back in New York they said to me, "Max, we like to work, but if we have to do it down there let's forget about the whole thing, because it's tough enough sometimes just bucking the weather."

They were referring to the time we had played upstate one winter. We had finished around 11 P.M., and just as we were leaving, a few flakes of snow started to fall. We were in two cars, Dick Cary's and mine. I'll never forget how wonderful Dick Cary was on these tours. He used to take half the men in his car, and since he knew I was hard up for money, he never charged me for the gas and mileage. Within ten minutes, the flakes turned into a raging blizzard and I lost track of Dick's car. I heard later he had to stop at a garage and buy two snow tires and chains. It took us twelve hours to drive the 350 miles through the worst blizzard I'd ever been in. At eleven the next morning, we were just coming into New York on Jersey's Route 3. It was so bad by now that all these cars were piled up in tangles on the side of the road and I was creeping along at five miles an hour and skidding all over the place; you could feel the back end of the car weaving and sliding as though it didn't belong to the front. And then when you approached a hill you had to get up as much power as you could because if you slowed down you stopped the traction. When we finally got to New York City, Keg said, "You did a Barney Oldfield today, Maxie. How you did it I'll never knew, and I was watching every inch of the way."

Chapter 13

It was through Louis Armstrong, the nation's greatest ambassador of good will, that I was selected for the jazz tours of Europe and the Far East. It all started, appropriately enough, in Washington, D.C., where every summer a group of concerts are given in the huge Carter Barron Amphitheatre at Rock Creek Park. For the 1957 season three jazz bands were hired for a week's engagement. Our band, with Jack Teagarden, Peanuts Hucko, myself, Lou Stein, Jack Lesberg, and Cliff Leeman, opened the show, then Errol Garner took over, and Louis Armstrong's band wrapped it all up. Although Louis and I had been acquainted for thirty years, this was the first time Louis had heard me play for any length of time. Louis would listen to our band each day over the speaker in his dressing room while he was getting ready for his own set, and reports came buzzing back to me so thick and fast about how much Louis liked my horn that I stopped in one afternoon to thank him and to return the compliment.

"Man, it's very similar, very similar!" Louis said, pumping my hand enthusiastically. I guess there is no higher praise from Louis. He meant, of course, let me add for the uninitiated, that the feeling was the same, not the licks.

Later that summer when the European promoters sent in a request to Joe Glaser's office for an all-star band to tour Europe, my name was among the several trumpet players listed as alternatives to Louis Armstrong, whose name headed the list. Louis couldn't go because of other commitments, but he said to Joe Glaser, "The cat to send is Max Kaminsky. He'll blow up a storm over there." Louis's recommendation of me meant as much to me as the trip itself, and the next most gratifying thing about the European tour was that I'd be playing with a crackajack group of superb musicians—the great Earl "Father" Hines, Jack Teagarden, Peanuts Hucko, Cozy Cole, and Jack Lesberg.

I first met Teagarden when he was working in Ben Pollack's band in the early thirties with Benny Goodman, although I had heard him on records long before that. Jack Teagarden is foremost among all the great trombonists, of whom there are many, many greats: Miff Mole, Tommy Dorsey, Jack Jenney, Cutty Cutshall, Urbie Green, Jay C. Higginbotham, Dickie Wells, Brad Gowans, Sonny Dunham, to name some. One trombonist who never had the acclaim he deserved was "Tricky Sam" Nanton in the Duke's orchestra. He was noted for his plunger work, but the few times I heard him play open trombone he had a wonderful fresh way of playing. It was right and good, not the kind of thing that became popular in the so-called Dixieland style with its slides and slurs and tailgate. The public today hears a trombone wail in tailgate style and to them that's jazz, and they think it's great, but it is simply regular marching-band style, and was used in marching bands long before jazz was born. But from an artistic and musical point of view it has nothing to do with jazz trombone.

The first thing about the great trombonists is that they had the quality of the tone. When Tommy Dorsey played a melody it was a very straight melody and it had a silken quality to it. When Teagarden played the same song he could interpret it more deeply in the jazz idiom, but he still had that wonderful tone and taste. That's where we seem to have the trouble today;

the quality of taste seems to have left most of the music. We had a standard in those days, so that when a musician played great he played great all the way—he didn't squeak by on tricky little things. He had to know his instrument and have the great ideas of what to play.

The trombone is an especially difficult instrument because, like the violin, it involves positions instead of a set note. You have to move the slide up to the right position to hit the right note. Most trombonists have to move that slide all around to get the notes, but there are "false" positions where a note can be hit, too, and Teagarden had figured it out so that whereas another player would be moving the slide like mad, Jack would scarcely have to move his slide to hit the same note.

Teagarden's tone is unmistakable and individual, and his pitch and intonation are so right that it's always a joy to play with him. And his ideas are so true to the jazz feeling and in such good taste that it's no effort to play with him. Most musicians play very sharp or flat or can't keep time or their ideas are corny, but Jack is always so simple and eloquent that from the beginning he has been revered by the great colored musicians. Louis Armstrong thinks the world of him. Jack has thousands of fans all over the world, but the greatest fan is Louis. Louis said that the first time he heard Teagarden he broke out into goose pimples. Once when I was visiting Louis backstage in his dressing room, the room was filled with people and Louis was talking to them and singing along with the tape of his own band records at the same time, but when it came to Jack's solo, Louis called out, "Shhhh, everybody—here's Jack!"

I had had many chances to go abroad over the years. The college bands I had played in during the twenties were continually offered summer jobs on boats bound for European or round-the-world cruises, but although like most Americans I dreamed all the time of going to Europe someday, when the opportunities arose I always seemed to be too interested in what was going on here to be able to tear myself away. And I don't know how much I was influenced by one of my mother's favorite remarks, to the effect that she had been all over Europe before she finally landed in America and, "Believe me, there is no place like America," but in any case I never did go. Now, when things were so upset at home, I was undecided at first about going, but the need for money and the prospect of playing in a top-notch band were too powerful to resist, and by the time we left I had worked myself up to a pitch of excitement at the idea that I was finally going to Europe.

The itinerary, covering seven weeks of one-nighters in Britain, France, Germany, Italy, Switzerland, Sweden, Norway, and Denmark, was rugged, but we were all seasoned travelers, and Earl Hines and Cozy Cole, who had been to Europe three or four years earlier with Louis Armstrong, were not only seasoned but knowledgeable. When we arrived in London on September 27th, the British fans had a band meet us at the airport, photographers took our pictures for the papers, and all day long there were visits and meetings with fans and reporters and friends.

We played our first two shows in the Royal Festival Hall the following afternoon and evening, and the next night we left for Glasgow by train. From there we played six one-nighters of two-a-night around the country, then back to London to the Coliseum Theatre, then on the road again for six more one-nighters (including one in Cardiff, Wales, where we couldn't understand the people even when they were speaking English), and then back again to London for another double-header at the Coliseum. We were in Britain for a total of sixteen days.

The first thing I couldn't get used to in England was the difference in traveling. Where in the States it would take us three hours to cover a one-hundred-fifty mile hop, in Britain it took us all day to do the seventy-five or eighty miles from one engagement to the next. Our tour bus was small, ancient, and unheated, the roads were narrow and winding, and after pooping along at thirty-five miles an hour on the open highway, the bus driver would slow down to a snail's pace when crawling through the quaint old towns and villages. The tour was laid out in such a way that we crisscrossed back and forth across the country, which isn't very wide to begin with, and it seemed to me that every day at noon we were driving through the same little village with its same, centuries-old, red-brick city gate and its cobble-stoned main street where the same uniformed woman was briskly directing traffic, and I'd always remark in great astonishment, "I'll be damned if there isn't that same lady traffic cop again!" The prevailing color of Britain in the fall, even in the country, was a misty gray, and I hadn't been off the plane more than twenty minutes when the sight of the mist-wrapped rows of dingy brick houses on the ride into London from the airport made me think of every English murder mystery I'd ever read.

In London, Ernie Anderson, my old friend from the Summa Cum Laude days, who was now working for John Huston, took me under his wing and walked me over every square inch of London, and it was all a vast confused blur in my mind, except for a few indelible impressions, such as the tired, listless, drab appearance of Londoners and of their bomb-racked city. In 1957, twelve years after the war, they were still in a lethargy from the terrible strain of five years of war and bombings. It was hard to realize that the British were still doing without so England could get the capital it needed to get on its feet again. These people are pathetically used to having so little and to existing on very little money. Not for them was the money we poured so lavishly into Germany, the cause of their poverty. Life is very strange. Germany was bustling and prosperous while London seemed so poor and sad and dirty, and the streets were full of raggedy-looking elderly people, bitter, lean-faced young men in turtleneck sweaters, and sharply dressed Teddy Boys. No one seemed to be going anywhere, they just loitered on the damp, cold streets. Speaking of loitering, this was before the authorities cracked down on prostitutes, and London at that time was filled with thousands of young girls, still in their teens, openly so-liciting. It was an astounding sight.

Another thing about London was the difficulty of finding any place after 1 A.M. where one could have a quick bite to eat. Everything shuts down at that hour, except for the private clubs, and I was always vaguely hungry during the tour. I never saw anyone so serious about their food as Europeans. They have very set hours for eating so they can give it their full attention, but since I'm used to being up at all hours of the night, I was completely stymied in Europe for lack of the corner delicatessen or the all-night cafeteria.

Our first performance in the Royal Festival Hall went over very well, but my lip wasn't in shape and I didn't play that first show as well as I wished. All the other guys sounded marvelous, while I felt lucky just being able to last through it. But at our next performance, in Glasgow, I was feeling and playing much better, and that was a better show. In fact, we were a sensation in Glasgow, and aside from Basel, it was the most successful show we did in Europe. The concert hall had been sold out and they had set up an extra hundred seats on the stage to accommodate the overflow, so we had an audience fore and aft and both of them gave us rafter-shaking ovations. I feel that we made this tour just before the fever pitch of interest in this kind of jazz slackened. Within a year or so, the promoters had run it into the ground and it began to lose its glamour for Europeans; they wanted to hear the latest rage—the boppers and modernists. But in 1957 they were still, except for the hard core of avant-gardists, madly appreciative of hot jazz and of the chance to see us, and I'll never forget the warmth and enthusiasm they accorded us. In Britain, Scandinavia, Germany, France, and Switzerland, wherever we played we were taken to a reception room right after the concert, where for at least an hour or two we signed autograph books and programs for a line of people overflowing out into the street. The European fans want something personal to commemorate the occasion, and this is a big ritual over there. Once, in Norway, we had to leave right after the concert to catch a train and it almost caused a riot because we couldn't stop to sign autographs.

Naturally, the foreign fans had been reading about and listening to the records of Jack Teagarden and Earl Hines and Cozy Cole and myself and Peanuts and Jack Lesberg for years and they were tremendously excited at seeing us. They are touchingly appreciative, and jazz to them is a much more serious business than it is to Americans, who naturally think of it as a more everyday thing than a rare art form. The European fan is highly intellectual and analytical, partly because with their main source of hearing jazz limited to recordings, they can't possibly get the whole picture. While the American grew up with it and can hear the real thing with very little effort, the European has, aside from local bands, which are improving but not quite right yet, only the jazz clubs, where the members gather to listen to the latest U.S. releases and then try to jam a little themselves. These jazz clubs also put out innumerable little magazines that contain very erudite and academic dissertations on the most minute aspects of jazz.

The English have always loved jazz and have formed many, many bands faithfully modeled after everyone from Kid Ory to Count Basie to Stan Kenton to Gil Evans. The "traditional" jazz band has long been their favorite, however, as it has been here, too, where every college has its stereotyped Dixieland band. In one city in England, I forget where, Peanuts, Lesberg, and I were invited by the jazz club of the local college to give a lecture on jazz. We were led into a large auditorium and as soon as we were seated on the platform one of the boys unrolled a huge map on the wall which looked like a family tree and bristled with names like traditional, neo-primitive, mainstream, urban jazz, modern, etc. After we were presented to the assembly, Peanuts stood up and said, "The first thing to do is to throw away that chart," and he went on to talk about how that sort of thing was the cause of the whole trouble in jazz, the attempt to pigeonhole every style and even every lick a musician might feel like playing and trying to rule on whether it was right or wrong. "It's not right or wrong," Peanuts ended up grandly, "it's just either good or bad!" and he sat down to thunderous applause and cries of "smashing" and "wizard."

On our one-nighter trips around Britain, the bus driver would always have to stop in the late afternoon for his cup of tea. I never cared much for this tea routine, so while everyone was having refreshments I'd walk around town with my camera. The weather was turning colder and I didn't have enough heavy clothes with me—in fact, this was the time of the Asian flu epidemic and all of us were coming down with colds—so on these walks I kept an eye out for a jacket to wear under my topcoat. One afternoon I came upon a shop which featured an olive-green twill riding jacket in the window. "Just what I've been looking for," I was muttering to myself when Peanuts came up behind me.

"It's awful!" Peanuts said flatly when I pointed it out to him.

"*I* like it," I replied. When I tried it on, it was so big on me that not even my fingertips showed, and the waist was nearer my hips than my ribs, but the shoulders fit perfectly.

"If you wear that jacket, I'll pay for it," Peanuts said when he had stopped ha-haing.

"Wrap it up," I said to the clerk. I was warm as toast in my oversize jacket for the rest of the trip and Peanuts said it was worth the price in laughs. Cozy Cole was another great one for making the trip fun. He'd pull his plaid cap over his eyes on the bus and appear to snooze, but he'd never miss a trick, and he'd see humor in everything. He really broke us up when he imitated Peanuts explaining to me how to work the German camera I had bought. I would listen carefully, nodding intelligently while Peanuts explained every facet of the complicated mechanism, and then when he was all through I'd say, "Great!" Then after a moment I'd say earnestly, "Uh, would you mind running through that again—a little slower?" and Cozy would collapse.

On October 14th, when we arrived in Copenhagen, we found both the Europe Hotel and the food a great improvement over London, where we had stayed in a pre-prewar hotel. The Scandinavian landscape at times reminded me of parts of Cape Cod, but with a grander, more barren and majestic sweep to it, and I could actually smell the cod and herring in the tangy North Sea breezes. The cleanliness and the great food everywhere we went in Denmark, Norway, and Sweden were fine, too, and the concert halls in Stockholm and Göteborg were about the most beautiful I have ever seen, with marvelous acoustics.

In all the Scandinavian countries, especially Norway, the people still couldn't get over the joy of being free again and were still talking about the dreadful times they went through under the Nazi occupation, with its daily horror of reprisals and hostages and calculated terrorism.

The Scandinavians were much under the influence of modern jazz. Among the enthusiastic audiences in Oslo and Stockholm and Bergen, we'd notice certain of their avant-garde musicians sitting there with scornful, dissatisfied looks on their faces because they thought we were old hat. It always amazes me how the Europeans could change so quickly with the fashions in this country. They never had any mind of their own about our music. They just follow us slavishly, or, rather, they follow our so-called critics, who don't use any critical judgment either. And to think it was Hans Christian Andersen who wrote the fable about the emperor's clothes.

In a Stockholm night club, I saw my first European beatniks, or existentialists, the girls with their long mops of hair and their thick sweaters, and the men with their beards and thick sweaters. The trumpet player in the band imitated Dizzy Gillespie even to the point of bending the bell on his horn skyward. One of the things that most appeal to them in modern jazz is the modern beat, which is looser and lighter than the older jazz beat, but although they do play it well they still can't get it exactly right. After hearing American jazz for thirty-five years, they still can't get it. In Oslo we heard a big modern orchestra styled after Stan Kenton's. Both the band and the audience were a little too wild for me.

At the end of October, we left Scandinavia for ten days of one-nighters in Germany, in Stuttgart, Düsseldorf, Munich, Hamburg, Bremen, Frankfurt, Wiesbaden, Passau, and Friedberg.

Germany jumps. After seeing the drained lethargy of the British and the still-dazed thankfulness of the Norwegians and Danes, it was startling to see the bustling prosperity of the Germans. They don't want to know anything about the war. They never heard of the Nazis. It never happened there, and if it did, there was nothing personal in it.

There were still ruins everywhere in 1957, but rebuilding was going on like sixty, with new buildings arising from the ashes—modern apartment houses, elegant new hotels with modern plumbing, and everywhere beautiful new concert halls. Germany was rebuilding overnight with American dollars, while battered old London, which had held on all alone in 1940, stayed in its rubble. In all the new hotels in Germany they proudly displayed framed photographs of the ruins they had rebuilt from. All along the lovely Rhine valley from Wiesbaden to Düsseldorf, the air was filled with the tang of grapes and our eyes marveled at the beautiful old castles. Castles are pure fairy-tale stuff to Americans; we think we would all have been princes instead of serfs.

All the cities in Germany have big night clubs and the people go out. In fact, all Europe has a lively night life. Munich, one of the loveliest cities in Germany, has a big swing section, full of beer halls and night clubs. We played for American Army bases all over Germany, as well as giving concerts for the German people. Our own men were wildly happy to see us, and the German audiences were just as enthusiastic. The avant-garde snobbery hadn't hit there quite yet and so they just enjoyed us. They liked us so much, in fact, that in one place they brought in movie cameras and sound equipment and without a by-your-leave they filmed our entire show. This piracy went on all over Europe and Asia, too, where we were taped repeatedly without our consent. Louis Armstrong's manager eventually became so fed up with it that he automatically would prowl around the concert hall before the show opened, pulling out plugs and cutting wires. One day in Brussels, I turned on my radio and out poured the sound of an American jazz band. I recognized Teagarden and Peanuts, but since I wasn't prepared to hear myself it was several minutes before I even recognized my own horn or realized that it was the tape of a concert we had played two nights earlier in another city.

We played only two dates in France, one in Orléans and the other in Paris at the Olympia Theatre. The avant-garde element in the Parisian audience was patronizingly tolerant of us but the rest of the crowd enjoyed it. I visited Mezz Mezzrow, who has been living in Paris for years now, and who is still the same happy, cocky guy full of projects and enterprises, and in the evening I caught his band, composed of French musicians playing in the traditional jazz style. The night club was a cave-like place which was formerly a dungeon, the authentic tiny cells and instruments of torture all part of the atmosphere. Jazz sure is being played in weird places these days. The club was full of beatniks and intellectuals and tourists from all over the world and it was very expensive. Everyone in Paris seemed to be cross and rushing around frantically; it wasn't the kind, relaxed, wonderful Paris I had always dreamed about, but it was more beautiful and more fascinating than I had imagined. Since we had only a couple of days there, I was soon acting just as frantic and trying to cram all my sight-seeing into a few hours. At one point I became so confused I went to see a Charlie Chaplin movie, but after a half hour I came to my senses and left when I realized I was sitting in a movie when I had only a short time to see this marvelous city.

From Paris we went to Amsterdam, a lovely clean city, and not expensive, but by the time we reached Brussels we began to get very tired. We were whisked in and out of Holland and Belgium so fast we had only the vaguest glimpse of them before we were on the plane to Naples, where we played at the Flaming International Club, a servicemen's club. We had about three minutes to see something of Italy on the drive from Naples to Rome and we gaped longingly at the semitropical countryside with the pastel-colored villas sparkling among the olive and cypress trees. From Rome we flew to Basel, where we had what seemed the best and most appreciative audience of the whole trip, and then we staggered on board the plane to fly home.

In January of 1958, it was all over as far as my marriage was concerned. It had never worked out, though not for lack of trying. I moved into the Hotel Bristol, and in the middle of the month I took a jazz band into the Duane Hotel. The job lasted until summer, but in the meantime the State Department tour of the Far East was in the offing, and I jumped at it.

The arrangements—for travel, hotels, setting up the whole network with the overseas United States Information Service officials and the local cultural affairs representatives—made through ANTA and handled by the Associated Booking Corporation, proceeded through the summer. I shopped for luggage and drip-dry shirts, the State Department gave us a pep talk and briefings of what was expected of us as "ambassadors" of our country, we had our shots, and in mid-September we left Idlewild on a sparkling clear day for Paris, the first leg of the tour.

Chapter 14

It took us two and a half days to reach Karachi, in West
Pakistan. Now you can fly there direct in twenty-four hours.
Our tour, which started on September 22, 1958, lasted four and
a half months, through the end of January, 1959, and covered
eighteen countries. The band, Jack Teagarden's Sextet, had Don
Ewell on piano, Jerry Fuller on clarinet, Ronnie Greb on drums,
Stan Puls on bass, and myself on trumpet.

We had time for only the merest glimpse of Karachi, an
Arabic-like Indian city with camels, snake charmers, veiled
women, oriental bazaars, and beautiful modern white buildings,
before leaving the next morning for Kabul, Afghanistan. The
plane, one of the ricketiest DC3's I ever clapped a nervous eye
on, rattled over a thousand empty miles of starkly barren desert,
to land us in an ancient, time-shrouded city where practically
nothing has changed for over three thousand years. By starting
our tour in Afghanistan, we were not only starting at the beginning of the alphabet, but almost at the beginning of time.
Kabul, set in a shallow valley in the foothills of the Himalayas,
commands all the passes north to India, and over the countless
ages Alexander the Great and Genghis Khan as well as hundreds

of lesser conquerors have rampaged through Kabul on their way to invade India.

Within an hour of landing in Karachi we had become aware of two of the most characteristic phenomena of the East—the peculiar rancid funk to the air, and the servant waiting outside your door to serve you. But in Kabul, where I had my first real taste of the incredible poverty of the East, and of its astounding caste system, I nearly flipped.

Since there is no modern hotel in Kabul, we were quartered in the homes of members of the American Embassy staff. In the afternoon, we were taken on a sight-seeing tour of the city, and that evening there was to be a reception for us at the Embassy. Driving down a street in Kabul was like seeing a page from the Bible come to life. And as far as the Afghans were concerned, we were apparently a weirder sight to them than they would be to us if they appeared on an American street in their native dress. Here the women were completely covered from head to toe in tentlike burkas. Two tiny holes in the face-covering allowed them to see where they were going, but I'll never know how they breathed in that stifling heat. Children of six and seven years old walked the streets with large tin cans tied to their backs, picking up camel dung and tossing it over their shoulders into the cans. These discarded fuel-oil cans were also very popular as cooking pots, and the filthy water in the gutters along the streets was used by the people to wash their clothes in. Since these people have no plumbing facilities, the air is acrid with the odor of both camel and human excrement. The shock to the American mind at the sight of this poverty is cataclysmic.

After the sight-seeing, I returned to Mr. Coulson's house, where I was quartered, and had a shower and a nap. The effects of the no-sleep routine we had been on since we left New York finally caught up with me, and I fell on the bed like a slab of granite. When I awoke at eight-thirty, there wasn't a soul in the house. Everyone had left for the party at the American

Embassy, which was scheduled for seven-thirty. I padded out-side to the garden and called again for the houseboy, and sure enough he came running out of the little house across the court-yard that he shared with the gardener. When I told him that I wanted to go to the party he understood at once, and replied in a sort of pidgin English that the gardener was a good man and would get me there. I dressed quickly and set off with the gardener down the dark, silent street. The night was cool after a long, impression-packed, blistering day, and the sight of the quarter moon riding high in the ancient Asian sky suddenly filled me with a mounting sense of excitement. At the corner, the gardener hailed one of the horse-drawn, gaily decorated wagons which are the local taxis. As I climbed aboard I heard the gardener say to the turbaned driver, "Embassy Polish," but I let it go, thinking maybe the party was over there, who knew? At the Polish Embassy, the gardener tried to rouse the gateman but it was obvious immediately that there was no party going on in that quiet, darkened building. Turning to the driver, I said, "America." The driver stared glumly back at me. After trying "U.S.A." and "Yankee," I finally hit upon "Eisenhower." That did it. The driver broke into a great, toothless smile, and nodding and chuckling he repeated "Eisenhower" several times, and then calling to the gardener to climb aboard, he flicked the reins and we jogged along to the American Embassy, where I arrived just in time for the entertainment. An Afghan musician performed for us on a native instrument built like a celeste, the fingerboard of which he operated with his right hand while his left hand worked the bellows to produce the sound. All the songs were typical Asian minor-key tunes. Back at the Coulsons' after the party, I worked on my packing again before hitting the sack. I was in a panic from all the stuff I had taken with me, but I finally solved it and crawled into bed to sleep only a few hours and then lie awake till dawn. This broken-sleep routine became a pattern during the entire trip as a result of the con-stant excitement and overstimulation of new, strange cities, the exhaustion of travel, and the grueling strain of trying to play well. We were always getting up at 5 A.M. to catch planes since there were few facilities for night flying.

The next evening, we played our first show of the tour at the home of the American ambassador to Afghanistan. The two hundred or so guests, composed of all the local high society and royalty as well as the ambassadors of all the countries represented there, seemed to like the music, and after the concert they congratulated each of us individually many times. The concert was taped and the next night I heard it over the radio. The Russian ambassador said that jazz was international. The Russians had gone all out in 1955 on a road-building program in Kabul, for which the Afghans are very grateful. The Russian road leads past all the embassies on the way to the airport, and is the only modern road in Afghanistan. The Russians also built a bread factory, but with American aid to Afghanistan going into invisible things such as financial loans and technical advice in development projects, the people aren't aware of the American money poured in there.

Don Ewell and I hired a horse cab to drive us around the Old City of Kabul the next morning before we played our second concert that afternoon for some four hundred people in the open field in front of a school. These were the poor people, and as I looked out over the crowd of bearded, turbaned, colorfully robed citizens and noticed that two of them were wearing eyeglasses, I suddenly realized that they were the only spectacled Afghans I had seen here. When I mentioned it to one of the Embassy staff, he said the people here didn't even know whether they had poor eyesight or not. They have very little book learning, he said, and consequently they never have the chance to find out whether they can see. That seemed to me an odd way of looking at it, but if they did need glasses I don't know where the hell they'd get them, anyway.

My next surprise came when I tried to tune up to the piano and discovered it was a whole tone flat. Of course, these people have no concert pitch to tune to, and not much use for a piano in the first place, since their music has no relation to the piano. While a piano player is lucky that he doesn't have to lug an instrument around, on the other hand he is stuck with lousy instruments most of the time. Poor Don Ewell—how he suffered on this tour. A piano player has to have great technique and a sturdy philosophic outlook to be able to play on instruments with keys missing or sticking, and still make it sound like something. But as far-out as were many of the places we played in, there was always a piano, horrible wreck though it often was. Up in Moulmein, I thought we had finally hit a place that couldn't scare up a piano, but just as we were climbing up on the bamboo bandstand, an oxcart came rumbling down the path with a piano in it.

In Kabul, when I spoke to the fellow who seemed to be in charge of the piano, I was so wrapped up in thinking of it in terms of being down to a 340 pitch instead of 440 that the way I phrased it was, "This piano is terribly low." The fellow gave me a dazzling smile and said in perfect English, "Oh, don't worry about that—we'll put some blocks of wood under it and raise it up."

The rapport between the audience and us when they heard us play that afternoon was equally nil. They had no idea at all of what we were playing. This experience was to repeat itself in many places in the Far East. But though it was obvious and understandable that the more out of touch with Western culture the people were, the less meaningful our music would be to them —just as theirs often pulled a blank with us—still I was bothered and uneasy whenever I felt we weren't playing enough for the common people. It was great, of course, when we played in the big, cosmopolitan cities where there were many jazz fans, and it was a tremendous thrill to have them clap the house down and follow us around as if we were celebrities, but it seemed to me that it was just as much our job to play for the common people, too, however little they seemed to get out of it. I couldn't get it through my thick head that the poor people in the East were not as hep as poor people in the West, and that perhaps in playing for the students and the elite and the culturally sophisticated our "message" was getting through where it would do the most good.

The next day we flew back to Karachi for a five-day stay before going on to Bombay. All in all, we spent thirty-two days in India; besides Bombay, we played in Calcutta, Madras, Poona, Patna, Ahmedabad, and Hyderabad; and Lahore and Dacca in East Pakistan.

It's hard for the American mind to get used to the great extremes of wealth and poverty existing throughout the East. Of course, in a hot country like India, much of the living takes place out doors, in the great open-air bazaars and the open-front shops, and you get a good chance to see how the people live. Business of all kinds is done right out on the sidewalk. I wasn't in Bombay more than five minutes before I found myself being measured for a suit. The shop owners do everything but lasso you. The streets seethe with humanity, and as in all hot climates, color is everywhere. A street scene in an Indian city is a knockout with its dazzle of brilliant-colored robes and saris and turbans, and all the things for sale in the shops, from the melons and fruits to the wood and ivory carvings, the silver bracelets and necklaces, the hand-woven scarves and bolts of shimmering materials.

Everywhere we went in India, the people were unfailingly kind and gracious to us, and the jazz fans were passionately devoted. Crowds of fans met us at the airports, and aspiring young trumpet players would come to my hotel room, and after presenting me with a gift—they are great on giving gifts in the Far East—they would ask for a lesson and I'd do my best to help them. But it was in Poona, a city of 260,000 people about 120 miles southeast of Bombay, that I met one of the most impressive and unusual fans I ever had the pleasure of knowing. He was the High Priest of the Parsis, and after the concert he asked to be presented to me. A slender, olive-skinned man with bright black eyes, he was dressed in a long white robe and a white turban and he seemed to me to be one of the original Three Wise Men. You had the feeling he knew everything, and he probably did. His name was Sardar Dastur Hormuzdiar.

This High Priest drove me all around Poona, which has a lot of beautiful temples and palaces, before taking me to his home, which was enormous and filled with magnificent carved furniture and rare antiques. I had never even heard of the Parsis before, let alone of their high priest, and it was strange to picture this stately man seated in his carved teakwood chair during the languid Indian night listening to a Summa Cum Laude recording of "Nobody's Sweetheart Now." I was told later that the Parsis are descended from the ancient Persians who emigrated to India in the eighth century and are adherents of Zoroastrianism, which was the Persian religion before Mohammedanism took over. The High Priest told me his position is hereditary; he also told me that the Parsis expose their dead to the vultures. As High Priest, he was the only one allowed to take the cadavers up to the top of special high towers—Towers of Silence, they're called— where within five minutes the bones are picked clean. The Towers of Silence have three separate tiers, for men, women, and children. The bones are cast into a well and washed out to sea. It's probably just as well that one doesn't know what one's fans are doing in their own time.

In Ahmedabad we had another exposure to Indian culture. We were staying in the home of a vastly rich Hindu family that owned many fabric mills. My room measured fifty by fifty feet, and had a porch at each end. In the morning I was awakened by the chattering of monkeys peeking in at me from the balcony. It was hot even in the early morning, and by the time we played our concert that afternoon in the local town hall, it was sweltering and our clothes clung to us like wet silk. It was at dinner that we ran into difficulties. It wasn't the fault of our hosts—they didn't understand that we didn't understand —but nevertheless it was very awkward for all concerned. We sat with the family at a huge, round, oilcloth-covered table. The food, which contained no meat since the Hindus aren't meat eaters, and on which the host kept pouring some kind of white sauce, was served in large aluminum plates with metal cups set on them. There were no forks or spoons and we just sat there in stricken silence while our hosts plunged their fingers into the concoction and scooped it into their mouths. They finally explained to us that their religion taught that God had given them their fingers to eat with. There was nothing to do but plunge in, too, and do the best we could. It was funny to consider that no doubt each was secretly thinking how barbaric the other was.

Ahmedabad was full of beautiful temples, palaces, and mosques, but it seemed to us a by-now typical Indian city of much poverty, full of sick and deformed people, and cattle roaming the streets at will, and we felt upset about the way the wealthy Indians just blew the horns of their big automobiles and drove through the street crowds as if the poor devils didn't exist. But if we were bleeding hearts in Ahmedabad, when we got a load of the poverty in Calcutta we were really rocked back on our heels.

Calcutta, the commercial center of India, situated about eighty miles up the Hooghly River from the Bay of Bengal, was the most heartbreaking place I have ever seen. Here in this "city of palaces," with one of the busiest ports in the world, the streets are filled with starving families, and empty lots are filled with shanty towns. The city attracts thousands upon thousands of illiterate workers, many of whom are driven from their villages by drought, but when these poor souls reach the city, they pour off the train and squat right in the railroad station and call it home. When they do find work, they are so undernourished that they have no energy, and it was explained to me that the people lying on lawns and benches and steps weren't doped but just exhausted.

I was so overtired when we checked into the Grand Hotel that I kept waking up all night and looking out the window on Chowringhee Road, which is in the midst of the shopping center of the city. The streets outside had a terrible fascination for me; it was like looking at a scene from Dante's Inferno. Around eleven there had been people lying all over the sidewalk. At twelve-thirty they were all gone, and then an hour later they were all there again, sprawled out on the sidewalk. I understand that the luckier ones who possess beds leave the bedsteads, which are just wooden frames with woven bottoms, stacked in hotel lobbies during the day and then they take them out and set them up on the streets at night. My eyes were drawn like a magnet to the sight of a man and wife and their six children. They were just sitting on the curb—no home, no food, no place to go. The father started to smoke a pod of hashish and three or four passers-by sat down and joined him. I guess they feel their only hope is to stay high. At 7 A.M., I awoke and looked out at the incredible scene again. Among the sleeping huddled forms on the sidewalk I spied a little boy, sitting up beside his still sleeping mother. I whistled to him, but since there was only one little open section on the window in my air-conditioned room, he couldn't hear me, so I picked up my horn and began to blow softly. He pricked up his ears then, and when he turned to face me I motioned to him to come under the window. He caught the rupees as deftly as Willie Mays and then he scampered back excitedly to show his mother the money.

A few days later, when we played for a small gathering out in a park, we had a more cheerful incident. The bandstand was a bamboo-carved little structure with one open side. All the guests were Indians. The microphone was far too low for Jack's height, so they brought a table and placed it on that, but it was still too low. They kept bringing out tables that were higher and higher until they found one tall enough. When it was my turn to solo I said, "I think they'd better bring back a smaller table." The audience laughed and applauded, and I said to Jack, "If we had more tables in our act we'd get more laughs over here."

From Calcutta we went to Hyderabad, the land of the Mo-

hammedans, and from there to Madras. After we were settled in
at the Oceanic Hotel, we had supper at John Wiggins' house.
Wiggins, the head U.S.I.S. man in Madras, was really worried
about the Communists in India, and he felt jazz was a great tool
in helping save the country from the Reds. Naturally, I was delighted to hear him say so, and if it is true, then the U.S.A.
should get a big movement of jazz to go there, but it seemed
to me that this poverty-ridden country is still so ignorant and
primitive in so many ways that it will be hard to steer it from
the Reds. "Wiggins is worried," I wrote in my journal that night.
"He has a tough job. I wish I could think of an idea to help him."
But these people have such a different way of thinking, just as
Asian music has a different thought behind it. Their music,
which is unwritten and is played by ear and from memory, does
have a sort of swing when they get going, but they don't have
any harmonic system to speak of. Just as Oriental painting has
no interest in perspective, their music has no interest in harmony,
and harmony is to music what perspective is to painting.

In Asia, melody is supposed to have reached its highest development, its most elaborate refinement. The rhythm isn't as complex as the African rhythms, but like the melody it is highly
refined. There is no underlying drive that stirs one into action.
Oriental rhythm and melody, with its quavering tones broken
down to quarter tones and eighth tones, have a hypnotic effect.
The music puts one into a languor, weaving a subtle spell of do-
nothing, as opposed to the "go" rhythm of the jazz beat. And
pitch, as we hear it, doesn't exist for them. They are continually
shifting and modulating the pitch; there is no standard pitch. All
over the Far East I was in a dither about the piano being off
pitch, and it probably sounded better to them that way.

In short, harmony involves order, the orderly building of a
piece of music according to the composition, progression, and
modulation of the chords, and they have no feeling for harmony
in Eastern music. We heard Asian musicians playing their butts
off, and you might say in a way that they were swinging, but

these guys were swinging without a harmonic system. In the West we built a whole musical civilization on the basis of the harmonic system—and a political one on the same principles of order, structure and compromise. It was the harmony between the white and black man that made jazz. So Wiggins has a tough job, trying to get the Asians on a more harmonious kick. I think a bop-type band would be a great hit in the Far East, especially since the modern jazz is getting closer to Asiatic melodics with its shifts in pitch and pantonality. If we can bend in their direction with bop, maybe they can bend in ours, too.

To get back to the trip, we left Madras on October 25th for a four-day stay in Ceylon. Colombo, the capital, is very old but very clean, and the gentle Buddhist monks look like walking pools of sunlight in their brilliant yellow robes. Our first night's concert held in Victoria Park in the center of town went over very well with the Singhalese. The next day, the famous Kandy dancers came down from Kandy to perform for us in Victoria Park. Their costumes are gorgeous, but their movements are very formalized and though the effect is breath-taking, I personally thought the best dancer I saw in the Far East was a fourteen-year-old Indian boy, a professional dancer who performed for us in Bombay. He could almost have cut my old friend Slappy Wallace, with his sensational ad-lib dancing, beating out time with his bare feet and shaking all over like Bojangles. He was something to see.

On Monday morning, we drove the seventy-five miles to Kandy through banana, tea, and rubber plantations to play at the Arts Theatre Peradeniya. We stopped the cars to take pictures of the elephants working along the road and the native mahouts very obligingly gave us rides on them. Jack seemed to feel safe as long as he held on to his trombone, and when he played a few bars while perched on an elephant's back, the animal must have thought he had a relative on board. Jack wanted to bring home a baby elephant in the worst way, but Mrs. Teagarden put her foot down.

On November 3rd, we started our swing through Burma. Rangoon, the capital, means "End of Strife," I was told. Let's hope they're right. A very large city, Rangoon must have been a very beautiful one before World War II, when it was given the works. Before they left, the British destroyed the oil works and transportation to make things tougher for the Japanese, and the Japs looted the place of everything that wasn't nailed down, and the bombings at the end of the war didn't help things. The wide boulevards laid out by the British are still there, although the sidewalks are filthy with betel juice. The streets are a fascinating hodgepodge of color, with the long, exotic-colored skirts and sheer blouses of the women, and the hundreds of little curbside stalls, the trishas and the gharries—the little dark-green shuttered wagons. The feeling here was more Oriental than Indian, and I was afraid to go out at night—the streets looked too dark and mysterious to me.

We played our first concert in a big open-air amphitheatre. The Burmese seemed to like us, but the bugs liked us even better. We played a concert in a stadium for the students of Burma University, and it went over very well. The following night we played for the President of Burma, U Win Maung. After the concert he presented us with tenderfoot Boy Scout badges, making us honorary members of the Burmese Boy Scouts. When we were told in the follow-up speech by a Burmese official that this honor hadn't been bestowed upon Adlai Stevenson or Vice-President Nixon when they were there, we really felt puffed up. The proceeds of all the concerts we played during our ten-day stay in Burma went to the Burmese Boy Scouts Fund, and at the end of our tour we were told we had made $25,000 for them.

It was expensive in Rangoon and prices were sky-rocketing. My room at the Hotel Strand cost twelve dollars a day, and every time you showed your nose on the street you were approached by somebody who wanted to make a deal in money or sell you gems. When we went shopping, the shop owners would offer you twice their money in exchange for yours, but they wouldn't take travelers' checks because they couldn't unload them. Burma is the land of jewels—rubies, sapphires, and jade—and when the Burmese women go out they deck themselves with every piece of jewelry they own. They have plenty of pieces and it's all the real thing.

From Rangoon we went out on two- and three-day trips to Maymyo, Moulmein, and Mandalay—real Kipling stuff. Moulmein, where we played two shows at the Palace Theatre, is full of pagodas and hard-working elephants. In Mandalay, the big town in upper Burma, the local Boy Scout troop turned out to meet us at the airport, but I wish they could have stayed around that afternoon and evening to help steady the bandstand and swat the bugs when we played at the fairgrounds. We were set up on a bamboo wedding platform that shook so badly we could hardly keep our mouthpieces to our lips. At night it was worse because when we took a breath we inhaled tons of moths and insects. Not only that, we were competing with a native orchestra that played at the same time we did. At Maymyo, forty miles farther up the mountains, our open-air concert for some four hundred people was easier to play, but the mountaineers didn't dig it very much. The hills were infested with Red insurgents and brigands and it was extremely dangerous traveling along the roads; nevertheless, I found the Burmese towns and countryside much more interesting and varied than the Indian ones.

Back in Rangoon, we received special invitations to a dinner at the President's official house. After dinner, we sat out on the lawn, which was glowing with the soft light of colored lanterns, and we and some two hundred other guests were entertained by beautifully costumed Burmese actors and dancers and two Burmese bands. One musician would play a few bars and another musician would pick up the melody from there, and they kept batting it back and forth between the two bands like a tennis ball. They have no written music and no leader; all their music is memorized and rehearsed. There were speeches afterward by Burmese officials thanking us for the fine work we had done there; our own Ambassador said we had done a great ambassador's job, while the U.S.I.S. man said we had helped them in their work of getting closer to the people.

On November 14th, we were up at dawn to fly to Bangkok, Thailand, where we found the Erawan Hotel, a brand-new modern building, to be even more expensive than Rangoon, up to eighteen and twenty dollars a day.

We hit another snag here, too, for it turned out that the chief Buddhist had died the day before and consequently we had to cancel all our big engagements, as the court went into heavy mourning. We just made a couple of television films and played a short concert at the Oriental Hotel's Bamboo Room. But the thirty-one-year-old King of Thailand, Phumiphon Aduldet, who received part of his education in the U.S., was a great jazz buff, and on Sunday he asked us to give a private concert for him at the palace. After we had played a few numbers, he took out his clarinet and jammed with us for four or five hours. "He doesn't have enough problems trying to run his country," Don Ewell said to me. "He wants to be a jazz musician, too!"

Bangkok was something to see with its mixture of old teakwood houses with red-tiled roofs and its modern buildings, and the streets are a madhouse of bicycle rickshas, autos, and buses. The wooden houses lining the canals that wind through the city are built on stilts and the kids just dive off the front veranda into the canal and swim around like puppies.

We went out to the university one afternoon to hear the college band, which played Western music. It was unbelievable to us that in a large university like this there was no music teacher. We thought the students had done wonders teaching themselves how to play. All of us, Jack, Don, Jerry, and I, were filled with zeal to have the United States invest in sending out teachers and music and books and instruments to these guys.

On November 23rd, we left for a twelve-day swing through Indochina. The Indochinese peoples—the Burmese, Thais, Laotians, Vietnamese, and Cambodians—seem gentler and calmer than the Indians, and less subtle and less complex than the Orientals. Laos is a small, very mountainous country with deep river valleys, and it is almost completely untouched by modern civilization. Most of its people grow their own food and spin and weave their own clothes. We played daily shows at a big fair in Vientiane, the capital, for five days, and we were a curiosity, if nothing else, although they seemed to like us. It was the first time in eight weeks that it had been cool, but my lip went bad and I had the shakes and couldn't enjoy it very much.

We were flown out of Laos by an Army plane on November 26th, and returned to Thailand to play at the University at Chiang Mai. This chief city of northern Thailand, set in a lovely valley surrounded by big wooded mountains, was perfectly beautiful at that time of year, and I thought I was in Shangri-la. I didn't learn till later that leprosy abounds in Chiang Mai and that there is a big leprosy asylum there. But I'm glad I didn't know that then, for the next day when we were back in Bangkok I came down with the Asiatic crud, and I felt miserable enough without being frightened out of my wits. However, it didn't stop me from enjoying a wonderful Thanksgiving dinner in the palace of one of the princes, attended by the King and Queen of Thailand. I never dreamed when I started the Shawmut Syncopaters that my trumpet would be the cause of my having Thanksgiving dinner in a palace, but I enjoyed every minute, in spite of the crud.

On the 28th of November we flew to Saigon in South Vietnam. Saigon, an Oriental city with a strong French flavor, is a very pleasant cosmopolitan city. Our four-day engagement at the Alhambra Theatre was well attended and well received by the citizens. We also played for dances at the officers' club and Army recreation hall and we did a radio broadcast before moving on to our next four-day stand, in Pnompenh, Cambodia. Cambodia, too, is largely undeveloped, with 75 per cent of its land still virgin forest. The high point here was our concert in the palace of King Norodom Suramarit. This was the last time we had a king for an audience, and although he wasn't as hep as the young King of Thailand, he seemed to get a bang out of our music, and we got a really big bang out of the medals he presented to us in honor of our visit. When he gave me my medal, he said in French that I was the greatest trumpet player he had ever heard. I knew as much French as he did English, but just to be polite I nodded vigorously and gave out with a loud "Oui," which broke him up and made me feel foolish when his remark was translated to me. Several months after our return to the States, a bomb was sent to the palace in a package. It killed one of the King's sons and maimed several court attendants. The King himself died in 1960. I was sad to read about his death.

And on to Singapore for three days, where we felt the audience had some idea of what we were playing, and then on to the Malay Peninsula for ten days. I was pulling out of my playing slump now and besides beginning to play better, I was able to enjoy the sights. Malaya is an incredibly beautiful part of the world. There are very few tourists, at least in December, and you get the feeling the natives live an easy-going, lazy life. The people are shy and unaggressive and very attractive looking, and their spacious tropical houses with red roofs and lovely carved woodwork are so handsome that I must have taken five rolls of snapshots of them. Rubber trees are the big things here. Though it was hot and there were lots of mosquitoes, the hotels were cool and the audiences enthusiastic and very receptive to our music. After playing at concert halls, Catholic schools, and theatres in Kuala Lumpur, Malacca, Seremban, and Ipoh, we flew to the island of Penang, off the west coast of Malaya. Penang, cool, quiet, and serene at this time of year, was the most heavenly place of all in Malaya. Our concert at the Rex Theatre pulled a full house, making our joy complete—and our letdown bigger when we opened in Manila two days later and drew only about six hundred people in a stadium that held four thousand. The story was the same all over the Philippines, where we played everywhere to less than half-filled halls. They have a chance to hear a great deal of American music in the Philippines, but since very little of our kind of jazz is fed to them, they had little interest in us. They'd love a big band, with lots of strings, and rock-'n'-roll bands, and ballad singers, and modern jazz—anything that is currently popular in the States would go well here. When Frankie Lane and Joni James were there some months before us, they packed the halls.

We arrived in Cebu on Christmas Eve, and a band met us at the airport. On Christmas Day, we played an afternoon and evening concert in the school gym, and I was glad to be working so I wouldn't miss not being with my sons so much. Outside of Warsaw, Manila was the most damaged capital city in the world during World War II, and though they have done an amazing job of reconstruction, there were still bombed-out ruins, and the harbor was still full of half-submerged hulks of Japanese ships. You get to feel there is no place on this planet left untouched one way or another by World War II.

Hong Kong was the right place to be on New Year's Eve, and a complete change of mood after the Philippines. What a fascinating city! Hong Kong harbor, chock-full of colorful Chinese junks and sampans, is one of the three most beautiful harbors in the world, and its atmosphere is absolutely unique. You can actually sense the intrigue in the air; it's one of those special cities that generates its own unmistakable flavor and excitement. In spite of the dreadful living conditions of the refugees crowded into unbelievable quarters, you can't help feeling strangely elated and stimulated. And you're always conscious that Red China is only some thirty miles away. The streets are noisy and colorful and extremely interesting, especially since the fetching cheongsams the Chinese girls wear are slit all the way up the thigh, making a stroll down the street seem as though you had wandered backstage at the Follies.

Jack Teagarden wasn't feeling well during our four-day stay in Hong Kong and he was out of commission entirely for two days. During this time we were scheduled to play for four

thousand Chinese youngsters, about six to eight years old, at one
of the schools. This was one of the biggest thrills of the whole
trip for me, even more gratifying than playing kings' palaces.
The children sat on the floor, quiet and attentive and good as
gold, their little heads shining like ebony and their round faces
beaming with good nature. We played for them in two shifts,
putting on one show for two thousand of them and repeating
the performance for the second group of two thousand. Through
the interpreter I told the children to answer me on "Jada" and
"The Saints," and they were perfect, coming in right on the beat
as if they had been hearing this music all their short lives. The
U.S.I.S. man was delighted, and all the guys in the band had a
ball, too.

On January 1st, we were up at 5 A.M. to fly to Taipei. The cool
air made us feel good, and so did the full houses we drew in
Taiwan, Okinawa, Korea, and Japan, for this was the part of
the Orient that not only had had the heaviest impact of American
ways but also, particularly Japan, was imitative of our ways in
many things and catered to Westerners. During the occupation,
the Japanese built huge, beautiful night clubs for the American
soldiers and the tourists.

When we arrived in Seoul, Korea, "The Land of the Morning
Calm," we were whisked straight into winter weather, with
temperatures of twenty degrees during the day that dropped
down to zero at night. The Koreans looked so poor in compar-
ison to the colorfully dressed Indians and Indochinese, and after
all the rich costumes in the warm countries their dark, heavy
clothes added to the feeling of drabness. In spite of the heater on
the stage of the Municipal Theatre in Seoul, it was about thirty
degrees in the hall, and the people huddled in their overcoats,
but their reception of us was very warm. They would have gone
wild if we had had some colored musicians in the band. Wintry
Seoul seemed dark and dirty and sad, and you sensed the anxious
spirit of the people, who are always in fear of new trouble. In
Pusan we were a big hit, too. Stan Puls had been taken sick a few

days earlier and we had to leave him in the Navy Hospital in Okinawa. We played five concerts without a bass, and we were worried about Stan, having had no word of his condition, but finally on January 9th we learned he had had an appendectomy and was doing fine. On January 10th, we arrived in Tokyo, and here we had the biggest reception of all.

The Japanese had been following jazz for a long time, and they knew all of us, and gave us the red-carpet treatment. We had a colored fellow, Lee Ivory, fill in on bass, and he played well and was a good attraction, too. We played in Nagoya, Osaka, and Hiroshima to full houses and great ovations. When we were taken to see the memorial tablet where the bomb hit Hiroshima, one of the Japanese officials said something about how terrible it was, but I got sore and snapped, "Next time don't mess around." There was a moment of coolness before the bland smiles took over again. The Japanese are very much aware of what is going on in the United States, and the bop bands and cool modern jazz bands would be extremely popular here, too, especially such musicians as Dizzy Gillespie, Miles Davis, Ornette Coleman, and Stan Getz.

On January 21st, we left for Los Angeles, and on the 22nd I arrived back in New York, having gone around the world. It is a beautiful world, and everybody should have a chance to live in it—all kinds of people, all kinds of culture, and all kinds of music.

Chapter 15

What will the sixties bring to jazz? Probably everything—more modern chords, more experimentation in atonal sounds, more jazz compositions in the classical forms of tone poems, fugues, chorales, concertos, symphonies, and operas. More blending back and forth between the classical and the folk elements of jazz. But I hope there will also be a place for the freewheeling, earthy, spontaneous style, and a renewed interest in the personal, direct approach to the music. And most important of all, I hope there will be some way for the new generation of musicians to make a living at this kind of jazz. The thing that worries me about any form of federal subsidy of popular music is that the "business" element, the promoters and critics and writers, will take it over as they have taken over so much of it already, and will end up as another force squeezing out the freewheeling types.

Jazz must continue to evolve, to change, to try out new forms and new sounds, and it needs places to be heard. It has always found them before, but more and more laws and restrictions, most of which are formulated with the idea of helping musicians, tend more and more to cut it off from the freedom it needs to grow and develop. Even in the late thirties and early forties there were places to play in New York where you could just sit in, or make an arrangement with the owner to try out a little band, and if it didn't go over, no hard feelings. Now a contract has to be signed ahead of time, and this scares off a lot of projects that would otherwise have a chance to be tried out. But one adjustment that could and should be made, that wouldn't interfere in any way with the jazzman's music, is a more understanding tax structure for musicians—for artists of all kinds. This is the kind of government subsidy that would be sure to get to the man it is intended to help. If a lower tax rate for musicians is too much to expect, at least there should be a reasonable setup whereby a musician, when he does have a chance one year to make some money, doesn't have an unfairly large share of it taxed away. A musician may have to work twenty years or more before he gets a break, and no consideration is taken of the years he was scuffling.

It's hard enough on the emotional level, being *in* one week and *out* the other. One month you're a representative of your government in a foreign country; you're cheered by thousands and thousands of people; you play in palaces and embassies— and then you're back in your hotel room, opening a can of hash for supper, waiting for the damned telephone to ring, and trying not to look at the pile of bills that covers the bureau. No matter how great is the job you're playing one week, next week you may just be a guy out of work.

After the State Department tour I was back on the open market again, and back at the old haunts, the Metropole, the Central Plaza, Eddie Condon's, the Roundtable, the Embers, doing club dates, gigs, and society parties, getting a couple of weeks at clubs in Pittsburgh or Toronto or Chicago, an occasional record date, and occasionally, too, having a ball, as with the Great Gleason Train trip the summer of 1962, when Jackie Gleason barn-stormed across the country to promote his new television program. Jackie Gleason is a trouper and a showman in the grand style and manner of the great entertainers of the twenties—a

one-man revival meeting. The train was met by cowboys in
Denver and by Indians in Phoenix and Albuquerque, and we
played at a baseball game in Pittsburgh. The trip was hard work,
especially trying to blow while the train was going fifty miles
an hour—and I don't know how Gleason kept up the pace—but
it was great. We played at railroad stations, where local bands
met us, and in parades and at receptions, but the funniest incident
was at Baltimore, where we were met at the station by a band of
fifteen accordionists. After they played, we had time for about
five bars of "Bill Bailey, Won't You Please Come Home," when
another reception band of ninety youngsters, which was waiting
nearby, burst into a march, and everyone marched after it. In
about two seconds the whole station was empty. "Some reception! Where did everyone *go*?" Bob Wilber asked, grabbing his
clarinet case. "They went after Bill Bailey," Cutty Cutshall said,
"and I'm getting back on the train for some sleep." And that's
how it went, and how it goes.

Index

Allen, Henry (Red), 47, 123, 176
Alvin, Danny, 123, 174
Ammons, Albert, 34, 123, 157
Anderson, Ernie, 108-109, 118, 121,
  127-129, 157, 166, 207
Angel, Miguel, 164
Aquarium, 176, 196
Arlen, Harold, 55, 118
Armstrong, Lil, 39
Armstrong, Louis, 10, 26, 27, 28, 56,
  72, 94, 174, 176, 193, 194, 203-206,
  style, 16, 17, 23, 32, 34, 36-37, 39-42,
  47, 53, 65, 100
  in Boston, 49, 74
  in Chicago, 32, 39-42
  in Harlem, 47, 48-50
  in Washington, D.C., 203
Aronson, Irving, 94
Asevido, Johnny, 19
Ashcraft, "Squirrel," 120
Auld, Georgie, 125
Australia, 149-151

Bailey, Buster, 176
Bailey, Mildred, 35, 69, 118
Bailey, Pearl, 176
Barbarin, Paul, 47
Barefield, Eddie, 199, 201-202
Barnet, Charlie, 121

Basie, William (Count), 56, 73, 80, 111,
  126, 160, 176, 209
Beach, Frank, 134
Bechet, Sidney, 123, 176
Beiderbecke, Leon Bismarck (Bix), 10,
  12, 27, 30, 35, 52, 55, 64, 88, 116,
  117, 120, 161
  style, 13, 15-19, 23-25, 32, 33, 36, 40,
  50, 193
  in Boston, 13-22
  in Chicago, 15-16, 17
  with Whiteman, 19, 20-21, 23, 64,
  69
Belafonte, Harry, 192
Berigan, Bunny, 86, 88, 89, 99, 118
Berlin, Irving, 55
Berry, Emmett, 123
Berton, Ralph, 117
Berton, Vic, 117
Best, John, 134, 138
Bigard, Barney, 39, 123, 129
Billings, Frank (Josh), 43-44, 52-53
Birdland, 190, 192-193, 196
Bland, Jack, 123
Bonick, Lou, 178
Bop City, 190
Bose, Sterling, 30, 80
Bowman, Dave, 108
Breed, Pearly, 10, 11

237

Brenner, Bobby, 199
Brick Club, 119-120
Brown, Vernon, 123
Brubeck, Dave, 199
Brunis, George, 31, 173, 176
Bryan, Mike, 125
Bushkin, Joe, 89, 90, 118, 123
Butterfield, Billy, 123, 176
Byas, Don, 123, 126
Byrnes, Bobby, 80

Caceres, Ernie, 76, 118, 123, 176
Calucci, Rocky, 134
Calloway, Cab, 78
Carey, Thomas (Mutt), 169
Carmichael, Hoagy, 14, 23
Carney, Harry, 14, 88
Carter, Benny, 63
Cary, Dick, 123, 188, 202
Casa Loma band, 78
Casey, Bob, 123
Castle, Lee, 91, 95, 125
Catlett, Big Sid, 71, 72, 84, 123, 174
Central Plaza, 177, 190, 235
Challis, Bill, 14
Chester, Bob, 153
Childs Paramount Restaurant, 198-199
Chocolate Dandies, 71
Clarke, Kenny, 102
Clayton, Buck, 88, 123, 126, 176
Cless, Rod, 32, 123, 156, 162-163
Cocoanut Grove, Boston, 74-75
Cole, Bill (Cozy), 120, 204, 206, 209, 210
Coleman, Bill, 123
Coleman, Ornette, 233
Commodore Records, 115-116, 157
Condon, Eddie, 30, 47, 50, 62, 63, 65, 66, 67, 70, 71, 89, 106, 107
    Summa Cum Laude, 108-121
    Town Hall Concerts, 127-130, 153, 167
    Condon Club, 164-167, 170, 172-173, 176, 190, 235
Condon, Pat, 142
Conniff, Ray, 123
Coonin, Tommy, 50
Corey, Irwin, 163
Costello, Tim, 158
Crawford, Jimmy, 199

Creole Jazz Band, 32
Crosby, Bing, 55, 68, 81, 121
Crosby, Bob, 84
Crozier, George, 14
Crystal, Jack, 122
Cutler, Ben, 182
Cutshall, Robert (Cutty), 118, 204, 236

D'Amico, Hank, 123
Daniels, Elliott, 11
Davis, Meyer, 183
Davis, Miles, 194, 233
Davison, Wild Bill, 123, 173
Delmonico's, 67, 69, 70, 73, 75
DeParis, Sidney, 75, 122, 123, 176
DeParis, Wilbur, 122, 123, 176
DeVries, Johnny, 117-118
Dickenson, Vic, 123, 176
Dickerson, Carroll, 39, 40
Diehl, Ray, 199
Dixon, Joe, 84, 166
Dodds, Baby (Warren), 39
Dodds, Johnny, 39, 50
Donohue, Sam, 134
Dooley, Bill, 186-187
Dorsey, Jimmy, 22, 81
Dorsey, Tommy, 13, 19, 22, 35, 77, 79-86, 90, 91-92, 95, 98-100, 153, 204
Drootin, Al, 70, 121
Drootin, Benjamin (Buzzy), 70
Duke, Vernon, 55
Duncan, Hank, 161
Dunham, Sonny, 204
Dyer-Bennett, Richard, 163

Eldridge, Roy, 88, 123, 175, 176
Elkins, Eddie, 74
Ellington, Duke, 14, 27, 46, 56, 58, 65, 73, 80, 111, 158, 160, 161, 167
Elman, Ziggy, 92
Epstein, Sidney, 59
Espíritu Santo, 144, 147-148
European tour, 203-214
Evans, Gil, 209
Ewell, Don, 215, 218-219, 228

Faber, Sam, 11, 12, 13
Faisioli, Bernie, 75
Famous Door, 86, 87, 89, 174-175

Far East tour, 215-233
  Afghanistan, 216-219
  Burma, 226-228
  Cambodia, 230
  Ceylon, 225
  East Pakistan, 220
  Hong Kong, 231-232
  India, 220-225
  Japan, 233
  Korea, 232
  Laos, 229
  Malaya, 230
  Okinawa, 232-233
  Philippines, 230-231
  Singapore, 230
  Taiwan, 232
  Thailand, 228-229
  Vietnam, 229
  West Pakistan, 215-216, 220
Farley, Ed, 78
Farley, Max, 30, 70
Feld, Morey, 73, 174
Fields, Kansas, 123
Fitzgerald, Ella, 101
Fontaine, Frank, 181
Foster, George (Pops), 47, 123
Francis, Panama, 123
Freeman, Arnie, 37, 70
Freeman, Howard, 21, 22
Freeman, Lawrence (Bud), 22, 47, 48,
    49, 50, 52, 62, 68, 70, 71, 123, 166,
    170, 173
  style, 35-36, 110-111
  in Chicago, 29-32, 34, 37, 43
  Tommy Dorsey band, 84
  Summa Cum Laude, 108-112, 120-121
Fry, Don, 123
Fuller, Jerry, 215, 228

Gabler, Milt, 115-116, 121-123, 152
Garner, Erroll, 203
Gershwin, George, 47, 55, 63, 117, 159
Getz, Stan, 192, 233
Gillespie, John (Dizzy), 175, 176, 211,
    233
Gleason, Jackie, 235-236
Gold, Sanford, 174
Goldkette, Jean, 12, 13, 14, 17, 18, 20,
    30, 64, 69

Goodman, Benny, 32, 35, 49, 73, 77-
    80, 88, 92, 93, 96-98, 100-101, 109,
    153-154, 204
Goodman, Freddy, 70
Gordon, Max, 163
Gowans, Brad, 123, 164, 166, 196, 204
  style, 111-112
  Summa Cum Laude, 108-121
Gozzo, Conrad, 134, 150
Grappelly, Stephane, 69
Grausso, Joe, 123
Greb, Ronnie, 215
Green, Bill, 30
Green, Urbie, 204
Greer, Sonny, 27, 73
Griffin, Chris, 92, 96
Guadalcanal, 144, 145, 146-147
Guarnieri, Johnny, 125, 176

Hackett, Bobby, 89, 123, 129, 176
Hackett, Kid Lips, 119
Haggart, Bob, 123
Hall, Al, 123
Hall, Edmond, 123, 176
Hall, Tubby, 40
Hallett, Mal, 13
Hamilton, Spike, 35
Hampton, Lionel, 176
Harriman, Benjamin, 191
Harris, Bill, 175
Harris, Tasso, 134
Hart, Lorenz, 45, 55, 118
Hawaii, 136-139
Hawkins, Coleman, 176
Heard, J. C., 176
Helbock, Joe, 84
Henderson, Bobby, 87
Henderson, Fletcher, 46, 76, 78, 79, 80,
    100, 102
Herman, Woody, 170, 173
Heywood, Eddie, 123
Higginbotham, Jay C., 47, 123, 176,
    204
Hill, Alex, 76
Hill, Chippie, 159, 163
Hines, Earl, 34, 39, 41, 50, 123, 203, 206,
    209
Hodges, Art, 123, 163, 174
Hodges, Johnny, 88

Holiday, Billie, 87-89, 97, 101, 105, 106, 129, 149, 157
Holmes, Charlie, 47
Hookway, Warren, 10
Hucko, Peanuts, 174, 203-204, 209, 210
Hyman, Dick, 192

Ives, Burl, 163
Ivory, Lee, 233

Jackson, Cliff, 123, 176
James, Harry, 92
Jenney, Jack, 89, 125, 204
Johnson, Bunk, 169, 173
Johnson, James P., 10, 47, 48, 129, 156-162, 166, 195
Johnson, Pete, 34, 123, 157, 176
Joindreau, Charlie, 27, 28, 29, 30
Jones, Jo, 56, 73, 88, 126
Jones, Jonah, 120
Jones, Maggie, 10, 11, 159
Julius's, 115

Kahn, Roger Wolfe, 69
Kaminsky, Matthew, 189
Kaminsky, Sam, 175, 189
Karle, Arthur, 11
Kaye, Sammy, 100
Kenton, Stan, 170, 209, 211
Kern, Jerome, 55, 136
Kincaide, Deane, 123
King, Wayne, 55, 100
Kirby, John, 63
Kirk, Andy, 78
Krupa, Gene, 22, 32, 47, 52, 67, 73, 92, 102, 176

Lang, Eddie, 34, 52, 69
Lang, Irving, 192
Lanin, Jimmy, 183
Lanin, Lester, 183
LaRocca, Nick, 17
Lawson, Yank, 91
Leadbelly (Huddie Ledbetter), 163
Lee, Sam, 150
Leeman, Cliff, 96, 203
Lesberg, Jack, 75, 123, 166, 174, 203-204, 209
Levitan, Sammy, 50
Lewis, George, 169
Lewis, Meade Lux, 34, 123, 157

Lewis, Ted, 2, 11
Lipkin, Steve, 125
Little Club, 7, 90
Lombardo, Guy, 55, 59
Lunceford, Jimmie, 78

Manone, Wingy, 32, 34, 35, 39, 40, 67, 68, 73, 84
Mares, Paul, 31
Margulis, Charlie, 19, 20
Marino, Don, 120
Marsala, Joe, 128, 152
Marsala, Marty, 123, 176
Marshall, Kaiser, 123
Marshard, Harry, 5-6, 180-183
Marshard, Jackie, 4-9, 60-61, 86, 177-182
McGarity, Lou, 123
McKenzie, William (Red), 50
McKinney's Cotton Pickers, 40, 46
McPartland, Jimmy, 32, 35
Metropole, 190-192, 235
Mezzrow, Mezz, 22, 50, 62-63, 71, 75-77, 123, 175, 213
Miller, Al, 198
Miller, Glenn, 52, 91, 100, 125
Millinder, Lucky, 78
Mole, Miff, 123, 176, 204
Monk, Thelonious, 160, 174
Monroe, Vaughn, 178
Moore, Big Chief Russell, 118
Moore, Freddie, 163
Morgan, Al, 123
Morton, Benny, 123, 129
Morton, Jelly Roll, 169
Mosier, Gladys, 94
Murphy, Turk, 170, 183
Murray, Don, 13

Nanton, Sam, 204
Navy Band #501, 131-154
New Caledonia, 140-145
Newman, Ruby, 183
New Orleans Rhythm Kings, 31, 32
Newton, Frankie, 75, 158, 195
New Zealand, 148-149, 152
Nicholas, Albert, 46, 123
Nichols, Ernest Loring (Red), 50-52
Nick's, 108, 109, 114, 117, 118, 121, 137, 157, 190

Noone, Jimmie, 39, 50

O'Brien, Floyd, 32, 33, 62, 71
O'Brien, Russell, 58, 59
O'Gorman, Bill, 155-156
O'Hara, John, 64
Ohms, Freddie, 166, 173, 195
Oliver, King Joe, 17, 32, 39
Onyx Club, 89, 90
Orchard, Frank, 123, 156
Original Dixieland Jazz Band, 17
Ory, Kid Edward, 40, 169, 173, 209

Page, Hot Lips Oran, 119, 121, 123,
    124-127, 192, 193, 195
Panassie, Hugues, 114
Panther Room, Hotel Sherman, 120-
    121
Parenti, Tony, 123
Parker, Charlie, 88, 175, 176, 192, 193,
    194
Pastor, Tony, 96, 105, 124
Persip, Charlie, 73
Peterson, Chuck, 96
Peterson, Pete, 50
Phillips, Flip, 175
Pied Piper, 156-163
Pierce, Charlie, 32, 33, 35, 42, 43
Pollack, Ben, 49, 204
Pollack, Henry, 2
Poor, George, 145
Porter, Cole, 118
Powell, Mel, 123
Price, Sammy, 56, 123
Prima, Louis, 86
Puls, Stan, 215, 232-233
Purnell, Keg, 201-202

Quealey, Chelsea, 70-71

Rainey, Ma, 10
Rank, Bill, 13
Rapp, Barney, 13
Rappolo, Leon, 31
Redman, Don, 46, 80, 100
Reed, Susan, 163
Reinhardt, Django, 69
Reisman, Leo, 53, 63-66, 79, 94
Renard, Jacques, 19
Riley, Mike, 78

Riskin, Izzy, 13
Roach, Max, 194
Robbins, Les, 96
Roberts, Luckey, 48
Rodgers, Richard, 55, 118
Rolfe, B. A., 52
Rollini, Adrian, 52
Rosenthal, Louis, 59, 181-182
Ross, David, 84
Roy, Teddy, 74
Royal Roost, 190
Rusin, Babe, 94
Rusin, Sunny, 94
Russell, Charles Ellsworth (Pee Wee),
    50-52, 62, 70, 71, 86, 123, 173, 200
  in Boston, 54-55, 164-165
  Little Club, 90-91
  Summa Cum Laude, 108-112, 118,
    121
  Condon Club, 166, 170
Russell, Luis, 46, 47
Ryan's, Jimmy, 121-124, 135, 171, 174,
    175, 176, 190
Ryker, Doc, 13

Saratoga, 143, 154
Schribman, Charlie and Sy, 12, 13, 17,
    80, 97, 98, 121
Schroeder, Gene, 123, 166, 173
Scobey, Bob, 170
Scott, Hazel, 76
Sedric, Gene, 123
Seeger, Pete, 163
Shapiro, Artie, 118, 123
Shavers, Charlie, 123, 176
Shaw, Artie, 76, 84, 92-105, 108-110,
    113, 124-125, 127
  Navy band, 131, 134-135, 136-139,
    141, 146, 149, 152-153
Simmons, Johnny, 123
Singleton, Zutty, 39, 41, 75, 76, 123
Smith, Bessie, 10, 15, 23, 32, 36, 159
Smith, Howard, 91
Smith, Kate, 55, 119
Smith, Pine Top, 34, 91
Smith, Stuff, 84, 120, 176
Smith, Willie the Lion, 16, 47, 63, 108,
    156, 157, 159, 161
Solomon Islands, 149
Solomon, King Joe, 74-75

Spanier, Muggsy, 32, 35, 119, 123, 176
Spivak, Charlie, 91, 153
Stacy, Jess, 32, 35, 123, 129
Stang, Arnold, 158
Stein, Lou, 203
Stewart, Rex, 176
Stordahl, Axel, 84
Straeter, John, 138
Stuyvesant Casino, 177
Sullivan, Joe, 22, 49, 50, 52, 71, 123,
    129, 166
Summa Cum Laude band, 39, 108-121,
    207, 221
Sutton, Ralph, 126, 183

Tatum, Art, 160, 176
Taylor, Herb, 50
Teagarden, Jack, 22, 52, 118, 152, 174
    style, 204-205
    European tour, 203-205, 209
    Far East tour, 215, 223, 225, 228, 231
Teschmaker, Frank, 32, 33, 34, 35, 36,
    43, 52
Thigpen, Ed, 73
Thomas, Joe, 123
Thomson, Virgil, 129
Thornhill, Claude, 134, 137-139
Three Deuces, 15
Tough, Dave, 47, 49, 50, 52, 53, 119,
    123, 125, 127, 175, 194-195
    style, 36, 72
    in Chicago, 32, 36-38, 43
    Tommy Dorsey's band, 84, 85
    Navy, 134-136, 138-139, 143, 146, 149-
    150, 152, 154
    Condon Club, 170-173
Town Hall Concerts, 127-130, 135, 153,
    166, 167
Tristano, Lennie, 192
Troup, George, 90
Trumbauer, Frankie, 13, 21, 52
Tucker, Sophie, 74

Turner, Joe, 157

United Hot Clubs of America, 115
Uptown Lowdown Club, 75-77

Vallee, Rudy, 11, 55
Venuti, Joe, 67, 68, 69, 70, 71, 73, 74
Village Vanguard, 163, 176

Wallace, Slappy, 57-59, 225
Waller, Thomas (Fats), 36, 47, 48,
    124, 159, 160-161, 188, 195
Ware, Munn, 192
Waring, Fred, 55, 85
Waters, Ethel, 15, 159
Watson, Ecky, 75
Watters, Lu, 170
Webb, Chick, 46, 63, 78, 101
Webster, Ben, 88, 176
Weiss, Sid, 123
Wells, Dickie, 75, 204
Weston, Paul, 85-86
Wettling, George, 32, 33, 35, 38-40,
    43, 95, 118, 119, 123, 192
White, Josh, 163
Whiteman Paul, 19, 20, 21, 23, 53, 64,
    65, 69, 125
Wilber, Bob, 236
Wiley, Lee, 117-118, 120, 121, 129
Williams, Clarence, 161
Williams, Sandy, 123
Wilson, Teddy, 87-88, 129
Windhurst, Johnny, 123
Wolverines, 10, 12, 17, 35, 116, 117
Woodward, Sam, 73
Wright, Edythe, 86

Yaged, Sol, 192
Yancey, Jimmy, 34
Young, Lester, 56, 88, 106, 123, 126,
    192, 193
Young, Trummy, 176

Format by Mort Perry
Set in Linotype Janson
Composed, printed and bound by The Haddon Craftsmen, Inc.
HARPER & ROW, PUBLISHERS, INCORPORATED